History of
My Own Times

Documents in American Social History
Edited by Nick Salvatore

A complete list of titles in the series appears at the end of this book.

Benjamin Henry Latrobe, *Ferrymen, Columbia, Susquehanna, January 14th, 1808.*
Maryland Historical Society, Baltimore.

WILLIAM OTTER

History of
My Own Times

EDITED BY

Richard B. Stott

Cornell University Press

Ithaca and London

First published 1995 by Cornell University Press
First printing, Cornell Paperbacks, 1995

Printed in the United States of America

Library of Congress Cataloging-in-Publication Data

Otter, William, 1787–1856.
    History of my own times / William Otter ; edited by Richard B. Stott.
        p.   cm. — (Documents in American social history)
    Includes bibliographical references and index.
    ISBN-13: 978-0-8014-9961-6 (pbk. : alk. paper)
    1. United States—Social life and customs—1783–1865.   2. Otter, William, 1787–1856.
3. Artisans—United States—Biography.   I. Stott, Richard Briggs.   II. Title.   III. Series.
E165.089   1995
973—dc20   94-24147

Cornell University Press strives to use environmentally responsible suppliers and materials to the fullest extent possible in the publishing of its books. Such materials include vegetable-based, low-VOC inks and acid-free papers that are recycled, totally chlorine-free, or partly composed of nonwood fibers. For further information, visit our website at www.cornellpress.cornell.edu.

3 5 7 9   Paperback printing   10 8 6 4

CONTENTS

ILLUSTRATIONS

Figures

Maps

ACKNOWLEDGMENTS

I n researching William Otter, I received the assistance of several histo-
rians and archivists. I especially thank Norman Creaser for researching
Otter's English background. Virginia M. Adams of the Old Dartmouth
Historical Society Whaling Museum, New Bedford, Massachusetts, aided
me on the historical context of Otter's whaling voyage. John Ward Willson
Loose of the Lancaster County Historical Society provided helpful informa-
tion about the local history of the region, as did Donna M. Shermeyer of the
Historical Society of York County; Rev. Msgr. George W. Rost of the Basili-
ca of the Sacred Heart (Conewago Chapel); Charles Glatfelter of the Adams
County Historical Society; and Dorothy V. Earhart of the Lititz Historical
Foundation. In Emmitsburg, Kelly Fitzpatrick was most kind and provided
copies of documents relating to Otter in the archives of Mount St. Mary's
College. Sister Aloysia Dugan did the same at Daughters of Charity Ar-
chives, St. Joseph's Provincial House.

The idea of republishing Otter was strongly encouraged by Roger Hay-
don of Cornell University Press, and his interest sustained the project.
Nancy J. Malone did a very thorough job of copyediting. I am especially
appreciative of the aid of Nick Salvatore, who offered encouragement and
very useful criticism on the Otter text and my commentary. Thomas Dublin
also read the manuscript and gave me helpful advice. I thank David Jaffee
for his comments on sections of the commentary. Other helpful suggestions were given me by Martin Bruegel and Adrian Srb and Jozetta Srb,
as well as by my mother, Marian Stott, who also helped proofread. I give
special thanks to Michael Weeks of the George Washington University

History Department for his invaluable aid in preparing the Otter manuscript. The support of the George Washington University Facilitating Fund is gratefully acknowledged.

RICHARD B. STOTT

Washington, D.C.

INTRODUCTION

"William Arter did the plastering of the Conewago Chapel when first built. He was a peculiar man and did some very foolish things. At one time he kept a tavern at Hanover, and was well known."[1] So wrote McSherrystown newspaperman John T. Reily in 1885. Fifty years earlier this "peculiar man," plasterer William Otter, published his autobiography in Emmitsburg, Maryland. At one time historians believed that ordinary Americans, and especially manual workers, were silent: there is little written evidence on which to base their history. Indeed, one historian even referred to such people as "inarticulate"—not because they had difficulty expressing themselves but because they left no documentation.[2] Although first-person accounts from ordinary people in the past are unusual, in the 1980s and 1990s a number of such accounts have been printed, and some of the most impressive work in American social history has focused on obscure men and women.[3]

[1] Reily, *Conewago: A Collection of Catholic Local History* (Martinsburg, W Va., 1885). This remark is almost certainly based on oral tradition. Not only does Reily misspell Otter's name, but the plastering Otter did was not on the chapel, built during the 1780s, but on the rectory in the 1820s. The Rev. Msgr. George W. Rost, the priest at the Conewago Chapel today and an authority on its history, believes Reily was unaware of Otter's autobiography (letter to Richard Stott, 16 June 1992).
[2] Jesse Lemisch, "Listening to the 'Inarticulate': William Widger's Dream and the Loyalties of American Revolutionary Seamen in British Prisons," *Journal of Social History* 3 (1969–1970), 1–29.
[3] See, for example, Alfred F. Young, "George Robert Twelve Hewes (1742–1840): A Boston Shoemaker and the Memory of the American Revolution," *William and Mary Quarterly*, 3d ser., 38 (1981), 561–623; and Laura Thatcher Ulrich, *A Midwife's Tale: The Life of Martha Ballard, Based on Her Diary, 1785–1812* (New York, 1990).

William Otter might well be called an extraordinary ordinary man. A plasterer in southern Pennsylvania and Frederick County, Maryland, in the first three decades of the nineteenth century, "Big Bill," as he was known, never prospered in life and, except for a brief stint as village burgess, achieved no elevated status. Yet, as Reily suggests, in his day Otter was well known, perhaps even something of a local legend. Certainly his *History of My Own Times* makes it easy to see why he might be considered "peculiar."

Otter's story is fascinating: born in Hull, England, in 1787, he ran away to sea, joining the town's whaling fleet. Seized by a press-gang and forced in 1799 into the Royal Navy, he escaped and returned to Hull only to discover his family had emigrated to America. Secreted during his journey across the Atlantic to avoid a second impressment, Otter was reunited with his parents in New York in 1801. In New York City he apprenticed as a plasterer and joined an urban gang, taking part in the violently anti-Irish Augustus Street Riot in 1806. In 1807 Otter broke his indenture by slipping off to Philadelphia. After working in the Quaker City for a few months, he began a series of moves west, settling in the town of Hanover, Pennsylvania, in 1809. There he lived and worked as a plasterer for the next twelve years, with the exception of a short visit to Cincinnati in 1819. After brief sojourns in Baltimore and on the eastern shore of Maryland, Big Bill moved in 1824 to Emmitsburg, Maryland, where he was a master plasterer, slave catcher, tavern owner, and notorious practical joker. The *History* was published in Emmitsburg in 1835. In 1849 Otter moved to Baltimore, where he died in 1856.

Otter's autobiography is, as his subtitle suggests, "altogether original." Big Bill is rarely boring; his tale is by turns exciting, humorous, and outrageous. *History* would not bear reprinting, however, if it was no more than a collection of entertaining anecdotes from Otter's life. I believe that it offers much more—it is a rare, perhaps unique, document in antebellum social history. Because Otter is open to different readings and because many of my conclusions are quite tentative, I have put my interpretation of *History* in a commentary at the end of the book. Readers can thus confront Big Bill directly, with only the aid of footnotes to identify obscure terms and to show where Otter's account can and cannot be verified by other evidence.

Nevertheless, I will suggest here, quite briefly, why I believe Otter's story is significant. First, his account of life as a rural plasterer is an addition to labor history. There have been fine historical studies of urban artisans, but we know much less about the considerably greater number of rural artisans.

Autobiographical writings by city workers are rare, and the life story of a country artisan in the early stages of the Industrial Revolution is even more unusual. *History* is especially interesting because Otter began as an apprentice in New York City, and he gives us an idea of the differences between work in town and countryside.

Second, and perhaps more interesting, Otter offers an "inside account" of the brawling and racism that was becoming increasingly common in this period. I know of no other document in which an artisan who engaged in attacks on blacks and the Irish describes, indeed boasts, of his behavior. Perhaps Otter's account will help broaden American social history by depicting a type of comportment that has not, I think, received sufficient attention. European travelers in the early nineteenth century were struck by the crudity and violence of American life—the fighting, drinking, swearing, and constant spitting. American genre painters such as George Caleb Bingham as well as regional writers such as Johnson Hooper (creator of "Simon Suggs"), T. B. Thorpe, and George Washington Harris ("Sut Lovingood") have left a sharply etched portrait of this masculine, coarse, even savage, aspect of American society. But for the most part, American social historians have not dealt with this subculture very effectively— much of the evidence was anecdotal and fitted awkwardly with the social-science approach that was popular. *History* is written in a quasi dialect with a large number of colloquialisms. It is proudly ungenteel, portraying a society of "jolly fellows," as Otter calls them, before the Second Great Awakening, when men of all social classes gathered in taverns and planned sprees. Unlike the temperance autobiographies of the period, Otter's is in no way written to denounce or renounce his rowdy life-style but instead seems to present it for approbation.

Obviously the value of *History* for historians will depend in large part on how true Otter's story is. Most of its anecdotes are too minor to leave any trace in the historical record. The question of Otter's veracity is discussed in more detail in the commentary, but it is obvious, as the evidence presented in the footnotes indicates, that this book is not a novel. The census shows that Otter was where he says he was, and the people he mentions are real. Newspapers and court records confirm several events. I believe that most of what Otter recounts actually happened, although the facts may be distorted by Big Bill's boasting.

Unfortunately, almost nothing can be discovered about the book's publishing history to shed light on Otter's motives or veracity. The 357-page original is now a very rare volume; so presumably not many were originally printed. How it was published is unknown; no other books were printed in Emmitsburg in the nineteenth century. It seems that Otter borrowed his title from a book published by a Catholic priest in Frederick, Maryland, in 1832, and though I suggest in the commentary what I think the significance of this might be, it is impossible to be certain what Otter had in mind. Big Bill's own preface, which he ends by stating that he is leaving readers "to their own conclusions," also offers little guidance, especially since its overly genteel language makes it difficult to know if Otter is serious.[4]

The only significant changes I have made to the text are to add chapters and footnotes. The original is completely without internal subdivisions. In the interests of readability, I have divided the book by the locations in which Otter was living. His very long paragraphs—one adventure per paragraph was the usual rule—have been retained. I have not changed Otter's unsystematic spellings, though I have corrected what are clearly typographical errors.

The footnotes I have added explain obscure terms and give additional information that is useful in clarifying points in the story and in evaluating Otter's truthfulness. (Cross-references to footnotes are to those in the text unless noted otherwise.) I have tried to identify every person named who plays a role in the story; I have not tried to identify names mentioned in passing. If a person who has a significant contact with Otter is not identified, it is because I was unable to find the name in the census, city directory, or other records.

---

[4] Only three copies of *History* are known to exist. at the Library of Congress, the New-York Historical Society, and the Maryland State Historical Society. In 1839 a single issue of an Emmitsburg newspaper was printed at Elihu S Riley's printshop, but before that there is no record of a printer in Emmitsburg, and Riley is not listed in the 1835 Emmitsburg tax lists. Probably he took over the shop from an earlier printer, but I have been unable to confirm this. Elihu Riley's name is given in the *Emmitsburg Gazette*, 17 August 1839, Newspaper Collection, Library of Congress, Washington. Commissioners of the Tax, Assessment Record, Real Property, 1835, Election District No. 5, Frederick County, Maryland, Hall of Records, Annapolis, Maryland.

HISTORY OF
MY OWN TIMES;

or, the

LIFE AND ADVENTURES OF

William Otter, Sen.

C O M P R I S I N G

A Series of events, and musical incidents

altogether original.

Originally published in Emmitsburg,

Maryland in 1835

Preface

The purpose for which the author principally intends his book, you will find in the sequel of this preface; that many words will not be spent to inform all those into whose hands his production may fall, that it is not expressly for the use and instruction of children—who, being as it were, blank paper, taking all upon credit; if that were the author's intention, the first comer might write saint or devil upon it, which he pleased.

To avoid such a verdict being pronounced, he does not intend either to labor very hard; that it was hastily got up, and ushered into the world before it was properly matured—as hasty publications are denounced by the public as a "crime." Our author is well aware that to brag and make professions in his dedication, as the practice of some writers of now a-days is, would be a digression upon the good sense and clear understanding of those into whose hands the work may fall if he were to endeavor to convince the world of his exquisite comical quirks; and in trying to convince them so far, as to get admirers of his hasty production, how little time and pains he consumed and bestowed upon it. He is aware that the public would take him at his word, and spare themselves the trouble of perusing the "History of his Own Times,"—which they reasonably could infer, as they would be assured before hand, that it is faulty through idleness, impatience, or wilful neglect in the author.

Well aware, in all his undertakings, never to do or say any thing which does not run smoothly and with the grain—knowing ourselves as we should do, so necessary upon all occasions; he will make his readers and himself too, as happy as a delicate and refined judgement is capable of; and in the plentitude of his own veracity he will give, free from coloring, a clear conception and precise account, of all the scrapes he had a hand in, jointly or severally.

Feeling assured, that those amongst whom he has spent the last twenty years of his life, would, if called upon, bear him out in the sincerity, and the sovereignty of truth, of the "History of his Own Times;" and as an intelligent and musical community will have the pleasure of judging for themselves, he confidently commits it into their hands with pleasure, leaving them to their own conclusions.

THE AUTHOR

England

I was born on the 19th day of July, in the year 1789, in the city of *Hull*, in Yorkshire, England.[1] As I intend to write a faithful history of my own times, I will not trespass upon the reader's patience, to give him the trouble of perusing the genealogy of my ancestry. Suffice to say, I was born of poor but honest parentage. One day my father ordered me to weed the garden, he being by profession a gardener. On his return home in the evening, he inquired into the matter, how far I had obeyed his orders, and having found that I had disobeyed them, he, in the plentitude of his goodness, got hold of me, and gave me a genteel wallopping. Upon the receipt of the flagellation aforesaid, being in the eleventh year of my age, I bade my father and mother a leg bail goodbye.[2]

After I had got away from my parents, I went to the dock in the city of my nativity, in quest of a master, and at length I succeeded in finding one, in a gentleman whose name was Gardener. To Mr. Gardener I represented myself as an orphan, whose feelings of philanthropy were awakened for my forlorn condition; to him I bound myself for seven years as a cabin boy, and sailed under Captain Clark.[3]

---

[1] Either Otter does not know his age or is lying about it, or this is a typographical error. William Ford Otter was baptized on 18 November 1787 in Kirk Ella, a village on the western outskirts of Hull. A November baptism for someone born on 19 July 1787 would be unusual but not extraordinary. The son of "Edward Otter, Gardener" and Mary Ashbridge, who were married in 1783, he was one of ten children. Rev. James Foord, ed., *The Register of Kirk Ella, Co. York* (London, 1897), pp. 178, 149–151, 160–163.

[2] "Leg bail" is English slang that means to escape from arrest or captivity.

[3] Hull, located on the River Humber, was one of England's major ports. A local census in 1792 showed its population as 22,286. Otter is joining Hull's whaling fleet, the main focus of the

Our first expedition was destined to Greenland, and after a voyage of about six weeks, we arrived at the place of our destination. The Greenland fleet having all safely arrived, after about eight days, our captain went on board the ship Jane, to dine; our chief mate, in the absence of the captain, amused himself in company with a few others, with the history of the four kings; the watch on deck was a little groggy, and I was in the galley putting on my tea-kettle for tea. The first thing I knew was, I was upset off my three legged stool, and the tea-kettle between my legs. I scrambled and succeeded in getting upon my feet, and the first thing that I saw, was a hole stove in the bow of the ship, about two feet long. All hands, (except our cook, who was in his bed and was lost,) jumped upon the mountain of ice, which had broken our vessel; and in short space of about five minutes our vessel went down about half mast high. We saved nothing belonging to her, only a part of the sails, the fore-top sail, the fore-top-gallant sail, the main-top sail, the main-top-gallant sail, the mizen-top sail. The crew was fifty-two in number; there we were in a most awful situation; upon a mountain of ice at least one hundred miles long, without provisions or bedding, floating ever and anon; to keep alive we wrapped ourselves in the few sails we saved from our sinking ship.

In this painful and perilous situation we remained about twenty-five hours. At length the ship Jane hove in sight; we hoisted signals of distress, and were taken in by her. Our captain being on board of the ship Jane, belonging to the Greenland whale fishery fleet. The crew was then shared out among other crews, to work their way home again, excepting nine boys, of which I was one of the number, our captain retained on board of the ship Jane. The prizes the ship Jane made during our voyage, consisted of eight whales, upwards of two hundred seals, and two Polar bears.[4] On our way

---

town's maritime activity—in 1800, 44 percent of English whalers sailed from Hull. On Captain Clark, see the following footnote. Edward Gillett and Kenneth A. MacMahon, *A History of Hull*, 2d ed. (Hull, 1989), p. 206. Gordon Jackson, *Hull in the Eighteenth Century: A Study in Economic and Social History* (London, 1972), p. 160.

[4] This account cannot be confirmed. Much of the difficulty stems from Otter's curious omission of the name of the ship he was on. Capt. Robert Clark of Hull was engaged in the whaling trade as the master of the *Truelove* between 1784 and 1798; there is no record of that ship sinking, however. One ship from the Hull fleet was apparently lost in 1797 and two in 1799, but missing newspapers prevent definitive identification. And which of the several ships named *Jane* was connected to Otter cannot be determined. Clearly Otter was a seaman (note the listing of sails). And I believe he had been on a whaler; the figures on the *Jane*'s haul are very plausible for a whaling voyage, even those on the polar bears. The sinking and rescue cannot be verified, however.

home we fell in with his Majesty's fleet, who pressed us into the King's service for life.[5]

In this new sphere of action my avocations became of somewhat a different character than that of catching whales, seals, and bears. My daily occupation was to feed about fifty prisoners, whom they had in chains, being a prison ship called the Nonesuch, carrying seventy-four guns, and having about two hundred prisoners in all on board, chiefly Americans.[6]

The first harbor we put in after I had been placed on the last named ship, was in Shetland harbor, in the Shetland Islands, to change water. After we had changed water, we put to sea, and cruised about in quest of hands. While employed in the occupation of feeder of prisoners, an altercation one day took place between myself and an old man, an American, whose name was John Wilson, a tarpaulin.[7] In our quarrel he had the audacity, as I thought, to call me an English bugger; by way of offsett I stigmatized him, *old rebel*, as the Americans were usually styled in the King's fleet. He told me if he lived to regain his liberty, he would kick me to where the old boy would not find me in a week. In reply to his, as I thought, vicious and rascally notions, I told him that I would feed him on the bony pieces on the platter; that the old boy could not chew him at all, and that was his daily rations; all the bony pieces on the platter fell to Mr. Wilson, as long as I was held in the office of feeder. After the lapse of about one year, from the time Mr. Wilson and myself had our confab, of which, in point of plain, hard swearing, he fairly outdone me, I was promoted to a *cabin boy*.

---

[5] In theory sailors in the Hull whaling fleet were exempt from impressment, but in reality they were often seized to meet the Royal Navy's need for seamen during the Anglo-French War. Peter Adamson, *The Great Whale to Snare: The Whaling Trade of Hull* (Hull, n.d.).

[6] The *Nonesuch* was a sixty-four–gun guard ship stationed in the late 1790s on the Humber outside of Hull, the commander of which in this period was Captain Woolley, also spelled Wolley. The *Nonesuch* was involved in a noted incident on 30 July 1798, when its press-gang attempted to board the whaler *Blenheim* in Hull harbor; two of the press-gang were killed as the attempt to seize the whaler's sailors was repulsed. Presumably Otter was impressed on the *Nonesuch* as the *Jane* entered the Humber on returning to Hull. The *Hull Advertiser* indicates that on 13 April 1799 the *Nonesuch* sailed for the Nore (the mouth of the Thames off Sheerness), returning to Hull on 6 July. Norman Creaser, my English researcher, whom I thank for this information, suggests that this trip was made to transfer impressed sailors to the naval base at Sheerness. The journey to the Shetlands may also have been to convey impressed sailors to a British fleet anchorage there. Though he has the name of the captain wrong, Otter's description of his service on the *Nonesuch* seems generally believable. Isaac Schomberg, *Naval Chronology* (London, 1802), 4: 534, 664; Thomas Sheppard and John Suddaby, *Hull Whaling Relics and Arctic or Historical Records of 250 Years, Concluded,* Hull Museum Publication no. 31 (Hull, 1906), p. 17; and Norman Creaser, letter to Richard Stott, 26 June 1992.

[7] Slang for a common seaman.

After my promotion to a cabin boy, we cruised about nine months; one moonlight night a sail hove in sight, captain Rodgers, commander of the Nonesuch, gave orders to bear down on her. As we bore down on her, she put out her lights. When within speaking distance the captain hailed her, "from whence came you;" to which question no answer was made; the captain gave orders to give him the two bow guns. My occupation was to hold the match, and that was the only time I ever said my prayers while at sea; after she had received our two shots given her from our bow guns, she hove to. We then boarded her, and made her captain come on board of the Nonesuch, and was asked by captain Rodgers, where he was bound to; he told captain Rodgers that he was bound for Europe. Captain Rodgers gave him a few for not answering his Majesty's ship when spoken to. Rodgers asked the captain of the small craft what his cargo was; he answered, sugar, rum, and coffee. Captain Rodgers ordered them to hoist out a hogshead of rum, and some coffee, and sugar, examined his books and then let him go.

The next port we made for was that of London. While there, the prisoners we held in chains on board the Nonesuch, were placed on board of the tender, being a guard ship. While at London, we supplied our stores with provisions; and while there I obtained liberty to go on shore every day in company with the officer of the day, to market, to carry provisions on board of our ship. One evening the officers were invited to a dancing party; after supper being over, I went to shake out the table cloth, on deck, it was one of the darkest nights I had ever seen, I heard three of the crew talking that they would desert the ship that night: I stepped up to them, and told them that I would go along. One of them swore and said if I said one word about their intention to desert, he would knock me overboard. After a considerable time spent by them in consultation, they came to the conclusion to take me along, provided I kept quiet. They instructed me to go and keep myself in readiness at the bow of the ship; and down the cable we went, one by one. I got on the back of one of the three who had thus far effected our escape; he had a head of very fine long hair, of which I availed myself: while on his back I conceived my situation to be somewhat perilous. I of course stuck close to him like a tick, and twisted my hands in his hair; he made several efforts to shake me off, but I would not let go my hold; after a considerable struggle, we at length arrived safe on the beach, after tugging about the distance of half a mile through the water of the river Thames. We then, after we got on terra-firma, walked along the beach till nearly day light; being exceedingly fatigued from the efforts we made to make our escape; weary and tired, we laid down on a sand beach to resuscitate our exhausted limbs, and by the alarm of the morning gun at the fort, in the vicinity of London, I was awakened, and found myself alone. I cast my eyes up and down the shore, not knowing which way to go. I crawled up the bank, and walked about one mile; I came to a place where two men were digging in a garden; I bade these codgers good morning. One of them, somewhat of an inquisitive turn of mind, inquired of me, where I was going to; in reply to his inquiry, I answered him, that I did not know; he then asked me where I had come from; I told him I came from off his majesty's ship, lying in the stream: he asked me how I got away; I told him that three men of the crew and myself had deserted; he then asked me where the three men were that had fled with me; I answered him, they had left me that morning on the beach. His companion observed that they could make five guineas on the lad if we take him to his Majesty. At his observation to his fellow-comrade, I began to cry; one of them asked me if I belonged to London; I answered him I did not; that I belonged to Hull, in Yorkshire, and that I wanted to go home to my father and mother. They then asked me how long I had been at sea; I told them about four years.[8] They then asked me how I came in his Majesty's service; I told them I left my parents, and sailed for Greenland; I was cast away on my return from thence, and placed on board of his Majesty's ship. He then asked my father's name, and what he followed; I told him his name was Edward Otter, and by profession a gardener. One of them said, he supposed that I was hungry; I told him I was; he took me to the house, and told the woman of the house to give me something to eat. I sat down and ate, and while eating, she asked whose lad I was; they told her that I had ran away from his Majesty's ship; and that they intended to take me back and make five guineas on me. She told them that that was too hard; she asked me where was my home; I told her in the city of Hull, in Yorkshire. She asked me if my parents were living; I told her they were. She then asked me, would'nt you be very glad to see them; I told her that I would; which idea so overcame me that I began to cry; she added, "I pity the poor lad;" John, said she to her husband, you ought to try to get the lad home. John told her he could, and that she should keep me safe till night. She took me up stairs, and told me not to be afraid, that they would do all they could for me. I thought that was the longest day I ever saw.

That night they took me down, and gave me my supper; and his wife said

[8] This was in 1801 (see footnote 21). If Otter actually was, as he says, aged eleven when he ran away, he would have gone to sea in 1798.

to her husband, that she thought it would be best to send me down in a coal boat, on the canal, and at the same time advised to strip me of my navy cap and jacket; that she would exchange them by supplying me with citizen's uniform. John then took me about three miles across the country, to the canal; he told the captain of the boat that here is a *Yorkshire bite*, meaning myself.[9] The captain inquired of my patron, what he was going to do with me; he told him that I had ran away from his Majesty's ship, and he wanted me to get home to my parents in Hull; he told the captain that it was hard for the poor lad. The captain's feelings were interested for me, and he told me that he would do all he could for me. The old fellow put in my possession a sixpence, and told me he now would leave me in the care of the captain of the canal boat, and bade me do the best I could, and bade me farewell. The captain took me down the canal, about forty miles, and asked me if I would go back again with him; I answered him no.

We landed at Newport,[10] a small town, and went into an ale-house; he told the landlord that here is a poor lad, ran away from his Majesty's service, and wanted to work his way down to Hull. O well, said the landlord, I'll try and work him on. The captain bought a quart of ale, some cheese and biscuit, and told me to put the biscuits in my pocket, and he then left me in the ale house. The landlord told me to walk about; that a hack stage would be along there, and to jump on behind; that it would carry me about ten miles. According to his directions, I waited about half an hour. I seen the stage coming; the landlord says to me, "now my lad jump on;" I put out, and rode about five miles, when one of the passengers got out to obey a call of nature; he came to the back part of the stage, and inquired of me, if I belonged to the stage; I told him no, I was taking a ride. The driver over-heard us, and asked who was behind; the gentleman who had stepped out, told him, a boy. Slapbang, came his whip, and off I came in short order; acknowledging payment in full for my five miles ride. I then started after the stage on foot, and went on till I came to an ale-house; I entered the house and inquired of the landlord the distance from thence to the city of Hull; he told me it was near forty miles; the landlord asked me where I came from; I answered, from the canal; he asked me if I lived at Hull; I told him I did I

9 "Yorkshire bite" was slang for a person from Yorkshire, with, it seems, the implication of cleverness, even slyness. Joseph Wright, ed., *The English Dialect Dictionary* (Oxford, 1898), vol. 1.
10 This reference is probably to Newport, York, a village on the Market Weighton Canal about 18 miles west of Hull and about 190 miles north of London.

asked him for a drink, he gave me a drink of beer; he then asked me if I was a runaway, I told him no, that I belonged to a collier, and was on my way home; he then observed to me I had a long walk before me; upon which I bid him a good day.

I trudged about four miles further, and came to a farm house along the road side. I there saw a man driving cattle; he says to me, high my lad, which way. I told him I was going to Hull, he asked me if I would hire; I asked him what to do, he said to mind cattle and sheep; I told him no. I travelled on and overtook a man who was driving a two horse cart, and he also asked me where I was going; I told him, to Hull; I then asked him how far he was going; he told me he was going to Beverly, a small town about fifteen miles from Hull;[11] he then asked me, how far I was going that day; I told him I did not know; he asked me where I came from; I told him as I did all the rest, that I came from the canal; he asked me if I lived in Hull; I told him I did; I then asked him how far he intended to go that day; he said about eight miles; I observed to him that would be as far as I would be able to go; his next inquiry of me, was, if I had any money; I told him I had sixpence; he laughingly observed that such a small sum as that would not carry me to Hull; I then told him that I had bread and cheese in my pocket; he then made an offer to me, that if I would help him to clean his horses, I might stay with him for that night; which offer I accepted.

We stopped at a widow woman's house for the night, and agreeably to our contract, I was to help to clean his horses, and having never in my life touched a horse before that time, I began to clean the horse at the foot; he came out and asked me how I came on, and seeing that his horses were not cleaned, he made free enough to tell me that they were not clean; I insisted on it they were, and referred him to take a look at their feet; after our confab had ended about the horse cleaning business, we went to supper. Our landlady asked him if I was his boy, he said no, that he picked me up on the road, she observed that I was a fine looking lad; and where was I going, addressing herself to me, I told her I was going to Hull; she asked me if that was my home, I told her yes, she also me asked where I had been, I told her what I told the rest of idle and inquisitive inquirers, that I was from the canal, the next inquiry was directed to me how I came at the canal; I told her that an uncle of mine had taken me there, and that I was tired of it and was on my road home. After supper being over, I sat myself down on a bench and fell

---

[11] A town eight miles north of Hull.

asleep, I had not slept long till the landlady awakened me, and observed to me that I had better go to bed, I answered her that I intended to take my lodging for that night in the cart: *Oh no!* said she, that will be too bad, I then told her I had no money, she said to me that made no difference, I should go to bed, money or no money. I then, after her kindness being proffered to give me a bed, under my embarrassed pecuniary circumstances, accepted her offer and slept very soundly; in the morning when I awoke and looked rightly around me, the man that drove the two horse cart, was gone. Having no money, I felt embarrassed, as I had not the means to remunerate my kind hostess, laboring under difficulties which my mind could not solace; in this moment of suspense, my landlady asked me if I would eat something, I replied and said to her, that I was not hungry, when the contrary was the fact. I inquired of her how far it was to Beverly; about five miles was her reply to my inquiry; I next asked her if I should keep on that big road that lay along her house, she told me yes; being ashamed to leave her house without making her any kind of recompense, I pulled out my sixpence, which I had received from John who left me in charge with the boatman. I told her, that that was all the money I had, offered the sixpence to her, she told me to keep it till I came to Beverly, observing to me that there I might want it; I put up my money and bid her a good-bye, she told me to stop, I did so; in the plentitude of her goodness she gave me some bread and cheese to put in my pocket, as a helper on the road, I thanked her for it very cordially, feeling quite rich, having as I thought the fat of the land safely stowed away in my pocket, and off I started for Beverly.

I arrived at Beverly at about 11 o'clock A.M.; I went to a tavern where I saw a man holding a horse at the door, I inquired of him which way led to Hull, he told me to go right down that street, until I came to the second square from there, then take to the right and keep on, that would take me to the pike. I travelled on about two miles, I came to a gate house,[12] I asked the gate-keeper to give me a drink of water, he gave me a drink, I then asked him how far it was to Hull—he told me ten miles, he asked me if I lived there, I told him I did; he asked me where I came from, I told him from the *canal;* he asked me how I came all that way, coming from the canal,[13] I replied that I knew of no other road, he asked me my name, I said my name was William Otter; a son of the Gardener? said he, I told him yes; said he how long have

---

[12] The Queensgate Toll Bar was two miles south of Beverly on the Analby Road.
[13] There was a road directly east from Newport to Hull; by going via Beverly, Otter had gone considerably out of his way.

you been from home, I told him I had been from home about four years. My lad do you know that your parents have left this country and have gone to America two years ago; he took me into the house and presented me before his wife, saying this is a son of Edward Otter; she said that cannot be possible you know that Otter took all his children along; he then said, he could not have done so if I was one of his children, she then asked me how many children my father had; I told her he had six, three boys and three girls, she asked me their names, I told her that the girls were named Harriett, Mary and Sarah, yes she said, catching the idea, that's right; he then asked me my brothers' names, I told him my brothers were James and Edward and mine was William;[14] he then touched me on a very delicate theme, for he asked me how I came to leave my parents, I told him the plain facts that my father whipped me and I ran away; where had I went to? I told him to Greenland, and had been cast away the first voyage, on my way home had been put on board of a man of war, and ran away from them in London, and am now on my way home. His wife said she did not know how I ever should see my parents again, yet has had now gone to America. That piece of intelligence was a damper to my feelings, I felt more down in the mouth about it, than any thing I had ever heard, he asked me if I would not eat something, I told him no, that I was not hungry, he told his wife to get me something to eat, she did so, I sat down and began to eat, and while I was eating she called in her two little boys, and told them that there was a poor boy that had lost his father and mother, that they should be good boys, always do as their parents told them, using me as a kind of bug-bear to frighten her lads into obedience, which so much affected me that I could not eat another bite; he asked me if I knew where my uncle lived, I told him I did not, he told me that he lived in Handleby a small town about two miles from the city of Hull,[15] that he taught school; I asked him how far it was to Handleby, he told me eight miles; I asked him if he thought that I could get there that day, he said oh yes, I bade him good bye and put out.

I walked six miles and my feet gave out, I met a boy, I inquired of him who lived in that next house, he told me William Wardel;[16] I asked him if he

---

[14] Baptism dates found in Foord, *Register of Kirk Ella*, are as follows: Harriet, 29 June 1794; Mary, 8 August 1784; Sally (the register lists no Sarah born to the Otters), 16 September 1792; James, 8 May 1791; Edward, 30 October 1785; and William 18 November 1787. Four other Otter children died before their first birthday.

[15] Analby, two miles west of Hull.

[16] Foord, *Register of Kirk Ella* shows a William Wardel witnessing a marriage in 1793.

thought that I could stay all night at that house, the boy told me oh yes, you can sleep with me. I told him my feet were so sore that I could not walk any farther; he then took me to the house, I told him to ask for me if I could stay all night, he told his father here is a boy come to stay all night; his father asked me where I came from, I told him from the canal; he asked me where I was going to, I told him I was going to Handleby, he asked me if I lived there, I told him no. I have an uncle living there, he then asked me my uncle's name, I told him my uncle's name was James Otter. What, said he, the school master, I told him yes, he asked my father's name, I told him Edward Otter; what said he, the gardener that lived in Hull; that can't be for he is gone to America and all his family, I told him that I was his son, though I had heard it too that they were gone to America, yet myself was here; he then asked why I did not go with them, I told him that I had been at sea; how long was you at sea, said he, I answered him I had been at sea about four years, he then asked me how it came that I went to sea and was so young, I told him my father whipped me at a time, and I ran away from him and bound myself for seven years in the Greenland trade; he then asked me how I got away, I said that I was cast away the first voyage, on my way home I was taken on board the Nonesuch; he asked me how I got away from her, I told him that four of us came away in one night, he asked me where the rest of my comrades were, I told him they left me on the beach, and I never saw them since, he supposed that I had been a middling wild lad, I told him I did not know; said he if you go to Hull the press-gang will take you again, I told him that I supposed that they would not know me, he said that it made no odds about that, if they see you they will take you any how, he told me it would be best for me to go to my uncle and stay there; I told him I intended to go to him; by this time we were called into supper; when I arose from the supper table I could hardly walk, he asked me if I was lame, I told him my feet were blistered with walking only, he told me he supposed that I was not much used to walking, I told him no; he ordered the maid to make some hot water, and told me to go to the kitchen and bathe my feet in the warm water the maid had prepared for me, and to keep them in about a quarter of an hour, I did so; he then asked his son Tom if he would sleep with me; he supposed that when my feet were well soaked that I should go to bed. In the meantime, the wife of Mr. Wardel had a curiosity to know if I carried about me any live lumber, such as seamen and soldiers are in habit of associating with, and to come to a point with me, she asked me if I had no other clothes than those I had on,[17] I told her I had the linen I wore, on my back about five days; Mr. Wardel told her she had better give me one of Thomas's as I had none to change, after I had made a fair exchange, the next thing they put me to bed in company with their son; I then asked Tom if he knew my uncle, he said yes, he added that he knew William and Edward both, he told me he was going to town the next day, he said that if I staid till after breakfast I might ride behind him, I told him that I could not that I had no money, he said his father would'nt charge me any thing, upon which assurance I agreed to stay. Being very much fatigued I fell asleep; the next morning breakfast was ready soon after we rose, we ate breakfast, and after breakfast I was for going ahead, I told him I had no money to pay him, he said he did not mean to charge me any thing; said he I have more respect for your parents to charge you any thing, he then inquired of me how my feet was, I told him that they were a good deal better than they were the evening before; he told me to wait, that his son Thomas was going to town, and you can ride behind him and he will take you to your uncle. The horse was brought, I mounted behind his son Thomas. Thomas asked me as we were jogging along the road, if I intended to live with my uncle, I told him no, that I should try to get to America; he asked me how far that was, I told I did not know that, he asked me if I could walk there, I told him no, I'd have to go to sea again; says he to me, then you would have to run away again, I told him I did not know, he asked me if we stopped every night while at sea, I told him no indeed; says he God I would'nt like to go; I then turned upon him and asked him what he worked at, at home; he said he minded the horses, cows and sheep, sometimes harrowed, carried coals, &c; he asked me what I had done at sea, I told him I waited on the table for the officers, he asked me if ever I got whipped, I told him yes, often; said he then I'd run off too.

By this time the town of Handleby lay before us to our view; I asked him whereabouts in town my uncle lived, he told me right on the main road on to Hull; I asked him where the school-house was, he said just at the end of town; then we came to the store, where we both got off, he shewed me the house of my uncle, I bade him good bye. I went to my uncle's, I rapped at the door, I heard a female voice saying walk in, I went in and found my aunt sitting in the room, I asked her how she did, she said she was very well, she

---

[17] "Live lumber" apparently refers to extra garments that were worn for the purpose of being pawned if necessary. "Lumber" was slang for pawn. Eric Partridge, *A Dictionary of Slang and Unconventional English*, ed. Paul Beale (London, 1984).

asked me to sit down, I asked her if my uncle was at home, she then asked me
my name; I told her William Otter; a son of Edward Otter? I told her yes—
my lord! she exclaimed, I thought you was dead three years ago; she told me
to stay there; she went out and fetched my uncle from school, when she
returned she was crying, my uncle came in and looked at me very sharp, and
the first word he spoke, he said, why Bill is this you? I said yes that it was; he
took me by the hand, and asked me where in the name of God did I come
from. The tears started in his eyes, I told him I came from sea; he said that
my father and mother had heard that I was drowned three years ago, he said
he could hardly believe it possible that it was me, he asked me if I had eat any
thing that day; he told me to wait, he would get a young man to teach his
school for that day; my aunt asked me if I would like to see my father and
mother; many an hour, continued my aunt, was your mother here, and cried
about you; she said she would give any thing in the world if my mother was
there now. By this time my uncle came in, and sat down by me, and told me
now to tell him where I had been, he told his wife he could not believe that it
was me; he asked me what made me leave my father, I told him my father
whipped me for not weeding the garden, my aunt said that was true, my
mother had told her many times; my uncle repeated, can it be possible, that
you are here yet? for your father heard it a many a time that you was lost in
Greenland, your father heard by the ship Jane, that the ship you sailed in was
lost and all her crew; I told him that our ship was lost, but the whole crew
was picked up by the ship Jane, off a mountain of ice, (all except our cook, he
was lost,) that we were shared out, a boat's crew on one ship, another boat's
crew on another ship, until we were all shared out, all but us nine boys; we
remained on board the ship Jane, and on our way home was pressed on board
the Nonesuch for life; I cruised about until we got to London, four of us run
away, then I came down the canal to Newport, from Newport to Beverly and
from Beverly here.

　　Well my lad, you have undergone more than ever I should like to undergo
said my uncle to me; my uncle observed to my aunt, we must keep Bill very
close, for if the press-gang find him out they will take him again; would you
like to stay with me, or would you like to go after your father and mother to
America? I told my uncle I would prefer to go after my father and mother, he
said he did not know how to contrive ever to get me there, but as I had so
much good luck, he hoped that there was more in store for me; I asked him if
he knew Captain Clark, in Hull; he said he did not, but he would try to find
him out if he could do me any good, he asked me what Captain Clark could

do for me; I told him I knew if I could see him, that he could help me *off;* he asked me if I could depend on him, I told him I could; he told me he would go to Hull the next day; he asked me if I knew where he lived, I told him the time I went to sea that he lived in Dock street. My uncle went the next morning; he went to Dock street; Mr. Clark had left there, and moved to a place called the Walls, near the garrison; he went to his house, asked for Captain Clark, his wife told him that he was on board the ship at the Dock, that she would send for him, he then waited until Mr. Clark came, he asked if ever he had a boy bound to him of the name of William Otter; he said he did not know, he would look at his sea Journal, that he could tell him in a short time; he looked at his Journal and found an orphan boy of that name; he then asked Captain Clark where he had lost me, or where I had left him; he told him that they were all cast away in Greenland, we were all taken on board the Nonesuch by a press-gang; he then asked my uncle if he knew me, he told the Captain yes, that he was my uncle; he then asked my uncle if ever he had heard of me since, my uncle told him yes, that I had arrived at his house yesterday; said the Captain, the devil he has! Captain Clark requested of my uncle to bring me to him some night, saying that he would try his best to get me off to America; my uncle told him that he would bring me to him.

After this interview had ended between my uncle and Captain Clark, my uncle returned home; I asked my uncle if he had seen Captain Clark, he said that he had, and related to me all Captain Clark said to him. I asked my uncle where the Captain lived, he told me that he resided near the Walls, observing to me that we would go there the next evening. When evening came, the day appointed to go, my uncle took me on the horse behind him, and took me to the Captain's house; on our arrival at his house he was not at home, the Captain's lady asked us to walk in; she told us that it would not be long until he would be in; my uncle told her that this was the boy that belonged to the Captain, she observed that I was a fine hearty looking boy; she asked me how long I had been on board his majesty's ship: I told her nearly four years: she asked me how I liked it, I told her not very well. By this time the Captain came in, my uncle arose at the entrance of the Captain, and bade him a good evening, and told him here is the boy: Ah! said the Captain, is this the lad; said he, come here my lad, asked me if I knew him, I answered him yes sir, he then asked me if I ever was in Greenland, I told him I was; I then told him I was cast away? where was I when you was cast away was his inquiry of me, to find out if I knew any thing of the Greenland fleet; I told him that he went to dine on board the ship Jane; he said that I was the very boy that was with him, he then got his sea Journal to see if my name was on the roll, and he asked me if I did not tell him that my parents were dead, at the time he had me bound, I told him I did; and had recourse to that mode of duplicity, being fearful, that under any other circumstances, that he would not take me; *said he,* ah you young rascal; he observed that I was an orphan now, that I had neither father nor mother to go to; his remark depressed my spirits very much, which he observed; and to divert my mind from dwelling upon the idea of my forlorn condition, he jocularly asked, how I liked it when we were on the mountain of ice; I told him not very well, for John Mills was going to throw me overboard; what for, said the Captain to me; because I cried, that was pretty hard Bill, said he. He then asked me if I would like to go to America, I told him yes; says he, if you do you will have to ship as an orphan again; how would you like to go to the East Indies a trip with me, said the Captain to me; I told him that if I could not get to America, I would go with him; my uncle then told him, that if I could be got to America, it would be a very happy thing for my parents to see me once more, for they are under the impression that I had been drowned three years ago, as the news had arrived in England, that the ship had been lost as also the whole crew; the Captain said yes, that was the report until I arrived; the Captain then said, that it would be a hundred to one if he ever gets to America, my uncle asked him why and what would be the danger. The Captain alleged that I might be put on board a man of war, before he is out two days, as he has no master and no protector; my uncle said that it was dangerous in that way, for the captain would have to take me as a strong hand; my uncle said he did not know what to do for or with me: the Captain said that if I would agree to go with him, as he had been my master, that he could be my master yet, that he would take care of me, till the times would change; that I could go at any time in peaceable times; that I could make my uncle's house my home every time that I came into port; that he could write to my father that I was yet living and under his protection. My uncle told him that would be a very good plan; the Captain addressed me by saying, what do you say to *that Bill?* I told him that if I could not get to America, that I would stay with him, but would rather than stay, go to America; the Captain said if he heard or saw a good and safe chance to send me there, that he would, as he felt disposed to do all he could for me; he said that I did not know the dangers I had to undergo; his ship he said would not be ready to sail for one month, and if he could or did hear of a chance, he would let my uncle know; he instructed my uncle to keep me very close, the neighbors might get to know that I had deserted, and that I would be taken up; my uncle assured him that he would take care of me; and that as soon as his ship was ready or any other chance for America, he would give him due notice thereof. Well said my uncle we'll be going home; the Captain invited us to stop and take a drink of good old brandy; after taking a drink we bade the Captain good-bye, and returned to Handleby; there my uncle kept me in his garret for fifteen days; at the end of that time, Captain Clark wrote to my uncle, that we should come on as soon as we could, that he thought there was a chance for New York.

We started that night, I bade my aunt a farewell; she told me if I ever lived to get to my father and mother, to remember her to them, and to give her best respects to them, and she could hardly tell me for crying.

Then we went to Hull, then to Captain Clark's; we went into his house and asked for the Captain, and found him at home; he told my uncle he had a chance for me to get to New York, he said his mate had been on board an American ship, that they had lost a hand on their passage here;—it will not do for me to smuggle him away; if he should be retaken, and I gave an account how I was put there, he might be broke of his commission; but my mate will go with him, said the Captain; he told my uncle to tell the captain of the American vessel my situation, and observed that then there could be no risk to run, only on my part; the mate accordingly went with us on board the American ship, introduced us to the American Captain, and asked the Captain if he wanted a hand; he said yes, that he had lost one coming in, that he got crazy and jumped overboard; he told him here is a boy that he wanted to send to America; he asked him if I was an American boy, the mate told him that I was not, but that my parents were in America, the American Captain asked me if I had ever been to sea, I told him yes, he asked me what I could do; I told him I could hand and reef a little;[18] he asked me if I could steer, I told him a little, but not much; he asked me if I could splice a rope, I answered him I could not; he then asked me what ship I had belonged to, and where I had been, I told him I belonged to the service and that I had deserted; he said that if you go along with me you will be taken again; the

---

[18] "The common saying [is] that to hand, reef and steer makes a sailor," wrote Richard Henry Dana, *The Seaman's Friend* (Boston, 1851), p. 162. "Hand" was to do the work of a common seaman. "Reef" is defined as the horizontal portion of a sail "which may be . . . rolled or folded up in order to diminish the extent of canvas exposed to the wind" (*Oxford English Dictionary*). Such was the task of the more experienced able seaman: see Marcus Rediker, *Between the Devil and the Deep Blue Sea: Merchant Seamen, Pirates and the Anglo-American Maritime World, 1700–1750* (Cambridge, 1987), pp. 85–86; and N.A.M. Rodger, *Wooden World: An Anatomy of the Georgian Navy* (London, 1988), pp. 164–182.

English mate spoke and told him way, said the American Captain. He then asked my uncle how he would like to send me, my uncle told him just as he and I agreed; and then he said to my uncle, if he goes, that it must be at my own risk, my uncle said yes; I told him that I had been at a risk all my life time; he asked me if I could do that man's duty if he would take me to America in safety, what would I ask him for the voyage; I told him I would ask him nothing, he said that was cheap enough; he then told my uncle that he would take me, my uncle said very well, that he was very glad of it, asked him when he would go; in about five days he would have his cargo in; he asked my uncle in what port of America my father was in—my uncle said he did not know exactly, but he believed near the city of New York; my uncle asked the Captain where his ship belonged to; said he New London, but the cargo was to go to New York; the English mate then asked what his cargo was, he told him chiefly dry goods; my uncle then asked the Captain his name, he told him William Leeds,[19] he then asked my uncle my father's name, he told him Edward Otter; the Captain put down mine and my father's name in a book; he asked my uncle if I had any clothes my uncle told him I had no suitable seafaring clothing, as I had deserted I dare not wear them, my uncle said he would buy me clothing; the Captain said no, as the boy had offered so generous, that he would rig me out; then my uncle asked him where I should stay until he should set sail: the English mate told him, that I had better remain at Captain Clark's, until he, the American captain would set sail; the Captain said yes, for I would have to be smuggled out past the custom house Officers; the English mate then gave him the number of Captain Clark's house, and gave him an invitation to call to see the Captain, that he could give him all information required about me; the American Captain told the mate that he would call, in a day or two. So then we went to Captain Clark's, and the Captain asked me if I had got the birth, I told him yes sir; he then said, you and the yankee for it; he asked the mate when she was to set sail, he told him in about five days, he told me I'd better be getting ready; the mate told him then that the Yankee would call up to see him in a day or two, the Captain said he would be very glad to see him; told me to stay with him until he was ready to go, I told him very well sir, and glad of it; my uncle then told the Captain he would go home, that he would call to see me again before I would start; he then went home; the Captain then ordered me to work for my mistress until I would start. Captain Clark asked me if my

---

[19] Captain Leeds's first name was actually Lodowick, see footnote 21.

uncle intended to buy any seafaring clothes for me, I told him no, that the Yankee Captain was going to buy some for me; he said that was very clever of him; he told the mate that this was the best chance I ever could get, he believed that the d—— young rascal was born to good luck; the mate answered, the bigger the devil the better the luck. The Captain said to me, well Bill, what will you do if you are taken again? I told him runaway again. Here ended our conversation, he ordered me to the kitchen to get my supper; after I had supped I went to bed; in the morning the mate called me up, and told me there are the Captain's boots to clean; after I had done with that job I got my breakfast; then the mate told me to tell the maid to give me the market basket, and follow him to market; I went to market, I came home again and gave the maid the provisions; she asked me if ever I cleaned any knives and forks, I told her yes; she then said to me, here is a good job for you, pointing to a lot of them; I fell to and cleaned them; she asked me if was done; I told her I was; she then ordered me to carry them up to my mistress; I carried them up to her; I asked if those would do, she told me they were elegant, she asked me if ever I had cleaned any knives and forks before; I told her O yes, many a time; she said she supposed I had been a cabin boy, I told her I had, ever since I had been in the navy; I suppose you know how to set a table, I told her yes; I asked her when I should set it, she said in about an hour; I went back into the kitchen, the maid asked me if I could peel potatoes, I fell to and peeled a small pot full; when I was done peeling potatoes, she asked me if ever I had basted any meat—I told her I never did, but thought I could do it if I saw how it was done; she picked up the ladle, and poured the gravy over the meat while turning on the spit; then I basted the beef till I was nearly roasted myself. My mistress, God bless her soul, relieved me by calling me in to set the table; I sat the table, carried up the dinner; and the Captain came home to dinner; I stood behind his back. Well Bill, said he, you got into business—yes sir, I replied; my mistress then said that he should look at the knives and forks; he asked me if that (meaning the knives and forks,) was some of my work; she answered him yes; indeed he observed to her, as he had done the work so nice, that she should keep me, she said that she would have no objections, if I would consent to stay, turning himself to me and saying, what do you say to *that Bill*. I told him I would rather go to America; he said that he supposed so. After the dinner was over I began to clear off the table, and about cleaning knives and forks as usual. The evening after that captain Leeds was introduced to captain Clark by the chief mate as the American Captain.

Captain Clark began the conversation with the Yankee Captain, by inquiring of him, to what part of America he was bound? he replied, that he was bound to New York; he asked him if he was acquainted about New York, he said he was not much acquainted about New York, as he belonged to New London.[20] He then asked Captain Leeds if he was willing to take me along to America; he said yes, that he would try. That he would do all for me he could, then told him that he was my former master, saying that I had been in his Majesty's service since he was cast away from him; that he could not say much about me, as I had been absent from him for two or three years; that it was his wish for me to get to my parents again, if it were possible for me to get there. He told him that he must be aware of the fleet on his passage going to America, if they get their eyes on him he will be re-taken as a stray hand. He answered that he was well aware of that, as he had several times been examined on his voyage to Europe. Captain Clark then asked him, if in case he came to America, and could not find my parents, what would he do with me? He told him that he knew no other way than, that if I ever got there, to advertise me, and if my parents were to be found, that I could then go to them. Then Captain Clark observed there would be no danger, provided his parents are yet living, and what would he do with me in case they cannot be found. He said, that in such an event he should give me choice to be bound to him, or to any body else; he then asked him when he thought he would set sail; he thought the next evening, if the wind was fair, and if the wind was unfair, he should sail the morning following, by high tide. Then Captain Clark asked me if I was willing to go with that gentleman, I told him I was. He then said that he would write a few lines to my uncle to come up that afternoon. He then took the Captain's name down and the date, and told him that if I was not a good boy he hoped that he would make one out of me; the Yankee told him that he would do all that lay in his power for me. The Captain asked him how it was about my clothing, who was to clothe me; the Yankee said that he told my uncle he would clothe me for the voyage. The Captain told me, now says he, boy you belong to Captain Leeds. Then my mistress told me to come into the other room. After we got into the room, she began to give me a lecture, by saying she hoped that I would be a good boy, until I got home to my parents again. She backed it with half a guinea, and sewed it in my pocket. She began to cry and enjoined it upon me never

[20] That Captain Leeds's home port was New London is confirmed by the (New York) *Commercial Advertiser*, 30 September 1801 See footnote 23.

to show it to any body until I came to America, and added a black silk handkerchief to her present, and then told me that was all she had to give me, and so ended the admonition of Mrs. Clark. We came out. The Yankee asked me if I was ready to go. I answered him I was. I shook hands with Captain Clark and his lady, and bade them a farewell.

I was taken down Dock street, by the Yankee Captain, he there bought me two suits of clothes, and from there took me on board the ship Charlotte,[21] and told his crew that he had cheated the English, he had taken an English boy, and observed to me to keep below until he set sail. The next day, after I had entered on board of the American ship, my uncle came on board our ship, and asked me if we were going to set sail soon. I told him yes, if the wind was fair, we were to sail that evening, and if not, that we would sail the next morning. He inquired of me where the Captain was. The mate of the ship told him that he went to the Customs House to get his papers, and that it would not be long before he would be on board. My uncle asked me if I had got my clothes, I told him I had, and showed them to him, he said that it was very clever indeed, of the Captain. The mate went on deck; my uncle asked me if I had any money; I told him yes, I had half a guinea, which my mistress had given me. He observed that she was very kind to me. He asked me where I had it; I told him that she sewed it in my pocket, he told me, if I would be a good boy that he would give me a guinea, and I should keep it until I got home. He asked the mate permission to let me go on shore about five minutes, the mate most cordially granted the request of my uncle. We went to an ale house, called for a quart of ale; while we were drinking the ale, he asked the landlady for a needle and thread, and gave her the guinea and requested her to sew it in my waistcoat pocket, along side of the half guinea which had been placed there by my mistress. She did so, and while she performed that office, she asked my uncle where I was going, he told her I was going to sea. From there we went out, and my uncle purchased a small chest for me, and told me to keep that vest in the chest until I got to America. In the next place we returned on board the ship Charlotte, and on our return the Captain was also on board. My uncle told the Captain he had purchased a chest for me to keep my clothes in, he observed all was right, and added he could have got one for me; then my uncle gave the Captain a letter with the request to give it to my father, if he got safe to America; he

[21] On 27 June 1801 the *Hull Advertiser* ran a notice for the "American ship CHARLOTTE," 180 tons, Lodowick Leeds, captain, bound for New York. It was to "sail in early July."

told him he would. The Captain then took out his brandy bottle, as a body would, and we all took a drink; my uncle then requested the captain to do all for me he could to get me home to my parents, inasmuch as I had a great many ups and downs. The Captain assured my uncle that on his part no pains should be spared to accomplish the object of my design, if his parents lived in the city of New York or in the vicinity, as he should advertise me when he came there, and if they cannot be found, why I might if I chose, take a voyage with him to the West Indies, and perhaps in that time they might be found out. My uncle then asked him how long he would lay at New York; the Captain replied to that inquiry, that his stay would be about two weeks. My uncle concluded by saying, that he could say and do nothing more for me; that he should do the best he could for me, and asked the Captain if he intended to set sail that night; he said he thought he would, if the wind was any way fair, and tendered his hand to me, and gave me a farewell and wished us a safe and pleasant voyage.

About eight o'clock at night the wind sprang up and blew a pleasant gale; we hoisted sail and put out, and I then bade my native land and the city of my nativity, a last adieu. The Captain ordered me to go up to the main top, and to lay there until we had passed the Custom House officers; we passed them safe, and sailed about one hour, the wind changed, we had to cast anchor till the next morning in the river Urnber.[22]

22 The River Humber.

New York

The next morning about 9 o'clock we hoisted sail. The Captain said that they must hide me until we had passed his Majesty's guard ship laying at the Capes, where we had to undergo another examination. They put me down between decks, and hid me by throwing potatoes over me, and got safe past the guard ship, and that was the last regular fiery ordeal we had to pass, as for the rest they were promiscuous. We were hailed on our passage from the city of Hull, England, until we came to the city of New York in North America, nine times by the English. In the mean time we had a pleasant voyage, and arrived in the month of September, in the 16th year of my age, in the Capes off New York.[23] Captain Leeds used me very well while in his service. We were, as it is technically termed, quarantined two days. The Medical board, under whose examination we fell, pronounced us healthy. We then got a pilot to pilot us into New York. We arrived at the wharf on a Wednesday about 4 o'clock in the afternoon. I jumped on shore. The next day after our arrival, the mate and I went to "Fly Market" to buy provisions,[24] after the mate had purchased as many provisions as we wanted, I carried them on board our ship. I stole back again into the market, and went up to a woman who had peaches for sale, and asked her how she sold them, she told me she sold them for twelve and a half cents per peck. The reader will please bear in mind, that peaches in the markets in England generally sell from a penny to two pence a piece. I then asked how much a

---

[23] (New York) *Commercial Advertiser,* 30 September 1801: "SHIP NEWS. *Arrivals—this morning,* . . . Ship Charlotte, [Capt] Leads, of New-London, 63 days from Hull, with dry goods, &c. to Wm. Nelson and Co."

[24] The city's main market, located at Pearl Street and Maiden Lane.

half a peck was, with a view to find what the value of 12½ cents was. She told me a fip,[25] and then I was just as wise as I was before. I pulled off my cap and told her to pour them into it. While she was pouring out the peaches into my cap, I took out my knife and began to rip the seam that enveloped the half guinea which my mistress had given me; I handed the half guinea to her and began to eat of the peaches. She said to me that I should not come there to fool her, that this is only a pocket piece usually denominated a counter, she not knowing the value of the half guinea handed it back to me. I took it again, and put it in my pocket, and pretty near at the same time we both made a grab at my cap, and she succeeded in getting it; she began to box it about my ears, and I began to let her have it. I made an effort and got my cap from her, and after I had my cap again, I began to let her have it for a Yankee. Our affray took place opposite an apothecary shop, the gentleman standing in the door came and asked what was the matter; she told him the young R— sc—l came to cheat her out of her peaches with a pocket piece. I, in defence of that charge preferred against me, denied it, and alleged it was half a guinea, and to justify my assertion, I told him to take a look at it, and handed the half guinea to him, he told me it was a good half guinea, and asked me where I had got it; I told him I had got it in England, from my mistress; he offered to change it for me if I wished it; I told him he should; he then weighed it, and gave me silver for it, and told me to go and demand my peaches. I gave the old lady a fip; she gave me the peaches, and told me that I was a good boy, after she had trounced me, at least I gave her no thanks for her courtesy.

I then started with my peaches towards the wharf, eating them, stones and all; after I had eat about two thirds of them, I began to avoid eating the stones, and was content with eating peach. After I had finished my half peck of peaches I went on board of our ship; the Captain asked where I had been, I told him I had been at market, getting some peaches, he asked me if I had got any; he asked me how many I had got, I told him half a peck, he asked me where they were, I told him I had eat them, when he heard that he observed, they will kill you,[26] and at his remark I began to be alarmed, and the fright

---

25 A fivepenny bit, "fip" usually meant a Spanish half real which circulated widely in this period and which had a value of about six cents. Mitford M. Mathews, ed., *A Dictionary of Americanisms on Historical Principles* (Chicago, 1951).

26 Peach pits contain a small amount of cyanide, and in a few cases children have died from eating them. Alexander Wynter Blyth, *Poisons, Their Effects and Detection* (New York, 1885), 1:170.

agitating my mind and a half peck of peaches in my stomach, I began to sicken, he told me to come into the cabin and he would give me something to work them off, and what he gave me I did not know, but in a short time the way that *them* peach stones flew was a *caution* to the world. He then observed that I had better not eat any more, as they might throw me into a spell of sickness, inasmuch as I was not accustomed to the climate.

He told me that the next morning he would advertise me in the Daily Advertiser, and he did so;[27] he asked me if I thought I would know my father, if I would see him; I told him I did not know, he told me to keep a look out at Market, as my father was a gardener, every day as I went to market. I, however, never saw him at the market as I knew of.

We were in New York about nine days, it happened to be on a Sunday that my father came on board our ship in company with some other man. I was laying on the deck, he asked me if this was the ship Charlotte, I told him yes; he then asked me if the captain was on board, I answered him he was, he is in the cabin, said I to him; he went down into the cabin and asked the captain if he had an English boy on board, the captain told him he had. My father then asked the captain for the name, the captain then told him his name was William Otter, he then asked him *his* name, he told him that his name was Edward Otter;[28] then the captain called me down into the cabin, and pointing to me, says he, there is the boy, and addressing himself to me, said, Bill there is your father; my father, upon this introduction of the captain took me by the hand, crying, asked me if I knew him, I told him yes, he then asked how I ever had got here, I told him I worked my passage, he then told the captain that he had heard that I was lost near four years ago; he thought from what he had then heard, that he never would see me again in this world. The Captain then handed to him the letter which he had taken from my uncle to my father, and gave it to him. My father read the letter which gave him a full account and explanation of my situation from the time

---

[27] I was unable to find this advertisement in the aptly named *Daily Advertiser* or in the *Commercial Advertiser*. The 13 October to 20 October issues of the *Daily Advertiser* are lost. It is possible that the notice appeared in one of the missing issues, but why would Captain Leeds wait two weeks before advertising Otter? If the advertisement did not appear, how did Otter's father find him? One possibility is that Leeds mentioned having Otter on board to the *Charlotte*'s owner, William Neilson, who knew and may even have employed Otter's father. See p. 30 and footnote 31.

[28] *Longworth's American Almanac, New-York Register, and City-Directory* (New York, 1803) lists "Edward Otter, gardener, Clinton," though this is more likely William's brother Edward.

I had got from my old master until I stood before him on the ship Charlotte, lying in the harbor, his next inquiry was of the captain, if he had any thing to pay, for bringing me to him, he said no, that if any pay was going, that it was coming to me. My father told my captain that he was anxious to take me home to my mother, he asked my father where he lived, he told him that he lived three miles from the city, at a place called Sandy Hill,[29] he requested of my father to bring me back in a day or two, that he wanted to see me before he sailed, as I had done him a particular kindness, which he could never forget. The captain told me to leave my clothes on board until I came back. My father bade the captain good bye, and off me and my father started together for Sandy Hill.

At my arrival in the bosom of my family, my mother, sisters and brothers were so overjoyed that language is too weak to express the sensations we labored under. My mother wept holy, pious tears of joy, and my brothers and sisters shook hands most cordially with me. It being evening, we went to supper.

My father began to ask me of my journies and travels; I related them to him the same as I have given them as related to my uncle; he said, the chances were as five hundred to one that I ever got to him, and added that I should never go to sea again while he lived, with his consent, although he believed I had the luck to go any where throughout the world, he asked me if while on the sea, I ever remembered the whipping he had given me. My mother then observed that whipping saved the rest many a whipping and hoped that he would never whip me again. I told him if he did that I would go to sea again. He asked me if I was never whipped while I was at sea? I answered, yes, sometimes. He asked me, why I did not run away from there. I told him I could not. He told my mother that he would take me and show me to General Nelson the next morning.[30]

---

[29] Sandy Hill, or the Sand Hills, was a group of low hills stretching from approximately where the junction of Spring and Hudson Streets are today to Lafayette Street. Sand Hill Road, sometimes called Greenwich Lane, formerly ran along the present Gansevoort St.; "thence north-easterly and easterly along the present line of Greenwich Ave. to Astor Place" (see Map 1). I.N. Phelps Stokes, *The Iconography of Manhattan Island, 1498–1909* (New York, 1918), 3:1001.

[30] William Neilson (also spelled Nelson) was a wealthy New York City merchant. The "General" is puzzling, for Neilson never held a military position. It seems that here and elsewhere in *History* Otter uses "General" simply as an honorific term for a distinguished man. The variant spelling "Nelson" is found in Helen M. Morgan, ed., *A Season in New York, 1801: Letters of Harriet and Marcia Trumbell* (Pittsburgh, 1969), p. 160.

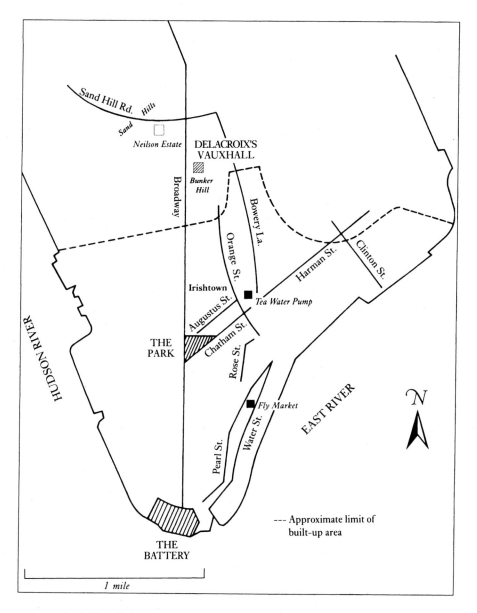

MAP 1. New York City in Otter's time, showing places mentioned in the text.

Accordingly, he took me to the General's house.[31] My father said to him, that here was his lost boy who had just arrived.[32] He asked my father if I was his son. My father told him I was. The general asked me where I came from. I told him that I came from England. He asked me how I came here. I told him that I worked my passage. He said that I deserved credit for that and asked my father what he intended to do with me. Father told him he did not know. Well, said the General, give him to me. My father, in reply to general Nelson said, That he would leave it all to myself.

When I found that I was to select a birth for myself, I inquired what I should have to do. He told me that I would be employed in the capacity of his waiter, ride behind his carriage for one year, and told me if after that I would prove myself a good boy, he would put me in his counting house and make a man of me. Taking him at his word, I consented that I would come. The general told my father that he should take me through the city and show me the different modes and fashions of this country. My father told him that he intended to do so, as I had to go back to the ship again on which I had left all my clothing. The general cautioned my father, and expressed the apprehension that the captain of the vessel might persuade, and take me from my father again. Father told him that he would take care of that, as he intended that I should never go to sea again with his consent. With that he bade the general good-bye, and off we started for New-York.

We then went to the ship to see captain Leeds, he the captain asked, how I came on, and how I liked the country. I told him I liked it very well. He

---

[31] Neilson, according to Joseph A. Scoville, had "one of the most extensive commercial houses in the city" in 1800 The Neilson firm engaged mainly in trade with Hull and Bristol and owned the *Charlotte,* the ship on which Otter crossed the Atlantic. Neilson was also a partner in an extensive marine insurance company.

As noted by Scoville, "the old gentleman resided in the country" with his house on Broadway and Sand Hill Road. His office was on Water Street. Citing "*Liber Deeds* LVII:108," I.N. Phelps Stokes located the Neilson estate at the southwest corner of Sand Hill Road and Greene Street (see Map 1). Scoville, *The Old Merchants of New York City* (New York, 1862), 3: 142–148, quotation p. 147. Phelps Stokes, *Iconography of Manhattan Island,* 5· 1365 (10 April 1799).

[32] Otter had just crossed the Atlantic on one of Neilson's ships and is now introduced to that very man. Perhaps Otter is confused or hiding something, but my guess is that these circumstances are simply coincidental. Neilson carried on an extensive Hull trade, and anyone sailing between Hull and New York probably had a fairly high likelihood of making the voyage on a Neilson ship.

The Neilson-Hull link probably explains the relationship between Neilson and Otter's father, a recent immigrant from Hull. Sand Hill was north of the built-up area of the city (see Map 1), and the fact that both Otter's father and Neilson lived there is unusual and suggests that Otter's father may have been the gardener at Neilson's country home.

asked me if I intended to stay with my father, or go with him a trip to the West India Islands. I told him I would not go with him as I had got a place. He expressed a happiness at the idea of my stay. He told my father that for my good conduct towards him while in his service he felt it his bounden duty to reward me. And applying the action to the words he reached into his pocket and pulled out eight dollars and gave them to me as a perquisite for special services rendered to him, he also requested my father to write to captain Clark in Hull to let the captain know that I had arrived in safety at my place of destination. Father promised him that he would do that by the first packet that would sail for England.

He next got out his bottle of Cogniac, inviting us to take a drink; we did so, and then I took my clothes, bade captain Leeds farewell, and put out on shore.

I left my chest in the grocery in market till the next day and went to my father's place of residence; the day after he brought my chest home, and I was safely moored in the paternal circle, surrounded by my brothers and sisters. I walked about for three or four days to and from the city, when I got tired of that I told my father that I would go to the general's. My father accordingly took me there that evening and told him that here was his son who had expressed a wish to come to him, the general asked me if I could wait on the table, clean knives and forks, shoes and boots. I answered him that I could do all these things. He asked me if I knew how to drink brandy, I said, yes, I knew that too. He said he liked me for that, as I had told the truth, for, said he, if I could not hide brandy, that I was no sailor. We took a drink, he asked me how often we got it at sea, I told him whenever the captain gave it to us, says he, That is exactly my rule, you are never to drink any unless I give it to you; and that was the first and the last drink of brandy we took either jointly or severally while in the general's service, by, and with the advice and consent of the general, I nevertheless, once in a while would take a horn with my own consent; yet I never consulted the general upon that subject. The general called up a footman, and the footman gave me an invitation to go down to the kitchen and take supper. I went down with him and ate supper, the footman asked me if I was coming there to be a waiter, I told him yes, he asked me if I had just come from England, that question I also answered affirmatively, he asked me if ever I had waited on a table before, I told him I had while at sea, he asked me how we sat a table in a storm, did the tables never upset. I told him that the tables could not upset as they were screwed to the floor. He then asked me if I knew how to ride a horse; I told him, no, I never rode much; he told me I would have to learn, that I would have to ride behind the general's carriage everyday to the city. I told him I should like that.

After a short time we went to bed; as I had been used to getting up on the morning watch, he asked what I got up so early for, I told him it was our watch, he asked me to come to bed, it was too early to get up. I went to bed again and laid there till he called me up. Then we all got out of bed, came down, swept the parlor and began to set the table for breakfast; he told me that would be my exercise every morning. When we all got done, he told me to come to the stable he would show me the pony which I would have to ride; when I saw the pony I said it was a very pretty little horse; he told me that I would have to take care of myself as he had a good many bad tricks about him. I told him I could ride him; the coachman said he would see; he saddled and bridled the poney and brought him out, to see me perform on the green; I told him that he should get on first, he did so, and rode him around the green, and then dismounted; then I got on the poney, I rode him about half way around the green, the coachman told me to give him the whip, when I applied the timber the pony began to rear and kick till overboard I went, to the amusement of the coachman and footman, for them my performance was rare sport; the poney ran to the stable, the coachman caught him; he jumped on him and rode him around the green as hard as the poney could lay legs to ground, saying he would let him know what he was about; he came to me and asked me if I was hurt, I told him I was not; he then encouraged me to try the poney again, accordingly I mounted him the second time, and when I was fairly planted on him he started off with me and ran two rounds around the green as hard as he could lay legs to the ground. The general in the mean time, stood in his piazza, seeing that the coachman had me in training, and seeing the poney perform—he called to me, saying, hang to the rigging, my lad; having fair wind before me I sailed right in the wind's eye, holding on to the reins and mane as hard as ever I could; and this was the first time I caught the idea by occular demonstration, that there was no stop in a horse-race. The pony after the second round, stopped short near his stable door, and over his head I went off again; the coachman came and picked me up, and asked me if I was hurt; I told him I was not; he then allowed that I had done very well for that time, that, in his opinion, I would soon learn to ride.

After our performance of horsemanship had ended, the footman and myself went to the house, washed ourselves, and then began to carry up the breakfast; the footman told me; I would have to stand at the General's chair, and he would stand at the madam's chair; the General observed to me, that I had a fair sail that morning; I told him yes sir; he then asked me, if the ships kicked up behind, as did the one I was on this morning; I replied that they did not; the madam asked the General where I had been that morning; the General told her that John was learning me to ride the poney; she asked him if I had a fall; I answered the question, seeing that the point of it was directed at me, that I only got two falls. She asked me if I got hurt; I told her no madam; she said I was very lucky; the General then observed, my dear, don't you know that a sailor cannot be killed on land? She observed, that it would be well for me, if I remained always on land. Breakfast being over, and the table cleared off, we went to the kitchen, and took our breakfast. The General called up the footman, and told him, that after we had our work done, he should take me to the city, to Mr. Nicholson's, to have my measure taken for two suits of livery, and to have them made in that week; he then hitched up a horse in a gig; we got in, rode to the city, got measured, and came back. I then went about my usual occupation, till the next week; when I got my livery suits, the General told me to be dressed, and prepared to ride to the city on that day, at three o'clock; at the hour appointed. I was ready; the carriage was brought before the door. I mounted my poney, and we started for the city. The General once or twice called to me, while on the road, if I was there: I answered him, yes sir. We went on very well, until we came to the foot of Bunker's hill.[33] I was a short distance behind the carriage; I met a negro on a horse, with a basket before him; my poney took fright, and away he went with me, took off the road, along the foot of Bunker's hill, and ran about half a mile, before I could stop him, when I had stopped him, I wheeled him about again taking after the carriage as hard as I could go. The general was waiting at the head of Broadway to see what had become of me, I rode up to him and he asked me where I had been, I told him that the poney, scared at the negro I had met with who had a basket on his horse, had run off with me. He laughed, and told me to stick close to the carriage and hold him as hard as I could; and the harder I held the little rascal the worse he behaved himself. From there we went on very well until we came to the head of Pearl street; as a carriage passed us by, going pretty fast, and I was looking about, he began to rear and pitch, and down I went; a gentleman on the pavement caught my poney by the bridle and asked if I was

[33] A low hill near the intersection of Grand and Centre Streets, three blocks to the east of Broadway.

hurt; I told him I was not, I jumped on the poney again and had not time to dust my coat; I rode along after the carriage, till we came to the general's counting house:[34] the general told me to get off and open the carriage door, and let the pony stand, who bye the bye knew his business better than I did, as he had been trained to stand by the carriage, at any place where it might stop. I opened the carriage door, the general got out and asked me how my coat became so dusty. I told him that the poney had thrown me at the head of the street; he asked me if I was hurt; I told him I was not. He admired my good fortune by saying that I was very lucky in my undertakings, and ordered me to go into the counting house to get the dust brushed off my coat. He then told the coachman to call for him at the usual hour, the coachman told me to come up on the box to him. I asked what I should do with the poney, he told me to put the reins behind the saddle and let him go; I did as he directed me and got on, he turned the carriage up Chatham street to the tea-water pump;[35] he told me to get down and give the horses some water; and he told me to look if the poney was behind, I looked and he was there; I watered him also, he told me after the horses had all been watered to get on the box again, that we would take a ride up to Bowery Lane, about one mile to a tavern; he asked me if I would take a drink of something, and not being in the habit of refusing those things, I told him I would; he drank some brandy, and staid there about one hour; then we started off from there and came round by the ship-yards to Pearl St. to the counting house; waited there about half an hour. The general stepped into his carriage and we went home, and went to my usual employment.

The next morning I had to undergo my usual morning drill, which was that of riding the poney. I succeeded very well on that morning.

About the month of October general Nelson changed his residence from Sandy Hill, and moved into the city of New York. I waited on the table about six months he one day asked me how I would like to take a birth in the counting house, I told him very well. The madam asked the general, what he would have there to do for me, he told her to go on errands and keep the counting house clean; accordingly I was placed in the counting house; my work was to keep it clean, help to hoist in goods, &c.; and remained in that occupation about four months; by this time I had contracted acquaintances,

---

[34] 46 Water Street.

[35] This pump, on Chatham Street (now Park Row), east of Orange (now Baxter) Street (see Figure 1), was a well-known city landmark in this period. It was famed for the high quality of its water, which New Yorkers used for tea.

FIG. 1. William P. Chappel, *Tea Water Pump*, New York City, 1807. The Metropolitan Museum of Art, The Edward W. C. Arnold Collection of New York Prints, Maps and Pictures, Bequest of Edward W. C. Arnold, 1954 (54.90.504).

who undertook to advise me to leave that birth and go and learn a trade; I did not know exactly how to get away with any kind of credit to myself; I began to neglect my business: the general gave me a scolding for my inattention to business, upon which I put out and went home to my father's. My father asked me what was the matter, I honestly told him that the general had given me a scolding upon the strength of which I had put out; he asked me what had I done, I told him I had not done any thing; which bye the bye, was the precise reason for which he gave me the scolding. My father said that he would go and see the general, I told him he need not give himself any trouble about it as I intended to learn a trade; he then asked me what I intended to learn; I replied I did not know as I had not spent a serious thought about it; he said that I had better stay with the general, that he would make a man out of me. I then told my father in plain terms not to be misunderstood, that I never would go back to him again. I knew that my father would not insist upon my going back to the general for fear I would go to sea again which idea my father had conceived an abhorrence for; he said that he must go and tell the general that you intend to learn a trade, and that he should not expect you to return to him; accordingly he went and asked the general what was the matter between him and myself, the general alleged that I had got into bad habits by running about at nights and neglected my business; and now, said he, is the only time to break him of them: my father agreed with the general, but was afraid of using prompt and coercive measures, lest I might go to sea again. The general replied, Yes, very true; but added, that some means should be taken to break me of them: he continued, that if I did not choose to come again that he did not wish me to return contrary to my will but would have liked to keep me very well.

My father then came home and told me all the general had alleged against me, said he hoped that I would be a good boy, and carry myself straight, and would get into some useful occupation; he then asked me a second time what I intended to learn, I told him I thought I would learn to be a shoemaker; he immediately consented if I could get a good master. I went to market with my father every day, at length I found for myself a master by the name of John Paxton, a resident in Water street in the city of New York, to him I went upon probation of a fortnight's duration, and staid with him a week all but three days, and then put out. From there I went home again, my father asked me how I liked the trade; to that enquiry I answered, that I did not like it at all, I had quit it; he asked me if I had told Mr. Paxton so; I told him I had; he asked me why I had quit; I told Mr. Paxton that it hurt me across my breast; my father asked me what are you going to learn now, I told him I did not know yet; I then walked about the city for two or three days.

I hunted for myself a master, in the meantime, and took a notion to learn the venitian blind making business, and found for myself a master in a man of the name of William Howard, who followed that business in Broadway, opposite the *park* he also took me on probation (as I had no notion to run a head of the wind) for two weeks; which is the established rule in the city, as to taking apprentices on probation. Mr. Howard put me at painting blinds; in that office I held out five days and found that the effects of the paint, on my part was intolerable; I told Mr. Howard I believed I would leave him, that I could not stand it, I would go home; he said, well you must know best yourself, I do not intend to persuade you against your own will,—and there, and in manner aforesaid, ended my second apprenticeship, and I put out home. When I came home my father was absent, my mother asked me how I liked my new trade; I told her I had quit; why, said she, William you learn your trades quick; I told her yes; and what are you going to do now, contin- ued my mother: I told her I did not know. In the evening my father came home; my mother told him that I had learned another trade; he then asked me had I quit again; I told him yes; he asked me if I had told Mr. Howard, that I intended to quit; I told him I had; he then said that was right. He then asked me what I would join next, I told him I thought I would try to learn the carpenter business; well, said he, seek for yourself another master, I told him I would; accordingly I went in quest of a master and got one, by the name of Gausman, a Scotchman, in Broadway:[36] he put me to sawing out boards all that week; on Sunday I went home; father asked how I come on, I told him very well, he said he was glad to hear it, hoping I would get myself bound the next week, I told him I would wait till next week was over before I got myself bound; I kept on sawing boards until Thursday; I told the foreman I believed I would quit it, that I had the back-ache and the work was too hard: and without any further ceremony I put out for home, and so ended my third apprenticeship. My father asked me how I came on at the carpenter's business; I told him I had quit it, he then gave me to understand that he entertained the thought that hard work and myself had had a falling out; I told him yes, that I did not like it much. He told me in good earnest to make up my mind and go to some trade and stick to it and learn it, as I was fooling away my time to no purpose, in the way I had been leaving trades; as bye the bye, I was master of none: and that after a while my name would become so notorious that I could not get a master, as he wished to see me do well; and if I got a master again to get myself bound straightway. If I did not do that, I would never get a trade.

I then took a notion to learn the bricklaying and plastering business, and went to hunt a master in good earnest, and found one by the name of Kenweth King.[37] I asked him if he would take a boy and learn him his trade; he asked if I was the boy, I told him yes, he then asked me my name and where I lived, which inquiries I answered; he told me to bring my father there the next day, I told him I would; the next day about two o'clock according to promise my father and myself called to see Mr. King. My father signified a wish to have me bound instanter as I had so many masters, and flew as often too; Mr. King told my father he had no apprehension about

---

[36] *Longworth's American Almanac, New-York Register, and City-Directory* (New York, 1802) lists "Gossman, Jacob, carpenter, 244 William."

[37] "King, Kenith, mason and builder, 18 Rose," in *Longworth's American Almanac, New-York Register, and City-Directory* (New York, 1803).

him; but that he could make a good boy out of me, as he had no less than eight boys at that time; my father told him if it suited, he would like to have me bound on the spot, to which Mr. King said he had no objections if I was agreed; I told him I was perfectly satisfied, and we went straight to a squire-shop and got myself bound for four years.[38] The next morning I went to work in my new birth, and worked on till Saturday evening; I asked permission of my master to go home and see my parents, he consented I might go provided I returned on Sunday evening; I told him I would; I went home, and father asked me how I come on. I told him very well; he asked if I liked my trade and my master, I told him I did; he said he was very glad to hear it, hoped that I would stay and learn my trade and make myself master of it. My mother said that she was glad that I had found a man and trade that I liked.

On Sunday evening, according to promise, I returned to my master and went to work as usual, and worked about a year at my trade; where my mother sent for me, being then afflicted with infirmity and sickness, she made a dying request, by saying she hoped that I never would go to sea again, that I would stay with my master, learn my trade, and be a good boy, I made the promise to her that I never would go to sea again, and staid at home until I had performed the last sad sepultural rights; I saw her interred. After my mother's death I returned to my master, and went to work at my trade; in about eight months after the death of my mother,[39] my father went to Charleston with garden seeds and fruit trees, returned home sick, to the house of Thomas Mills, a brother-in-law of mine, who had married my eldest sister, with whom my father resided; Mr. Mills, by profession a lawyer,[40] drew an instrument of writing, purporting to be the last will and testament of my father, in which said instrument Mr. Mills was the sole heir, as it afterwards turned out; which will be referred to more particularly in the sequel, meaning to return to the history of my father whom we have left sick at the house of Mr. Mills, intermarried with my eldest sister Mary. When my

[38] "Squire" meant justice of the peace.

[39] Otter was in New York City considerably longer than is indicated by the chronology he presents here. The time he specifically mentions sums to less than three years, whereas he actually spent five and half years there.

[40] There is no lawyer named Thomas Mills in the city directories. But there is a "William Mills, grocer," who resided at "Broadway and Vauxhall gardens," listed in *Longworth's American Almanac, New-York Register, and City-Directory* (New York, 1804). Given the Otter family connection with the Vauxhall Gardens (see the next note), it is possible that this is the Mills to whom he refers. It is also possible that Otter is using a fictitious name because of the unflattering things he is saying about his brother-in-law, as he seems to have done in a later episode involving "Dr. Vanpike" (pp 123–125).

father felt that the hour of his dissolution was approaching, he called us around him, and told us that he had made such a disposition of his worldly matters as to leave us all a small patrimony to begin in the world; and in two days after, he closed his eyes in death and sleeps the sleep that never endeth. After my father had been interred, as usual upon such occasions, his will was brought and ushered into the presence of the family, and read, in which my brother-in-law, lawyer Mills, was left sole executor; and he, not content with that, also made himself sole heir of my father's estate, personal and mixed, and dealt with accordingly; he went on and took possession of all my father's property, and converted it to his own use, cheated myself and the rest of my brothers and sisters out of every cent, which my father was possessed of. Having for myself in the meantime, conceived an opinion of my brother-in-law using towards us a mal-practice of which I never could be reconciled to, from the declaration made by my father in his dying moments, of the disposition he had made of his worldly affairs, the fraud used by him towards us was too glaring to acquiesce in silence, and resolved in my own mind to chastise him for the outrage committed upon us by him whenever an opportunity should present itself.

In the meantime I went to my elder brother whose name was Edward, he then being the head boss of Vauxhall gardens at Bunker's Hill,[41] and intimated to him the idea that I was apprehensive that Mills was going to cheat us out of all we had to get; his apprehensions on the subject was not as sensitive as mine were, he observed that it looked a little like it, yet did not think that he, Mills, intended or was capable of such a bad design; I told him that I was fully convinced in my mind that he was both capable and willing, and alleged my reasons for my suspicions, which were that he, Mills, became savage to my sister, he used her in a manner different from what conjugal affection and matrimonial ties would warrant, I intimated to my brother that if any opportunity would present itself I would inflict upon him a proper chastisement usually denominated "club law," my brother told me I should be quiet until I became of age as I could do nothing during my years of minority, I told him by that time he might have it all spent; I then urged my

---

[41] Taking the name of the famous London pleasure garden, the New York Vauxhall was located on the former Bayard family estate, the area today bounded by Grand, Broome, Crosby, and Lafayette Streets (see Map 1). Noted for its summer fireworks displays, it opened in 1798 and closed after the 1804 season. Thomas Myers Garrett, "A History of Pleasure Gardens in New York City, 1700–1865," Ph.D. diss., New York University, 1978, pp. 217–244; and W. Harrison Bayles, *Old Taverns of New York* (New York, 1915), pp. 399–401.

brother, as he was of age, to see to the affair of Mills' conduct; and make him account if his administration is in accordance with the requisitions of the law of the land; my brother Edward thought I had better wait until the term of my apprenticeship had expired, we then could see into the matter jointly, I found that my brother's inclination led to a different point from mine, and became a little excited at the tepid manner in which he treated the subject; I gave vent to my feelings and concluded in my own mind that I could put the first impressions into execution, and swore I would wallop him the first chance I got. I then told my brother that I would go to Mrs. Mills and hear from her what she had to say; and accordingly that evening I went to my sister; I inquired of her if Mr. Mills was at home, she told me he was not; I asked her if she knew where he was, she said she supposed that he was at the Cross Keys, a tavern which he frequently haunted, and in my sister's own language "the place where he always is." I then asked her if she thought that Mr. Mills would lend me ten dollars, she said she did not know. I then requested her to ask her husband that question, and I would call the next evening to receive his answer. This was the plan I had resolved to try him upon, was to get him to lend me ten dollars, for I was sure on my mind, that he would refuse me the favor, and then I would open for myself an avenue for hostility with him; according to appointment the next evening I went to my sister, and he, Mills, was out again; I asked her if she had asked Mr. Mills the question I had proposed to him, she told me that she had, and said that he had no right to give any of the money to any of us until the nursery, the house, and garden were sold, and the youngest child had arrived at full age, he asked my sister if she knew what I wanted with the money; she told him she did not know; he told her he thought that I had no business with any money while I was an apprentice, but I was too wild as things were; his way of thinking ill comported with my way of thinking, and added fuel to the fire, that was burning in my breast against him and accelerated my design upon him. I plainly told my sister that I thought he would have the money all spent before the youngest child would become of age; she told me she hoped not; and in general terms observed to her I would see about it;—bade my sister good evening and went home.

Spring of the year was coming on, my brother Edward asked me if I would hire myself for Sundays, to wait upon ladies and gentlemen, whose fancy led to amuse themselves in visiting Vauxhall gardens. It may not be unacceptable to the reader to give him a description of the Vauxhall gardens. The location was, at that time, on the top of Bunker's hill on the North

Point; and contained from four to six acres of ground; the enclosure was a board fence elevated above the view of any person, and white washed on all sides, and occupied by a gentleman of the name of De Lacroix, a Frenchman;[42] and the reader may form some idea from the proprietor being a Frenchman, that the garden was fashioned accordingly. The garden was nearly square, and it contained six gravel walks, running north and south, and six running east and west, elegantly gravelled; the garden being out into thirty six nearly equal squares; at each square was erected images representing saints, and in the central square was the image of the blessed Virgin Mary, carved out of wood as large as life.[43] The summer houses were placed at easy and regular distances apart, elegantly fitted up, the ground was occupied in the rearing of flowers and shrubbery generally. The rules of the gardens, which every visitor had to observe, were, pulling a flower fifty cents fine. My brother Edward, whom I have already stated was the chief gardener of the said garden, offered me a dollar a day to assist him in the garden in waiting on visitors, as aforesaid, I told him that I would, and accordingly assisted him on Sundays, and every Sunday night Mr. De Lacroix paid me a dollar for my services, rendered during the day. I continued for some time in this employ, waiting on the gentry visiting the garden, on Sunday; and working for my master at my trade until my brother Edward and Mons. De Lacroix's daughter took it into their heads to make a runaway matrimonial match of it, which stung the old fellow, and he, out of spite, discharged me out of my Sunday employment.

The reader will please to bear in mind, that the garden which I have described is not now in existence.[44] However there is a garden of the same name, and owned by a man of the same name in the Bowery. Being in the seventeenth year of my age, my brother Edward being gone, gave me an uncontrolable opportunity of executing my original design I had upon my brother-in-law. I went to see him one evening, he was a little intoxicated; he

[42] Jacques Madelaine Delacroix was a French immigrant distiller and confectioner who was the proprietor of several pleasure gardens and restaurants in the city in the late eighteenth and nineteenth centuries. Garrett, "A History of Pleasure Gardens," p. 177; Bayles, *Old Taverns,* pp. 399–401; and Phelps Stokes, *Iconography of Manhattan,* 5:1382 (9 January 1801).

[43] Actually the statue in the center of Delacroix's garden was a bronze equestrian one of George Washington. Smaller statues of other patriotic figures were found elsewhere in the garden. (New York) *Daily Advertiser,* 2 July 1803.

[44] After the 1804 season, Delacroix closed the Bayard Vauxhall and opened a new garden at the Bowery and Astor Place which continued to operate until 1855. Garrett, "A History of Pleasure Gardens," p. 279; and Bayles, *Old Taverns,* pp. 401–402.

asked me what I wanted, I told him I did not want anything in particular more than to pay a visit to my sister; he then said that he had heard that I was going to give him a walloping, that he intended to acquaint my master of my conduct; I found from the threats he made that he was of a cowardly disposition but did not then feel in a disposition to pummel him although I was conscious that I was able for the lad. I, however, told him that I would give him a lacing, upon that declaration he got his cane, and when I saw that he armed himself for combat I made at him, and at this juncture my sister interfered and begged me to go home. I obeyed my sister and left his house, and went home to my master. The next day my lad came and made his complaint as he had promised, to my master, of my conduct towards him; and by way of threat told my master that if he did not take care of me, he, Mills, would take care of me. My master said he would talk to me about it, and told me when I came to dinner the charge preferred against me by Mr. Mills. My master said I had better stay away from Mills's until I became of age; I promised my master that I would follow his council, that I would not go there any more. In the mean time, although I made a promise to stay away, which I did not intend to fulfil, I resolved in my mind to be revenged on him, and it so much inflamed my already heated imagination, that I was determined to give the lad a lacing.

I submitted the matter existing between Mills and myself to an acquaintance of mine by the name of John Lane, a baker by trade; when I had told him all I had to say about it, he said he knew Mills very well, and observed that he would not be worth one cent by the time all his debts were paid; that if he was me, he would give him a genteel and good walloping, for that would be all I ever would get; I told him if I did so, that I would be under the necessity of putting out; he said that he would not care for that, for said he I intend to put out myself in march next, I asked him where he intended to go to, he said he intended to go to Philadelphia; I told him that I would go along with him, then he enjoined secrecy upon me so that our plan should not be frustrated,[45] I asked him how much money it would take to take us there, he allowed it would take about five dollars a piece; I told him I could easy raise that sum by that time; from that time out, Lane and myself associated under every possible circumstance; and on Christmas eve we went to amuse ourselves at a dance; it being very common to make merry on holidays; while

---

[45] Otter would be breaking his apprenticeship indenture, hence in part the need for secrecy (see p. 38).

there and in the act of dancing we heard of a riot that had been raised at the Catholic Church near the park;[46] Lane and myself left the house and went to the church and on our way to the church, Lane observed that we would stick close together, when we came to the theatre of action; the church was surrounded with a motley crew of Irish and sailors, we inquired what was the matter, we were informed that the Irish had killed a sailor. The Irish and the sailors were engaged in deadly conflict, and without farther ceremony we entered the list of combatants and espoused the cause of the sailors, and the mob fought from the door of the church to Irish town, being the distance of about one fourth of a mile, and kept on fighting all that night, Lane and myself, in company with three or four more who came with Lane and myself from the dance, went into a grogshop in Irish town asked the keeper of the shop for a half pint of rum; he told us to clear out for a set of rascals; without farther ceremony upon any account, we fell to and waled the grogshop keeper and two more hands who seemed to espoused his cause, most elegantly; his wife went into the cellar and we shut her down in the cellar, and took possession of the shop; having by this time cleared out all hands, we fell to and drank as much as we pleased, and while we were refreshing ourselves the mob came in and began to break bottles, glasses, pitchers, barrels, and all and every thing they could find in the shop; and fought on till day light throughout Irishtown;[47] laying all Irishtown waste; a great deal of property was destroyed by the mob, and a great deal of human blood shed; it was sometime in the afternoon on Christmas day before I got home, and when I was at home I was far from having a sound skin, for in the affray somebody let me have a lick on the left side of my head with a cudgel and laid it open about one inch; and by way of uniformity I received also a tap on the right side of my head not quite as big as the first, and a black eye into the bargain;

---

[46] This was the Augustus Street Riot of 24–25 December 1806. On Christmas Eve a street gang known as the Highbinders gathered outside the Catholic church on Barclay Street, with the intention to taunt those leaving the midnight mass. The watch prevented serious disorder at the church, but on Christmas Day the Irish, fearing a Highbinder attack, armed themselves and gathered in the streets of their neighborhood. An attempt by the watch to disperse the Irish crowd on Augustus Street (later City Hall Place; see Map 1) resulted in a melee, and a watchman was killed. As news of his death spread, an anti-Irish mob formed. The nativists attacked George Coburn's Augustus Street grocery, broke his windows, and destroyed his liquors. Paul A. Gilje labels this riot "one of the most violent . . . of the early national period."

Otter's account is accurate, except that it was a member of the watch, not a sailor, who was killed. *New York Post*, 26 December 1806; and Gilje, *The Road to Mobocracy: Popular Disorder in New York City, 1763–1834* (Chapel Hill, N.C., 1987), pp. 130–133.

[47] The area to the north of the (City Hall) park; see Map 1.

as for my part, all I had to do with that spree ended just here. My master asked where I had been, I told him I had been in Irishtown; he said, I thought so, for you wear the Irish "Coat of Arms," about you, and added that it was a wonder that I had not my brains knocked out into the bargain.

The next scrape I got myself into, long before my head was healed, and not exceeding four days after the mob in Irishtown, was at a dance at a Mr. Green's. Being a notorious dance-house,[48] we went for the express purpose of raising a row and were gratified to our heart's content,[49] for we had scarcely got into the house, until the crew of the English packet came in, and they scarcely had time to touch bottom, when we let them have it, and the way it went there was nobody's business only those whom it concerned; we had a battle-royal, and the first thing I knowed of myself I was in the hands of a watchman; as he was taking me on to the watch-house, he treated me, uncourteously he had me by the collar, I told him I had occasion to obey a call of nature; he let go his hold by my collar, and as soon as he let go his hold, I put out, and the way I scampered off was just the right way, and he had no other than legbail for my appearance; the next night, however, I had the bad luck to fall a captive into the same hands I had been in the evening before, and my captor was a good old Dutchman, no doubt of the strain of those good old and venerable burghers of the old school; when he laid hold on me he said "I dinks as you are de lad as I had a hold of last night," I told him I thought not, that I never was here before, he said "No, but I dinks I ketched you down at the Greens;" I told him I did not know the Greens. I then called my comrade who had attended me to French John's, the place where I fell into the Dutchman's hands the second time, my comrade vouched for me to the watchman, that I had not been up town for a week before, he was staggered at the information my comrade gave him about me; he said, "I might be mishtaken as dere ish so menny poys;" he then let me

---

[48] *Longworth's City-Directory* for 1804 lists two Greens as tavernkeepers: Abraham, at the corner of Charlotte and Henry Streets, and James, at 10 Broad Street.

[49] Gang attacks on taverns and dance halls were beginning to become common in this period according to Gilje. Typically a group of men would force their way in while yelling and shouting, smash the liquor and glasses, and tear apart the furniture. In addition to taverns, houses of prostitution were often targets, in 1805–1806 the Highbinders "produced several riots, making the demolition of houses of ill-fame the ostensible object of their disorderly practices" (*New York Post*, 26 December 1806). Because Otter refers to Mr. Green's as a "notorious dance-house," I suspect that it was a bawdy house I do not think, however, that Otter is always using "dance-house" as a euphemism for a house of prostitution; it seems clear from the text that many of the dance-houses he mentions were just that. Gilje, *Road to Mobocracy*, pp. 236–239.

go, and off me and my comrades started for Greens, and after we had been at the Greens as the watchman said, about one hour, and in our tantrams, Green's being in the same ward and in the same street, and under the jurisdiction of the same watchman, he came down there, and said, "well my lads you ish here now," we told the watchman that we had just come there to become acquainted, he told us he thought that we would very soon become acquainted, and enjoined good behavior on us; we told him we would try and do that, nothing more happened of any consequence, and we scampered off to our respective homes.

The holydays being over, I was put to night-school by my master, and I happened by some means or other to miss attending school as often as I happened to attend it; one night that I failed in attending school having business at a Mr. Francis Drake's in Orange street,[50] in lending a hand to a dance that happened to be there, when we came to the door, a shilling was demanded by the door keeper as an admittance fee, we told him we had no small change about us, but when we came in we would pay him; he said he was not quite so green; that he had been sucked in too often for that; we found we could not get in by stratagem, we went out to the front door at the street and began to kick up a row amongst ourselves which was merely done to call his presence and attendance there, and we succeeded in the design, for he came as we wished he should, to the front door to see what was the matter, while we had him there we surrounded him and we kicked and knocked him about till we had all slipped in; he came and reported his case to Mr. Drake, how we had maltreated him, and that we were a set of audacious rascals, and had not paid our entrance. Mr. Drake asked him, if he knew any of us, he said, he did not know, that it was too dark to be sure, yet he thought he could point some of us out, he said that, at any rate, none of us had any tickets. Mr. Drake came up to me, and asked me for my ticket, and by this time I had ingratiated myself into the good graces of a young lady, to vouch for me certain facts, to clear myself, which she consented to, and accordingly she bore me out; I replied to Mr. Drake's inquiry, that I had got a glass of punch at the bar for the ticket, and that me, and the young lady I was in company with, had helped me to drink it. She was called upon to verify my assertion, and she confirmed it, by answering the appeal made to her, in the affirmative, and said that I was clear; and Drake catching the

---

[50] *Longworth's American Almanac, New-York Register, and City-Directory* (New York, 1805) lists "Joseph Drake, tavern, 57 E. George." George Street is now Market.

word, well then you are clear; in the mean time, snug as I felt, still I believed
that I was the biggest scamp among the whole bunch, for, in justice to
myself, I was the original inventor of the plan to get the door-keeper into the
street, and to kick and cuff him in the manner we did, and was one among
the first who commenced the exercise on him. Mr. Drake asked several
others for their tickets, some had one excuse, some had spent their tickets at
the bar, &c. &c.; at last he inquired of a lad of the name of Dick Turner for
his ticket, Dick told him it was none of his business; that reply of Dick's, was
paramount to a declaration of internal wars. Drake then told him that he
believed that he was one of the rascals. Dick told Drake, he was a liar. Drake
drew his club at Dick, and Dick seeing the storm gathering to burst over his
head, and to avert it, he availed himself of this advantage of pugilistic
science, let Drake have a Kenset and felled him;[51] we all took the hint at
Dick's performance; chimed in, whipped Drake and the door-keeper, cleared
the ballroom of stray hands; blew the lights out; drank as much as we
wanted, and cleared the gangway, before time could be allowed to call upon
the watchman for aid; and dispersed and went to our respective homes; and
took care not to visit that part of the city for about two weeks. Dancing was
in them times so very fashionable, that it was no difficulty to get to one any
night in the week; the dancing fever began to rage in Harman street, there
being a gang of about eighty strong, where all hands attended to the bellows.
We heard that a dance was to be at Mrs. Cunningham's, in Harman street;[52]
we repaired there, and our force mustered strong. We learned from a girl that
no boys would be admitted; we told the girl we would get in any how, but
that she should say nothing about our intention. We laid a plan to get Mrs.
Cunningham away, by telling her, that her sister, who lived about one square
from her, had fell and had broke her arm, and requested Mrs. Cunningham's
immediate attention; when we had delivered our message to Mrs. Cunningham, away she went post haste to see her sister. In a short time, a lad
went to the door-keeper, and told him that a lady was at the door, and wished
to speak to him; he told the boy to ask the lady in; the boy told the door-
keeper that she had not time; he came out, and as soon as he came to the
door, the way we pummelled him was a caution to door-keepers, and the

---

[51] George Kensett was one of America's first prizefighters. He fought two widely publicized
battles with Ned Hammond in 1824 and 1826. Elliott J. Gorn, *The Manly Art: Bare-Knuckle
Prize Fighting in America* (Ithaca, N.Y., 1986), pp. 40–41.

[52] *Longworth's City-Directory* for 1805 lists a "Mary Cunningham, tavern, Cherry [Street]."
Harman Street is now East Broadway.

whole posse of us slipt in; by this time the old lady came back in a wonderful splutter, she began to scold the door-keeper for letting us all in. Yes, by G—, said he, we had got him out, and almost killed him, which assertion of his savored strongly of the truth,—in confirmation thereof, she, Mrs. Cunningham, said, we had made up a lie to get her away. She told the door-keeper to call the watchman; she would shew us what we were doing; accordingly two watchmen were brought, and they came in, and when they entered the domicil, she addressed herself to the watchmen, that here were a gang of boys who had come with an intent to mob her house; the watchmen asked us who had let us in. We told them that nobody was at the door when we came in; we heard a noise on the street, we came just to see the dance; they then asked the door-keeper if we were the ones who had him out on the street; he said, he did not know, it was too dark to tell any one, but his belief was, that we were the fellows; the watchmen told him, if he could not discriminate who they were, that it was impossible for them to tell, and as long as we behaved ourselves well, that they could do nothing with us, and by way of interrorum, told the old lady and her door-keeper, that if we did not behave ourselves to give them a call; and after they had given the above charge, the watchmen retired; my comrades danced among the rest, and things went on smooth for a while. I, for my part, never did dance, and to amuse myself, I walked up to the bar and called for a small glass of punch, which I drank, and paid the old lady for it. I observed to her, that she had a full house, with a view to court the good graces of her ladyship; and to let her have it the more amply in the outcome; she observed, that there were too many boys, more than she wished, and asked me if I knew any of them; I told her, I did not, I only knew one or two, that I, for my part, did not reside in the city, that I lived on Long Island, and merely called to see the city fashions. She said, she thought she had seen me before; I replied, that might be, as I was in the city nearly every day. She then told me to try to get acquainted with some of the girls. I told her I would after a while. The boys began to get their blood a little warm from dancing, and as that got up, they began to get glad, and as their gladness increased, of course they began to get too loud. She told the boys, that if they did not keep less noise, she would call for the watchmen. I told them that they ought not make so much noise; one of them told me, it was none of my business. The old woman told me, I should say nothing more to them; she believed they were a very quarrelsome set, which was very well. Little did she dream of Indians about in me. She next wished that they were gone, that nothing could be made while they were there. I chimed in with her ideas, and thought not. She asked me if I would take another drink; I told her I did not care much; she then gave me a small glass of punch; I drank the punch, and after that I walked round to a girl, who sat beside one of my comrades, and informed him, that I had got on the good side of the old woman. I told him how she had given me a glass of punch, and told me she wished these boys were gone, that she would make nothing while they were here. G——, says he, I'll go up to her, and I'll knock something out of her too. I told him I would go along, and I would ask him how he liked the dance: so we both went up to the bar, and he called for a glass of punch, and began to feel into his pocket for his ticket; after having searched awhile for it, (like hunting a needle in a hay-stack, for he never had any,) he said he had lost it. She said, it was immaterial, that if he had had it, he could have his glass of punch; so up he picked the glass, and drank the punch. I then asked him, how he liked the dance. He said, that nobody could dance for them boys, that had got in for nothing. She said, yes, and that she would have them put out, and she went and gave the door-keeper her orders. The door-keeper came and told the boys, that they had now danced long enough, that they now must give up the floor to other people. The boys quaintly replied to the door-keeper's mandate, that they would dance just as long as they pleased, that their money was just as good as that of any other body. The reader must be now informed of the location of the room we were in; we stop here to give an account of it, as we presently will have to describe the row that ensued.

The room had been formerly occupied as a store room, with two folding doors in the front, closed by a large bar in the inside; the door of egress and ingress was at the partition of the house; in the mean time as I was on excellent terms with madam Cunningham, I drew the bar that bolted the folding doors, in the event that any watchmen should make their appearance amongst us; and I told the boys that I had removed the bar, and that, that way was clear to make our escape in a quarter which they least expected. Some of the company told the boys that they wanted part of the enjoyments for the evening, that they, (the boys,) should not enjoy and engross the whole of it to themselves; the boys told them that they would do just as they pleased; and with that I walked up to Mrs. Cunningham, and I observed to her that the boys were acting too bad; that they felt disposed to give nobody a chance to participate in the sport, but themselves, she said, that she really would not suffer it any longer, that she would have them put out. She went to the doorkeeper a second time and told him he must absolutely put out them boys; the doorkeeper said, Egad I'll soon have them out; he accordingly went to the door and got in hand a club, and when armed, he stept in amongst the boys, and peremptorily ordered them out; and laying hands on one of our gang, and no sooner, than the violation on his part of that sacred right, of invading the privilege of personal protection, than the person assaulted in his person, made a happy return of attack; and with a short tap, laid the gentleman doorkeeper sprawling on the floor. Then the spree began, the old woman ran out for the watchman; by the time she came back, reinforced with watchmen there were a good many men laying in the floor; and the girls cleared themselves in the best way they could. We had extinguished all the lights in the room, save one; by the time the watchman came in, as they, the watchman entered by the door at the entry, we threw open the folding doors leading to the front, and out we put, the whole gang of us; and acting possum with the old lady, I went in again to see how things looked, after the affray was over. She was just in the act of giving the watchmen a drink as I entered. One of them advanced upon, and seized me, saying to the old lady, here is one of the boys now; said she, NO INDEED, that young man was here all the evening, and was one of the most civil of all that was in the house, and asked me to come and take a drink. (Yes, indeed, thinks I to myself, my old lady, you are rightly fixed now.) The door-keeper was most horridly hammered; and he was raving and cursing, as I thought, scientifically; he had, at least said of it, some system about it, as he laid it down thick and strong, saying, if he knew who they were, how he would fix them. In the mean time, I let the old woman have another of my left handed spangs. I told her it was the worst spree I had ever witnessed. She said with a good deal of self-satisfaction, that she would be bound, that the next ball they would make, that them rascals should not get into the house. I inquired of her, when she would likely have the next dance. She said on Saturday night next, at the same time she gave me a cordial invitation to come, and that's the time she missed it. I promised her, that if I was in the city that I would attend. She said, that some nice girls then would be there. I went, after our conversation had ended, in quest of my comrades, and found some of them. They asked me, how the land lay; I told them the watchmen were gone, and how our landlady had given me a grog. They inquired also, how the door-keeper looked; I told them that he was pretty much battered, and the rest of the hands that had attended were gone, and that she would have another ball on next Saturday evening, and there was the end of that spree.

One evening, a parcel of us lads went to the house of a certain John

M'Dermot, keeper of a victual and oyster shop, in George's street, New-York, with a view to set things to rights in his establishment, as he deserveed it, being of an overbearing turn of mind, and saucy as mischief itself; and we came to the conclusion to put him where he ought to be. After we had got our gang together, and thought ourselves strong enough, we began to play, what was termed "patent billiards," for drink and oysters. We played about one hour. We began to quarrel amongst ourselves, as he thought, to lead the lad on the ice, and as we became too loud for Mr. M'Dermot, he appeared amongst us, and told us, that if we did not keep less noise, that he would put the whole of us out. To this menace of his, we just told him, that he could not do that. No sooner than he had heard our answer, than he laid to grabbing at some of us, and we took the hint, and let him have it. The first thing that he was conscious of, was, he found himself sprawling on the floor, received the hearty kicks of every one who could get foot on him. Some of the spare hands fell upon the negroes who were employed by him to shock oysters, and drove them into the cooking room, and beat them, poor d———ls, into a jelly; being in a cellar, this whole performance was conducted in silence, unknown to the watchmen. After we had laid Mr. M'Dermot and his hands speechless, the way his geese, chickens, oysters, hams, &c. were slashed about, was nobody's business.

After the glories of the several sprees, as I was a very apt scholar in this kind of street etiquette; in the mean time I would attend night school by time, to keep up what may be termed a liberal attention to classic lore. What I forgot to learn one night, I'd be sure to learn the next. I attended night school for ten nights in regular succession.

One evening, fancy led me to the house of Cunningham, son of my old hostess, who kept a grocery store, in the basement story of the house, and the second story of the house was occupied by some ladies of my acquaintance. I called in to see them; while there, some other young men came in, and they began to kick up a row, one of the young ladies went down and apprized Mr. Cunningham of their bad conduct; he came in with a club in his hand, and hit me a lick on the side of my face and knocked me down stairs, heels over head; and as I fell he gave me another blow on my back to help me falling, which I did not get well of for two weeks; his mal-treatment so incensed my spirit for revenge, that I watched my opportunity for six or eight nights to retaliate on him, as he was by no means justified in, to chastise me in the manner he did, as I behaved myself orderly. One evening, a chance presented itself, I was standing on the pavement with seven stones in my pockets; as he was walking round the counter, I let slip a war-hawk and missed him, the stone took a keg, and spent its idle force there; he came to the door and looked up and down the street; by this time I was standing in the street; he did not see me; he went in again, and went up to the desk, and while he was standing at his desk, I prepared for another shot, and let slip another, and hit him on the jaw and knocked him down; they raised a noise in the storeroom, and I went in to see how things were, and there was Mr. Cunningham knocked stiff as a board—by all I could hear and see, I found that his jaw was fractured and pretty much shattered; after I saw how he was, I walked off, and allowed that his jaw and my jaw and back would have a race to see which would get well first. After this achievement of mine, I went to night school for some time after quite regular.

One Sunday, my particular croney, John Lane, and myself, we took a walk on the Battery, with a view to devise plans, to make our exit as the month of March was approaching, and it being the time fixed by us for our departure from New-York for Philadelphia. He told me that he would be ready about the tenth of March. I told him, that the tenth of March would be too early for me, that I could get no work at that time. He told me that should be no objection, as he was sure of a job as soon as he came there and we made a permanent vow to one another, to maintain each until we were both permanently fixed in a birth. I told John Lane, that I intended to try Mills for the ten dollars which I held in reserve as a trial cock for my brother-in-law. He said, it was not worth while to ask him, but to give him a good whipping. I told him I intended to ask my sister, I did not even let Lane know my secret design I had upon Mills; yet he advised me to what I intended to execute. He told me not to deceive him, as he depended on my accompanying him. I told him he might depend upon me, if I lived—by this time we came to the wharves, walking up town, and there we parted. The next week I went to see my sister Mary married to Mills, and he, Mills, was from home. I asked her to lend me ten dollars for a while. She told me she had no money then, yet allowed she would get some by Sunday. I had parcel of ornaments and pictures, I carried them to my sister on the Sunday she allowed to have the ten dollars for me, I told her to keep them for me until I was out of my apprenticeship, as I had no way of keeping them. She took them from me, and gave me the TEN DOLLARS and forbid me saying any thing, for fear Mills might get to hear it. I assured my sister there would be no danger. I went home to my master, laid my money away, and made it my business to see John Lane the next evening, and told him I had made the raise of ten dollars, at which he expressed his glad feelings, and added, that by the time fixed by us to put out, he would be able to raise fifteen or twenty dollars. I told him I would do all I could to get more. The next week, me and another boy got a barber's shop to plaster, for which we got fourteen dollars, which we divided equally, so that I had seven dollars more to add to my stock to scamper upon; and while we were at the barber shop, a man living two doors from the shop, he had a partition to plaster; he asked us to come up to see it, and see what we would do it for. We went up and took a look at it, and told him we would do it for three dollars. He asked us, how much we would have, if we found the mortar. We asked him how many coats he wanted it to have; he said one would do it, we could make it smooth enough for papering. We told him we would do it for six dollars, and do it well. He asked us when we could do it; as soon as we are done with the barber shop. We told him we would have to do it at night; he said he did not care, and in that week it should be done, and accordingly we did the plastering. However, we used finese with the barber, we made him make more stuff than he wanted; we bought it from him, and fixed the partition; he paid us the six dollars, we divided it, and by this time I had twenty dollars, for expenses on our contemplated journey. I made it my business to see John Lane on Sunday following, and I reported my success in making another raise of ten dollars more. He asked me how I made it. I told him by plastering a barber shop, and the partition, and other work. Upon which deliberation, we came to the conclusion to hook it. We were to get our clothes ready, have another blow out by way of a clear up shower to our sprees, and then put out between two days. We accordingly put our clothes to a certain Mrs. Paxton, a widow, whose occupation was that of wash-woman, to have them all ready for a go. We met our comrades one night to have the farewell spree at Mr. Drakes, and according to appointment, about fifty of our gang met, and made a contract for our admittance fee. We agreed to go and make an appearance, ten in number, and the rest of the gang were to rush in, when the ten who had paid went in. We called Mr. Drake out, and asked him, if he would let ten of us in for a dollar. He said he would, if we would be civil, and make no disturbance in the house. We made a promise we would not make any noise; that we would behave ourselves quiet and orderly. We went and gave notice of our proceedings with Drake to our comrades, that the bargain was struck and that we would go up to the door-keeper, and that they should lay shoulders to, and begin the push forward, to force the door open, and some should lay hands on the door-keeper, and pull him away from his station, with a view to prevent him of knowing who was who;

and the door was cleared of its keeper, and the portals were soon forced as wide open as the hinges of the door would allow, and in we all went. Mr. Drake allowed, that we were a very long ten and confessed that we caught him napping that time, and gave us assurances that we would never catch him again. The door-keeper called for the watchman, two of them came in and asked what was the matter. He told them, that a parcel of boys came in, and kicked him out of doors. The watchmen asked him which were the boys that had kicked him. The door-keeper picked me and four others as the offenders. We called on our comrades to prove our innocence, and that we had paid our entrance fee, as we had contracted for with Mr. Drake. This information, and verification of our comrades for us, completely unhinged the door-keeper's accusation against us, which fell to the ground in the estimation of the watchmen; and they told the door-keeper, that he must make the best of a bad bargain he could; and as long as they (meaning us boys,) behaved ourselves, that they, the watchmen had nothing to do with us. The boys began to dance, and danced for about an hour, and then we began to set things to rights; we broke every glass in the whole house, and cleared it of men, women, and children; and after that performance, we cleared ourselves from the premises. We scampered off to a grog-shop, and there we took our farewell drink together; and the shaking of hands in the last farewell being over, Dick Turner was to take us over the North river in a pleasure boat, together with about a half dozen of choice spirits, to accompany us by way of escort.

Philadelphia

The time for our departure had by this time nearly arrived; I went to the washer-woman, and got our clothes, and gave them to Dick Turner, and told him to wait there for about an hour, when we would be back and then we would set sail. I had a small affair to settle with Mr. Mills, which I could not leave undone; accordingly, accompanied by John Lane, we went up the bowery to the "cross key's" tavern; I told John to go in and inquire if Mr. Mills was in; he went in and found Mr. Mills there, he told Mr. Mills that there was a gentleman in waiting at his house to see him; Mr. Mills came out with Lane, and did not let myself be known to him until we come to a part of the city where the watchmen are not too handy; I then fell upon him, and I hammered him until I thought I had the worth of principal and interest out of him for my share of my honored father's estate; and that was the only share I ever had from him, and depend upon it I did my last job well; after I had dressed the lad, I did not hear from him for about two years afterwards. We then went to Dick Turner and the lads who were to go along with us over the North river, and found them at the wharf at their post like men; we got into the pleasure boat and we sailed across the river; John Lane and myself took our final adieu of the city of New-York. We landed in safety on the Jersey shore, and went to the ferry-house, and made promise to write to one another to tell of our adventures; in our final exit, the city of New York lost two very fine boys, in John Lane and myself; however, I may be premature in my opinion, I will leave the reader to judge for himself. John Lane and myself were on the road from New York to Philadelphia about three days and a half; and arrived in the latter named city in safety about the middle of March; we called a halt in a tavern in Market St. at the

FIG. 2. J. L. Bouquet de Woiseri, *Philadelphia from the Ferry at Camden, New Jersey*, ca. 1810. This is the view Otter, coming from New York City, would have seen as he entered Philadelphia. I. N. Phelps Stokes Collection, Miriam and Ira D. Wallach Division of Art, Prints and Photographs, The New York Public Library, Astor, Lenox and Tilden Foundations.

sign of the black horse;[53] my comrade inquired of the landlord if he knew a man of the name of John Kline, a baker residing in Cambden, Northern Liberty, in Philadelphia;[54] he told John Lane that he did know him, and said that one of his (Kline's) hands was in the markets every day; that he would shew him to us; and the next morning our landlord did as he had promised, he shewed us the boy; we went to him and asked him if he lived with Mr. John Kline in Cambden; he said he did; after he had disposed of his market-

[53] Presumably March 1807. (See Figure 2.) The Black Horse Tavern was located on Market between Fourth and Fifth Streets. Willis P. Hazard, *Annals of Philadelphia and Pennsylvania in the Olden Time* (Philadelphia, 1857), p. 346.

[54] James Robinson, ed., *The Philadelphia Directory, for 1808* (Philadelphia, 1808), lists a "Kline William, baker, 268 north Eighth," and a "Cline William, baker, 485 north Third." Otter's geography is hazy here: Northern Liberties was a northern suburb of Philadelphia; Camden was across the river in New Jersey.

ing, we went with him to Mr. Kline's; Mr. Kline expressed himself as being very glad to see Mr. Lane, as he had come on, Lane introduced me to him as a plasterer, gave my name, &c. Mr. Kline was a man that preferred a life of single blessedness, and had to board abroad; John Lane inquired of him if he knew any place where I could get boarding. Mr. Kline said he would speak to his landlady, perhaps she would board me a week or two; he spoke to Mrs. Smith for me, and she gave me boarding. John Lane told Mr. Kline, that he felt fatigued from our walk, that he would rest a day or two before he would go to work; in the mean time we would take a look around to see the city, and to see if I could a get a birth to work. We did so, and I went into every building that I could see going on, inquiring for work; at length I came to one, the master's name was Timothy Currans,[55] I asked him, if he wanted a hand; he said he would in the course of a week. He asked me where I had learned my trade; I told him in New-York. He asked me who I had learned my trade with. I told him with a Mr. King. He said I looked young for a journeyman. I told him I had bought my time; he next said, then I suppose you call yourself a master work-man. I told him, I did, at any kind of plain work. He asked me what I would be asking a day. I told him, I did not know the rules of the city, and asked him what was generally given; he told me from one and a quarter to two dollars per day; and said if I could cornish,[56] that he would give me two dollars a day. I told him I could not cornish. I asked him, if he boarded any of his hands; he said he never had boarded any. I told him, if he would board me, I would come two weeks upon trial to see how he liked me, and how I liked him. He asked me in the next question, if I had any tools. I told him no, I had none; he then said, that I should go to Rose's factory across from Schuylkill, and buy myself a set of tools, as I could get them cheaper at the factory than any place in the city; in the mean time, John Lane and myself, we cruized about the balance of the week, to see and learn the fashions, and we were apt scholars, being members of the old school in New-York; and I thought, learned pretty fast, for we became perfectly acquainted in Southwark, being the lower part of Philadelphia, where all the lads with specks in their characters lived.

---

[55] "Curren, Timothy, plaisterer, Juniper Alley"; James Robinson, ed., *The Philadelphia Directory, for 1807* (Philadelphia, 1807).

[56] This word means to make cornices, an ornamental plaster molding run around a room at the junction of ceiling and wall. According to Edward Hazen, "all well-finished rooms" have cornices, so Otter's inability to "cornish" would have been a considerable handicap. Edward Hazen, *Popular Technology; or, Professions and Trades* (1836; rpt., New York, 1850), p. 126.

On Monday, I then repaired to the house of Mr. T. Currans to fall to work, and worked for him the two weeks we had agreed upon; as the time for trial to see how we liked one another; at the end of that time, I asked him what he thought he would be able to give me for a week's work. He said, that if I would engage myself to him for the season, he would pay me at the rate of eight dollars per week. I told him I would engage myself to him for the season at that price, provided he would find me in boarding; he agreed to my proposition, provided I would pledge one weeks work as a security for him, which I assented to; and to confirm our contract, we entered into an article of agreement, at the prices set forth above for the season; having now a whole summer's work before me, and a birth secured, I fell to and began to work.

I worked one month, and being handsomely fixed, and so was my companion, for he made about twenty-five dollars a month. I seen him, and urged upon him the necessity of writing to our comrades in New-York, to let them know how we fared, and to let them, in answer to our letter, let us know how the land lay. We accordingly wrote the letter, and in it, we inquired how my brother-in-law came on. Dick Turner, he answered our letter, informing us that Mills and my master were both on the hunt for me, one to have me to atone for the violation of the law, the other to get me to work, and Mr. Drake he also had joined in the hunt. He was successful in his watch, for he caught three of the gang, of which we were honorary members, and they had to pay the sum of twenty-five dollars, to make fair weather with him. We of course, found ourselves bound by the ties of friendship to help our mates, and sent our quota to our cronies to help them out of the scrape in which they had been caught. Nothing of any importance happened worth noticing, being every day occurrences, with the exception of a fondness I found insensibly stealing upon my affections, occasioned by a young lady with whom I became acquainted, for about three months, all which time I worked faithfully at my business. Now to talk of what my feelings were, when I found myself in love with a lady fitted by nature to fill my eye to a fraction, can be better felt by the reader than described by me, as it is a thing which in its very nature is inherent, and we all like it, and I began to feel queer, very queer; and one day being full of it, I spoke to my companion about it, and he gave me my castle which I had built in my imagination, a death blow, by saying, he would be bamboozled if he would marry any girl with red hair, of which my dulcet dear had a very beautiful head full. Mr. Master too found out where I had come to, he wrote a letter to me, to learn from me, if I would come back and work for him, he would clear away all difficulties which were hanging over me, and allow me a dollar a day besides. I wrote to him in reply, that I would be back in the course of about two months, and consulted John Lane about the matter; he gave me his opinion, that I had better stay where I was; this idea was in unison with my own, on the subject, and of course it was adopted by me. I earned money fast, and I expended a reasonable share of my earnings in good clothing, of which I had got for myself a very decent set, the balance of my money went for the first three months, light come, light go. Having always a propensity for fun, an opportunity presented itself to give loose to, and gratify it, and as all things have beginnings, the following scrape in which I participated, had its origin in the following manner: A number of FRIENDS[57] purchased a suitable lot of ground in Cambden, on which they erected a house of worship for Africans,[58] who, after some time, became so numerous as well as clamorous in their worship, that they were estimated (at a fair calculation) by the neighborhood as a nuisance, and to rid themselves of their noisy blackies, they fell upon the plan to get the boys and let them make a set upon them. The boys were as ready as willing, as they had assurances from the neighbors to see them safe through. A conspiracy was formed, and my friend, John Lane, gave me notice; so one Sunday night, the evening in which the darkies had worship, we repaired to the theatre of action, when we were about fifty or sixty strong, we had formed a plan, moving systematically, and the watchword was "Glory." We consisted of butchers, ropemakers, carpenters, plasterers, and bakers. The ropemakers were armed with weapons called colts, which is a short rope with a heavy knot at the end; the rest were armed by the butchers, they had calves' tails with bullets twisted in the hair. The first thing we done, we got an old he-goat, put a dog-chain round his neck, and had him chained ready for action; he was prepared by some of our hands in the most ludicrous manner imaginable; he was blind-folded, and had a part of an old sheet stripped over him, and goats are not the most pleasing smelling animal at best in a natural way, and his smell was exceedingly heightened, insomuch so, that he outstunk the devil himself, being daubbed all over.[59] All things being now in readiness, we

---

[57] Meaning Quakers.

[58] I have not been able to identify this church. Camden was very sparsely populated in the early nineteenth century, and I can find no record of a black church there this early. Otter in the text at note 54 uses the phrase "Cambden, Northern Liberty," which suggests that he may have been confusing the two places. According to the *Gazette of the United States*, 11 July 1807, there was a black church, the African Episcopal Church, either being planned or under construction, but the location is not given.

[59] The goat is a traditional symbol of the devil.

got the door-keepers away, by telling them that some boys intended to disturb their meeting, and if they would come to one side, we would help to catch them; while we decoyed the door-keepers, the rest of the gang brought up the goat to the door, and as the words fell from the mouth of the venerable preacher, "Don't you see the devil a coming," into the meeting-house they popped the blind-folded goat, and he seen the light at the altar more distinctly than any thing else, he made for the altar moving along the aisle, straight-way, and as soon as he was safely moored in church, they fastened the door on the outside; and all the screaming and hallooing that fell, these exceeded all things I ever heard. A rush was made for the door, and it was fast; the blackies forced the windows, and as sure as any set foot on the outside of the church—bip, a calf tail or a colt would take him, and down he'd go; and they kept on until nearly the whole of the darkies were stretched out. No particular regard was paid to sex, they levelled them indiscriminately.

The next day, a general search was made to find out who had been concerned in the spree, and several butchers were taken up on suspicion, and that was about the amount of the inquiry, as nothing could be proved against them; they came out clear, yet the costs for defence was about twenty dollars, which sum was raised by the citizens. This was the first spree I had a hand in since my arrival in Philadelphia.[60]

The next day I went to my usual avocation, and worked for about two weeks, and in the evenings we would walk out in the market-house, that was the place of general rendezvous for privateering, and among the first things that threw itself in our way as an object of diversion, was an old woman who frequented the market-house and the adjacent neighborhood, who was in the habit of making some kind of soup, called pepper-pot. She was as cross-grained as the pepper-pot itself. We concluded to have a little fun at her expense. We got a ball of twine, and waited our old lady's arrival in the market-house; at length we heard her usual note of pepper-pot. My com-

---

[60] A search of Philadelphia newspapers for 1807 reveals no mention of this episode. However, records exist of attacks on black churches quite similar to the "spree" Otter describes, so it can by no means be ruled out. According to Edward Raymond Turner, in 1825 "several young men entered a negro church in Philadelphia, and . . . threw a mixture of pepper into the stove. The suffocating fumes and cries of fire caused a panic among the congregation in which some members were trampled to death." In 1834, black churches in Southwark "owing to their noise and disorder, had come to be regarded as a nuisance to the neighborhood" and were the targets of white mobs. Turner, *The Negro in Pennsylvania: Slavery—Servitude—Freedom, 1639–1861* (1911; rpt., New York, 1969), pp. 145, 161.

rades stopped her to buy of her a bowl of her soup, and while they were drinking it, I tied the twine around the handle of her kettle. After she had made all the sales she could, she put her kettle on her head, and started off; and as she went, I paid her steps with twine as she was going down the market-house; and as she was going along, she met two young men to sell some of her pepper-pot; and as she was preparing to take the kettle off her head I gave the twine a sharp pull, and down came kettle and pepper-pot on the floor of the market-house. She began to curse the lads for a set of rascals, for knocking her kettle off her head; and without more ado about it seized one of them; she being under the impression, that it was them who had spilled her soup, and began to call upon the watchman for assistance; by this we ran up to them, and while the scuffle lasted between the old lady and the lad with whom she had grappled. I cut off the twine I had tied around the handle of her kettle. The watchman he came to her assistance, and asked the old lady which was the lad. She was not able to distinguish the one in the lot, and they thought that it looked as if there might be short holds about for them; being taken by surprize they put out, and no doubt thanked their stars, that they got off as well as they did. The watchman asked her, if it was any of us that had demolished her pepper-pot. She said no, and praised us as very clever young men, that we had just bought some from her; and that was the time she was mistaken.

My companion, John Lane and myself, took a few days to ourselves, as a kind of blue-Monday. We went to the wharf, and while there, a number of butchers being assembled, in the act of buying calves, I seen a pick-pocket, he made free enough to ease the pocket of one of them of its contents. He took his pocket-book and walked down the wharf, quick time. I went to the man he had robbed, and asked him if he had not lost his pocket-book. He told me, he had not. I asked him to look, as I had seen a man filch it. He searched, and it sure enough was gone. I pointed out to him the man who had it; he pursued him, and the villain got on board a packet, and we followed him; when we came on board, he had got into the cabin, and laid upon a settee resting himself. The butcher, after I had identified the thief, charged him with the theft, and the thief denied it, and they seized one another, and raised a rumpuss. I became somewhat frightened, and the captain he came to see what was the matter, after he learned the accusation, and the pocket-book not being found on his passenger, he rather sided with the thief. The butcher told him, he was no better than the passenger, or he would not take his part; and they, the accuser and accused went on shore. The butcher he went on board the packet again to search for his pocket-book, and at length found it lying under the settee whereon the lad lay, and the pick-pocket being a lad who understood things better than the butcher did, effected his escape. The butcher asked me what my charge was for the information I had imparted to him. I told him, nothing at all, Sir; he pulled out a five dollar note and handed it to me, and insisted upon my taking it, which at length I did to oblige him.

Strange as it may appear, (there is some things in the affairs of man, always calculated to lead to detection,) I was made the instrument by which the butcher regained his stolen property, and by his bad management the thief escaped punishment, and that same interposition by the same means, I was made the instrument of detecting another villain in the fact of theft, which happened as follows:—One day, as we were coming from our work to dinner, in company of two carpenters and a plasterer, we were met by a negro man in Market near Chestnut-street, he appeared distressed and feigned to raise a cry, saying he had a rent to pay, and no money where with to discharge it, and asked us to buy from him a watch he pulled out from his pocket, and offered to sell it to raise money to pay his rent, as he said. We asked him what he would take for it; he said he would take ten dollars for it, (being worth about fifteen dollars,) it had no chain, key or seal to it. We asked him about them; he told us, he had them at home, and allowed to keep them. The carpenters allowed it was cheap at the price he offered it; I bid seven dollars for it, upon condition he would furnish the chain and key to it; he promised he would. I borrowed three dollars from the carpenters, and took the watch at the seven dollars. At dinner, I shewed my purchase to my boss, and told him the price I had bought it at. He said he was sure it was a stolen watch, as it was quite new, and wanted chain, key and seal. My boss asked me permission to have it, and shew it to a certain watchmaker in the city, whose shop had been robbed a short time before. He took the watch to the man who had been robbed. The man, he said it was his, as he had the number of the watch in a book kept for that purpose. He asked my boss after me; he told him where I was. The watchmaker and my boss came, and he asked me how I got the watch. I told him, and called upon the plasterer and the carpenters to vouch for me; which they did; he asked me, if I thought I would know the man I had bought the watch from, if I seen him. I told him, I was certain I could recognise him, if I could get sight of him. He said, if I would go along, he would pay me per day my usual wages. I told him, if my boss was agreed to it, I had no objections; my boss immediately consented, and off we started. We walked about that afternoon, and all next day, and part of the third day, when I got my eye on him. I pointed him out to the watchmaker; he asked me if I was sure that he was the fellow. I told him I was. We were on the opposite side of the pavement, and to convince the watchmaker, I went across to the negro, and asked him for the chain and key; he reached in his pocket, and said he had not got it with him; upon which the watchmaker felt satisfied he was the bird; he seized him, and at the same time tore from his fob a gold repeater, gold chain and seal; and the negro being too strong, tore away from him, and ran down street among a parcel of carters on the street, he hallooed "stop thief." The carters knocked him down, and we secured him, and carried him to the sheriff's office. Mr. John Hart was then the high sheriff of the city and county of Philadelphia.[61] The sheriff called him to an account how he came to the watches. He told Mr. Hart, he got them from a man up in Cambden. The sheriff enjoined on him to tell the truth, that nothing would happen him, provided the watchmaker got his watches again. After a little pause upon the subject, he said, he would tell the sheriff the truth, that he had the watches in Southwick. The sheriff said, we must all go down there, and off we all started together for South-wick to get the watches. He led us up one street and down another; at length we came to an alley where the villain lived; at length we came to a house which he acknowledged to be his habitation. He entered the house and we all followed him, and we went upstairs to the room which he occupied, and he pulled out a trunk from under the bed, wherein he had secreted his stolen treasure, consisting of watches and parts of watches, silver spoons, and sundry other articles of jewelry. The sheriff took his pocket handkerchief, spread it upon the floor, and began to put in the aforenamed articles, and while the sheriff was employed as I have related already, he, the thief made a bolt at the window, forced it, and jumped out of the window and in liting upon the pavement below, the black villain broke his leg by jumping on the curbstone. The sheriff and watchmaker ran down to prevent him from escaping their vigilance to bring him to punishment, which he endeavored to avoid, no doubt that was the inducement for such a bold adventure to effect his escape. As soon as the sheriff seen how matters was with him, that his escape was impossible; he returned to his room, and laid all the jewelry in his handkerchief he could find, and stated that his leg was broke; upon which piece of intelligence, the woman we found in the room began to make a

[61] "Hart, John, high constable, 125 north Sixth," Robinson, *Philadelphia Directory, for 1808.*

dreadful lamentation about him. The sheriff told her not to be alarmed, that she must go along. The sheriff then began to search farther into the fellow's trunks which were in his room, and found some silks, shawls, shoes, &c. After we had every thing that savored of stolen goods, which those above-mentioned, no doubt were, the sheriff hired a cart, and hauled the black man and woman to the Mayor's office. A Mr. Wharton who filled that office at that time,[62] examined the prisoners, and committed them to jail for trial; while under examination, a surgeon was called upon, who bandaged his leg in the office. I had to enter into recognizance for my appearance as a witness against him. When this was done, the sheriff hoisted them off to jail. In two or three weeks after, the court term commenced, and during its sitting their trial came on. He was tried, found guilty, was convicted, and sent to the penitentiary for five years. All the time I attended court, I was allowed my per diem as the witnesses are allowed, and the watchmaker he received his goods, and I got the watch I had bought from the black man, as a present from the watchmaker, and the farther sum of twenty dollars as a fee for my service, in detecting the robber and bringing him to proper punishment for his transgressions. This brings this matter to an end. I forgot to name, that the woman was sentenced to the same punishment, and for the same time that he was.

My boss, he observed to me, when the whole job was ended, that I had made pretty well by my watch.

My boss in this time got a raw Irishman to carry the hod, something of a green lad; he had a half guinea, which we found out by way of a slope.[63] We began to make contrivances to draw him out on the field of honor, to get his half guinea laid as a wager. Accordingly I made a proposition to John M'Clay, my fellow plasterer,[64] that the Irishman could not carry a certain number of hods of mortar upstairs in half a day. M'Clay bet five dollars he could, which so tickled the Irishman's vanity, he went M'Clay's halves in the bet. M'Clay, he bought a pint of whiskey for his share, and I got two doses of jalap,[65] and mixed the jalap and whiskey together, and M'Clay and the

[62] Robert Wharton (1757–1834) served fifteen terms as mayor of Philadelphia between 1798 and 1824, including 1806–1807. *Dictionary of American Biography.*

[63] "Slope" means trick, a usage found in nineteenth-century Yorkshire dialect. Joseph Wright, *The English Dialect Dictionary* (Oxford, 1904), 5:534.

[64] "M'Clay, John, plaisterer, 211 St. John's"; Robinson, *Philadelphia Directory, for 1808.*

[65] A purgative drug made from a variety of morning glory. In Spanish it is called *purga de Jalapa,* after the Mexican town.

Irishman were very great cronies; he gave him the bottle of the mixture to strengthen him; he liked the stuff raw and otherwise; he took a hearty swig and began to work, and he worked with a great deal of spirit; the more he exercised, the more his dose was likely to prove burthensome, inconvenient, and unhandy to him, as he had not time to idle; nay, he even had not time to attend to the most pressing calls of nature, and did not, which had been exceedingly heightened by artificial means, and his blood was raised, with a view to win the bet and achieve athletic honors; he unheeded all the pressing calls; however, he at last had to yield, he became so much exhausted by labor and the operations of the medicines were so very active, that he gave fairly out, and I won the bet. The Irishman's half guinea we got it snug enough, which was exactly what we wanted. After that Irishman's spree was over, our boss sent Jacob Smith[66] and myself to whitewash the Spanish ambassador's house; a black woman of uncommon size carried blackberries about for sale. I told Jacob Smith, if he would engage the black woman in a conversation, that I would pour a bucket full of the whitewash soup over the blackberries; he did as I requested, and when they were in full glee in their conversation, I let slip my whitewash souse upon her blackberries, and gave them a decent whitewash coat. The whitewash found its way through the berries and basket, and finally upon the black girl, which made her inquire in this manner into the matter: Who the hell done that, meaning who had poured the whitewash over her; and by that time I had got down stairs, and I inquired of her, what was the matter. She took the basket from her head, and she said that some rascal had blinded her, for the lime got into her eyes. I told her that it was lime, that somebody had poured into her basket, and in commisseration for the poor wench, we took her to one of the hydrants and washed her; but before we washed her, she put one in mind of striped molasses, white and black appeared alternate; at last, however, we got the lime out of her eyes, and she was restored to her usual vision. I began by pitying her, and told her, that it was a tarnel shame for any body to play such a trick upon her, and proposed to pay her in part for the berries. Some of the by-standers followed my example by giving her some little change, and we made up as much money as to pay her for her blackberries. She washed her blackberries at the hydrant, and gave Smith and myself about half a peck of them for the money raised for her, as a mark of respect and reciprocity for our kindness.

---

[66] "Smith, Jacob, plaisterer, 179 Cedar"; Robinson, *Philadelphia Directory, for 1808.*

I worked away, and things went on smoothly in the usual way until about the latter end of the month of September. A gentleman from Valley Forge, in Chester county, Pennsylvania, came to Philadelphia in quest of hands. He inquired of John M'Clay, if there was any chance to get hands in the city. John M'Clay gave him, the gentleman, a vague answer, with a view to elicit from him, what wages was going in Chester county, at that time. He replied, that he would give to a good hand seven dollars a week, find him in washing, boarding, &c. all the balance of that season. John M'Clay invited him to call at the building the next morning, that he would inquire, and let him know if he could find out for him any hands. So according to appointment, the gentleman called the next day at the building, where we were at work. John M'Clay in the mean time observed to me, that there was a good chance for somebody. I told M'Clay that if he would pay me every week that I would go along with him. M'Clay said to me, that he supposed that he would pay, and observed, that my better plan would be to draw an article of agreement with him, which would set forth our contract. In reply to M'Clay, I told him, that if the gentleman from Valley Forge would do that, I would go with him the next week. M'Clay in conclusion predicted, that I never would stay with him. I told him I would, if he gave me work for the fall season, and keep me over winter. M'Clay then got off from the scaffold and went into another room to meet the gentleman from Valley Forge, and acquainted him, that there was a young man in the building who was willing to go along with him, if he would observe the several requisites made by me. He inquired of M'Clay, if I was a steady young man. M'Clay said I was perfectly a sober man, all that ailed me was, that I was full of devilment; to which he said, that he did not mind that; he inquired if I was a good workman, to which M'Clay said for me, that I was a very good plain workman, and that he could show him some of my work in the building, which the gentleman examined, and said that he did not want any better work done than that. After he had examined my work and approved of it, he authorised M'Clay to call me into the room where they were, and asked me how I should like to work in the country. I told him, I thought that I should like it very well, if I could get wages enough. He told me, that he would give me seven dollars a week, wet or dry, for all the fall season, as also in the spring. I next asked how about the boarding during the winter; to which he replied, that if I would lathe one house, that he would not charge me boarding during the winter. I asked him how large that house was, to which he had reference. He replied, it contained about eight rooms; to which proposition I assented. I then asked him, how the boarding was in that country; to which he replied, that it was first rate. My object in inquiring into that subject, may be easily guessed by the reader, as I thought that I might help out with some of the good things of this world, and found he had not exaggerated, when I came to test his country. I never lived better in my life, than in Chester county during my stay, which was about six months. We agreed to meet at the Black-horse tavern on that evening, to conclude our contract, and to ratify the same by an article of agreement. When I came home, I acquainted my boss of my intention of leaving him, and going to Chester county for that fall and the following spring. To which piece of information he observed, that I must know my business, and added, that he wished that he had known it sooner to have made his affairs meet the case, but did not throw any blame upon me, that it was all fair sailing for every body to do the best for themselves they could. Agreeably to appointment, when evening came, I repaired to the Black-horse tavern to meet the gentleman from Chester county. When I came to the house he was there in waiting for me. We reduced our bargain to writing; after the contract was ratified and confirmed according to Hoyle, I told the man that I would be at the Valley Forge by the middle of the following week; allowing myself a few days for a genteel blow out, by way of a city good-by. I had by this time just seventy dollars in money, and it was deemed by my companions, as well as myself, too much money for any journeyman to carry away from any place. We held a kind of jury over my purse, and the verdict was, that fifty dollars would be sufficient for any decent use for any body who was in the habit of daily earning money; accordingly twenty dollars was convict to sustain the cost, damages and charges of a spree, which my comrades helped to sustain at my expense. We kept the pegs moving for two nights, and the way it wound up was just nobody's business.

Pennsylvania

Early in the morning I took stage, as railroads was unfashionable at that time of day; it since, however, is deemed the top of the fashions; in them days for a fellow to be rode on a rail was not considered the tip of the TON by any means, as I myself heard, those luckless wights whose bad luck took them to the rack, say, that if it wasn't for the name of the thing, that they would prefer to walk. The driver of the stage cracked his whip over his horses, and away we went, leaving the city of Philadelphia behind us.[67] When we came to Chester county, I stopped at Mr. Clark's tavern, near the Valley Forge. I inquired of Mr. Clark, if he could tell me where Mr. Ford the plasterer lived; he told me that he lived about two miles from there. Mr. Clark asked me, if I was acquainted with Mr. Ford. I told him I was not, and asked him if he was, to which inquiry he answered me, that he was. I then asked Mr. Clark what kind of a man Mr. Ford was. He in reply told me, that Mr. Ford was a very clever fellow; a few friendly remarks expressed by Mr. Clark towards Mr. Ford, I told him my business, he then took the hint, and said that Mr. Ford was there on Sunday, looking out for a young man from the city, and Mr. Clark supposed that I was the man he was looking for. I replied to him, that I was the man who had engaged with Mr. Ford. I concluded to stay all night with Mr. Clark, being in part weary from the journey, and in part worried from our spree which we had put through, and after having made an arrangement with the hostler to go to Mr. Ford, to let him know that I had arrived, which office he performed in the evening, for

[67] The time period is probably the fall of 1807.

which I paid him. I gave myself up for that night, and the cares of the world were lying dormant at my feet. In the morning, Mr. Ford came to the tavern with his (tarry-all, as old Jesse Martin calls them,) to remove me and my baggage, and off we started, and in a little time we came to Mr. Ford's house. I told Mr. Ford that I would prefer not to commence work so late in the week, that I felt somewhat fatigued from my spree and jaunt, that I would like to see a little of the ways of the world, &c.; all which he assented to in a minute, and observed, that he had a job about five miles from there, we would go and see it; by this we got on horses and rode over to see the house and the country, and a little of the fashions in our way; we travelled along the Schuylkill in the direction of the Black Rock, a most delightful section of country. We rode about the country, and my particular object was to feel my bosses pulse, to see what kind of a lad he was. I proposed to him to go past the tavern and take a glass of ale, to which he agreed as soon as the proposition was made to him. We set our horses heads for the Bull-head tavern, kept by Mr. Clark, and when we came there, we began to touch upon the ale modestly, and I topered off on ale. Ale is, as you know, an Englishman's meat, drink, washing, and lodgings, as the Irishman said to an Englishman. The Englishman said, that the ale of his country was so delicious, that it was his meat and his drink, and so they parted; in the evening the Irishman came along the same way, and found the Englishman laying in a ditch, along a hedge-row. He looked at the Englishman and saw that the lad was tight on ale; he concluded, that it was not only his meat and drink, but his washing and lodging too. When we had drank as much as we wanted, and more too; in the evening, we took horse and rode home to Mr. Ford's house; went in a reasonable time in the evening, retired to rest for that night, and the next day I got the loan of Mr. Ford's gun, and went gunning to get a little better acquainted with the Valley Forge settlement. The day after being the Sabbath, my boss gave me an invitation to go to meeting; being a dry kind of a gathering, which I had not got much in the habit of attending them, and I feel a pretty strong predilection never to get myself much into that habit, being a kind of motley crew of all sects of Christians. We, however, made out to go; but before I consented to go, I inquired if the meeting-house lay in the vicinity of the Bull-head tavern. He told me it did not, and added that a great many fine girls would be there, and it would afford me an opportunity to become acquainted, as that was my wish. After the meeting was over, we went home, and I joined work on Monday morning, at a Mr. Pennypecker's

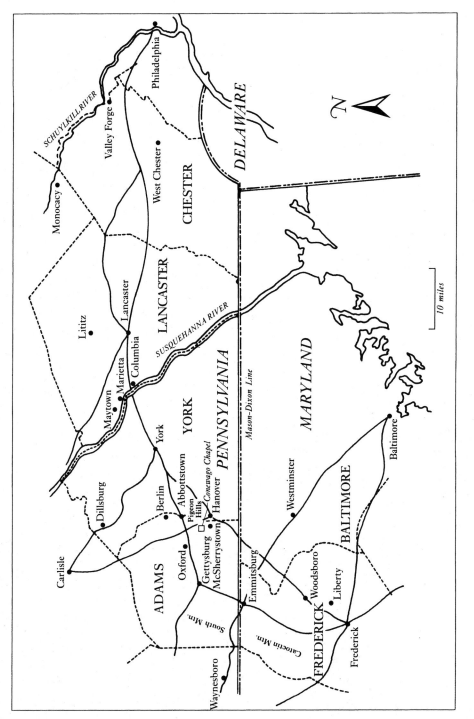

MAP 2. "Otter Country," ca. 1820, showing places mentioned in the text.

house.[68] My boss put me there for one week, by myself, as I supposed to try me. I worked like a Turk, for I lathed and first coated seven rooms in that week. Mr. Pennypecker inquired of me, how long it would take me to lathe and first coat his house. I said, I supposed it would take me a week or two; at which piece of intelligence he seemed to be satisfied, by saying, if I could do it in two weeks it would afford him entire satisfaction, as he had to find the laborer; and when I had it lathed, I put on the first coat in two days. Mr. Pennypecker to explain himself to me, the reasons why he made those inquiries of me was, that he was going to the city. I told him that I was glad that he mentioned his intended journey to the city, that my intentions were to first coat his house all, except one room by Saturday night, and that he would have to hire another laborer; to which he said it was impossible, that I could not do that. I told him, I thought I could; to which he acquiesced and said, that I knew best, and said he would get me another hand, if I could keep them at work; to which I told him, I would insure that part of the performance; he accordingly hired another hand, and then he started for the city; and after I began to plaster, the second day at noon one of my tenders gave out, and he swore that he would not work at that kind of work, and at that gait for five dollars a day. I went to Madam Pennypecker, and informed her of the facts, that one of the hands had given out, and that I must have another, or the work would be entirely stopped. She said she would go down to the mill, and see if the miller would give his hand which he had in the mill, until Mr. Pennypecker would come home. The miller consented that his hand should go to supply the place of the one who had yielded up the ghost. When he came, he said, he would be damned if he wasn't just the lad, that could keep me a going if the other one could temper it fast enough for me. I told him, that he was the very lad I wanted. The building was a stone-house, and the way I slung the mortar against the wall was a caution; some times I would have a hod full thrown against the wall before my man got

68 Probably Matthias Pennypecker (1742–8 February 1808). Pennypecker is a common name in Chester County, but this identification is possible because of a comment in Mary M. Meline and Rev. Edward F. X. McSweeny, *The Story of the Mountain: Mount St. Mary's College and Seminary, Emmitsburg, Maryland* (Emmitsburg, 1911), 1:376, that a former "Governor of Pennsylvania, whose ancestor figures in . . [*History of my Own Times*] paid a large sum for a copy." This statement almost certainly refers to Samuel Pennypacker, the Republican governor of Pennsylvania from 1903 to 1907 and an amateur historian and book collector. Samuel's great-grandfather Matthias Pennypacker was a "wealthy farmer and miller" who lived in the village of Phoenixville in Chester County near Valley Forge. George Swetnam, *The Governors of Pennsylvania, 1790–1990* (Greensburg, Pa., 1990), p. 47; and Samuel T. Wiley, *Biographical and Portrait Cyclopedia of Chester County* (Philadelphia, 1893), quotation p. 642.

down stairs, and I kept him under whip and spur until Saturday at noon, when he also gave out, and fully convinced that he had barked up the wrong tree; when he bragged of his being all sorts of a man, and when he was gone, Dick, he swore that me and the house might all go to the devil, for all he cared for us, by way of a decent offset. I by this time had all first coated the whole house, except one room. My progress in my profession had astonished the folks in the neighborhood; as I was determined to give myself a reputation amongst them, a good many folks to called to see the wonders, and among the rest was an old codger, who, when he learned that the second hand had given out, and but one room to finish, he volunteered his service to finish the last room, and to keep me a going. I told him, if he would keep me a going for that room, that I would give him a dollar; and if he did not keep me going, that I would give him no pay; our bargain was struck, and we went to work. The old fellow was a sucker, I gave him a good dram, and suffered him to keep the board full, as long as I worked at the ceiling; the old fellow began to feel himself a man, when he found he could keep the board full of mortar while I was at the ceiling; and said, that he had before now carried the hod for masons, and that HE could always keep two a going, and then he began by taking a wider range in conversation, observing, that some men did not know what hard work was, that he understood all these little notions to a T. I kept him in conversation and work too, until I took the scaffolding down, for fear he would give out too soon, and I then could not accomplish my design. When I had the scaffolds removed, I began on my old lad; by this time the miller, he came from the mill to the house, and says to him; well, John, how do you come on. Oh, my God, said he, I never seen the man yet, that he could not keep a going. The miller observed to me, that I would loose my dollar. I told him, I thought so, for this man, said I, works like a horse. I told the miller to wait awhile till I would shew him how he could keep me a going; the miller said he would. He brought another hod full of mortar in, and I had that daubbed against the wall before my old lad was clearly out of the room. He brought me two or three hods full of mortar after that, some of which I had laid on the walls before he had his hod cleaned. He made a remark, that I was altering my gait. I told him, yes, I had altered it a little; and he took the hint, and made every exertion in his power to keep me a going, to verify his declarations as to his capability to keep one man in employ at any gait. He still found it necessary to increase his exertions, as was demonstrated to him, beyond the possibility of a doubt, for what his eyes saw, his heart was bound to believe; and he came in a very great hurry, and in the act of stepping into the entry, his toe struck the sill of the door, and down went my John, hod and mortar, and broke the hod into splinters and his neck nearly into the bargain, splash upon the entry floor. The miller he pronounced the sentence on my John, that he had fairly lost the dollar, to which he replied, he did not care, that he was determined to carry the hod no longer for any man; and concluded his speech by saying, that I worked like a damn fool. I made out, to put my job to an end about five o'clock in the afternoon on Saturday, as I did not like to leave it, until I had entirely finished it, as a small degree of pride pervaded my breast in the rapid progress of my work. I was thought in the neighborhood of Valley Forge, to be a jam hand at my business, and I labored hard to get up that opinion in my favor, as it was a theme on which my self-pride owed its whole existence. On that evening, Mr. Pennypecker returned from the city, a few hours after I had finished my job. He asked me, how I came on. I told him, that I had done all, excepting one room. He said, that cannot be possible, that I could have done it in so short a time. I told him that it was a fact, upon which he went into the house to see, and to his astonishment his incredulity dissipated before him, as I had asserted only what he had actually beheld with his own eyes. He, in continuation of his surprise, asked me, if all hands worked with such extraordinary speed in the city—to which I replied, that they did not, only some of them. He asked me to tell him honestly, how long it would take me to finish his house, as near as I could guess at it, by myself. I told him, that I thought that I could finish it in ten days, out and out, as the saying is; to which he brought Mr. Ford's opinion in contact with mine; as he, Mr. Ford told him, it would take eight weeks to finish it. I asked him, how much he was to pay Mr. Ford for doing of his house. He said, that he was to pay him eighty-five dollar for it, and allowed that it was too much for doing it, if I could finish it in the time I had said I could finish it; to which I replied, that I would be very sorry to work eight weeks for eighty-five dollars; upon which he asked me what wages I got; I told him I got seven dollars per week; to which he allowed, that I was very foolish to work at that price, seeing that I could work as I had done at his house, all which was done by way of a slant to become acquainted, and to establish a reputation. In answer to his remarks, I told him that I worked journey work; he then wanted to know what I done with my money. I told him jocularly, that I generally spent it in any way it suited me; then he had learned a secret, and said, he believed that the mechanics in the city were generally in the habit of spending their money, nearly or quite as fast as they earned it. I told him, yes, indeed, and some had a knack to spend it even faster than they earned it. He then said, he hoped that I would not leave Mr. Ford until his house was finished. I assured him, that I would stay with Mr. Ford all the fall, as I expected, and during the winter too, added he, if you can leave the city that long; to which I coolly observed, that I would do that and not distress myself in the least about it.

On Tuesday evening I finished the eighth room, which finished the whole house of first coat; after I had done with Mr. Pennypecker's job, I went home to Mr. Ford's, my boss; when I came home, Madam Ford inquired of me, what was the matter; I told her that nothing was the matter, that I was done, and had first coated my job, Mrs. Ford said, that Mr. Ford told her, that it would take me three weeks to finish my job, which I perceived from her inquiry of me when I came home, as my appearance quite surprised her, as I perceived. I asked her if the boss was home; she said, he was not, that he was about ten miles from home. I told her that I was out of work, and what to do for another job we did not know. I adroitly observed to her, that it all went in my week's work; however, on Friday Mr. Ford came home; asked me, how I came on at Mr. Pennypecker's. I told him I was done with the lathing and first coating of that job; to which he observed, that if I worked at that rate, his jobs he had on hand would not last him till the cold weather. I said all the better for that; I asked him where and at what I should work at to-morrow; he said no where, since I had got done with that job so quick. My boss took his horse the next day and rode over to take a look at it; when he came back, I asked him if my work would do; he said, yes, very well, and he paid me fourteen dollars the number of days I then had been with him, amongst which I had worked eight.

On Monday morning after, he took me to a widow lady, by name Madam Taylor, to lathe and plaster two rooms for her, for the purpose of keeping a store in them, it was a log-house. He asked me how long it would take me to do that job. I told him I thought I could do it in about five days. Mr. Ford allowed that it would do very well if I would finish it in a week, that perhaps that the rest of the jobs might not be ready. I began work, and began to become acquainted with the widow, and put over that week quite agreeably to myself, finished her house, which afforded her entire satisfaction, praised my dexterity as a mechanic, and observed that I worked very smart according to her notion of things; and on Saturday noon I took leave of absence and repaired to my boss to our general place of rendezvous, as I had occasion to bring into notice the house of Mrs. Taylor; justice demands that I should let the reader know, that she was a lady of unquestionable character, and as such maintained that dignity of character amongst her neighbors.I spent the Sabbath as usual and at the tavern of Mr. Clark drank a few glasses of his ale, and in the evening I repaired to my home, and on Monday morning my boss he put me at a job at a certain old quaker who resided near the Black Rock. The Black Rock is a place of some notoriety in that neighborhood; it projects about one half over the Schuylkill, is a soft kind of stone, similar to the Jefferson Rock at Harper's Ferry, Virginia, and visitors are in the habit of carving their names on it as memorial of their visit to that place, and is the greatest curiosity in that part of Chester county. Well, then, I began at my work at my old quaker, and put over with him one week quite agreeably, and by way of a slope, I also formed an intimacy with one of his daughters, who in some degree filled my eye, being young and a little inclined to feel as young folk do about those matters, and the old man chimed in with our mutual views on the subject; for his part he permitted his daughter and myself to take the horses and ride out among their neighbors when we pleased, which opportunity we on several occasions embraced, and in the fullness of her kindness towards me, she betrayed herself and developed in her character a weakness which is utterly unsufferable in the female; she was a little fond of the drops, which she out of kindness towards me let me have shared, and yet thought to hide under the cloak, by saying it was her brother's, and by the by that kind of apology would have done to tell marines, but the sailors would not believe it.

Mrs. Taylor, on my way home to my boss, gave me to understand, that I was the lover, so she had learned from my little quaker girl and the beloved, and gave me to understand, that she labored under an infirmity of which she thought to apprize me, and ended by saying, that if I would be quaker, that I would get a fortune by marrying her; to which I replied that I was a quaker long ago. After leaving Mrs. Taylor's store, I put out for my bosses house.

On the Monday morning following, I went to Mr. Pennypecker's to finish his house; just as I was finishing the house I informed him, that he ought to have a centre piece in his entry for an ornament; he being quite lost at the suggestion of mine, as the man had not the least idea in the world how they were made, nor even how they looked, as he had never seen one in his life. I asked him, if he had never been in any gentleman's house in the city, and if he had ever taken notice where the lamps hung; he said, yes, but he thought that they were made of wood; of which I told him that they were not, and that I could make them out of plaster of paris.[69] He then asked me what I

---

[69] Plaster of paris is made with gypsum instead of lime and is considerably stronger than ordinary plaster.

would charge to make one. I told him, that if he would have one made, being it was the first one made in that part of the country, I would make it for five dollars, the usual price in the city was from eight to ten dollars for making them. He asked me how much plaster of paris it would take; I told him that about half a bushel would make it, and how long it would take me to make it, some would take two and three days, but promised him to make his in a day or two; after he had the whole theory of the centre piece business fairly demonstrated, he told me to make one for him; in the night I began my hocus-pocus in boiling the plaster, and in the morning Mr. Pennypecker started off for Westchester, the seat of justice for Chester county, I began my centre piece after dinner, and in the absence of mine host, and finished it in the space of two hours. Next morning he came home, I stood at the mortar-box; he asked me if I had began my centre-piece; to his interrogation I replied, that it was up already. What, made too, said he, quite surprised and amazed at my declaration; yes, said I, finished out and out. He went in to take a look at it, and sure enough it was there; he asked me how I had put it up, and whether it was nailed fast; I told him it was not nailed, that it was nothing but the plaster fastened, and by way of a brag, told him, I would give any body five dollars to pull it down; to all that, he listened with an attentive ear, and expressed a desire to see the operation; finding that his curiosity was excited, I told him, to heighten it still farther, that I did not show those things to every body. Mr. Pennypecker paid me the five dollars, my boss paid me seven, and them two sums added, made my week's earnings twelve dollars, and in the space of fourteen days his house was just finished to his hand, where my boss calculated on an eight week's job of it. After he had paid me, he allowed that if I had and could earn money as I did with him, that I would soon have a house of my own; to which I replied quite gravely, yes; I lay all my money out in houses, and he took it for granted that I was expending my money in the purchase of houses, and oh, he labored under a sad mistake, although I laid out my money at that time in houses, his ideas never carried him so far as to think that the houses in which I laid out my money were ornamented with a sign and sign-post [see Figure 3], those were the houses I alluded to, and he took it for granted that I meant buying houses—He allowed that I was making good use of my money, and I entertained the contrary opinion. The following week I went to my friend Mrs. Taylor, to finish that job of her's, being a place so much like, O 'twas love, 'twas love, I nursed the job a little, for I made out to stretch it seven days before I got done with it. Within those seven days my little quaker girl came

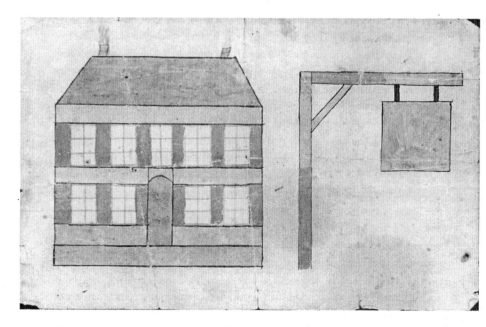

Fig. 3. Anonymous fraktur artist, *Tavern and Sign*, probably Lancaster County, Pennsylvania, ca. 1820. Courtesy of Lancaster Mennonite Historical Society, Lancaster, Pa.

there with some marketing, knowing that I was there, Mrs. Taylor prevailed on her to stay and take tea with her, and on my account she consented, knowing that after tea we would necessarily or rather complimentary be thrown in each others company, which by the by was a little finese on the part of Mrs. Taylor, and in the esteem of my little quaker girl was deemed a courtesy, and when tea was over, I gallanted my little quaker girl over the beautiful lawns along the Schuylkill to the Black Rock mansion, staid all night, and in the morning I returned to Mrs. Taylor's, she quizzingly asked me how I had spent the last night. I told her quite agreeably. She then allowed from my manner, as she had drawn her inferences from my answer, that I would as she supposed remain in Chester county for a long time; to that quiz I began to anticipate her manouvres. I replied, I did not know how that would go as yet. She said, she supposed that when I would be done with her house, that I would go back to finish the house of my little quaker girl's father's. I said I did not know how that would be, that depended altogether on my boss, if he would direct me to do it, of course I would do so; I continued the conversation, by expressing my wishes that I should like to have the doing of that job myself; she said she supposed that if the right one was there, I did not care how long it would take me to finish it, but manifested a share of fear that the right one had been left in the city; that epistle of her's brought me to the rack, fodder or no fodder thinks I, this is a pretty spot of work; and said that I had left the city free as air, and had came into the country to seek amongst the fair a partner for myself; our confab, as to these little matters, of which we were both candidates in the field in a matrimonial point of view, was brought to a close, and in the end of the week I also ended my job and bid Madam good bye, and made tracks for my bosses house.

The following week my boss took me ten miles in a different direction from the one I had in my mind's eye, to a small job, we did not quite finish that week, but at the end of the week I was sent home to finish the job near Black Rock for my old quaker; and on Monday, on my way to my old friend the quaker, I called a halt at Mrs. Taylor to see how the work stood, and how she came on; she, after the ceremony of hands shaking, and how-do-ye-do was over, she asked me if I was on the road to the old place, as she called it. I said, yes. She next inquired if I had a mind to finish the job myself, which question was also affirmed; she allowed that I was cunning enough; after which I went on to my good old quaker and began work after a friendly greeting with all hands. He asked me if Mr. Ford intended to come to help along with the job. I told him not, that he had gone up the country to work. He said he was very glad of that, that he had learned that I was able to keep one hand a going myself, and that he had but one hand to spare. I worked on that week, and the next week his sons got an invitation to a corn-husking frolic, and they asked me to go along. I told the lads I did not know what that was, as I never had seen a thing of the kind in my life; I however consented to go to the husking frolic, to get an idea what it was; so when evening came, the boys, myself, and my little girl, we all started off together to the place where the husking frolic was, and all the corn I husked that night two men could easily eat at one meal; first I did not intend to hurt my fingers husking corn, where I had such delightful notions as country girls to romp and sport with, but at the supper table I guess I counted myself a full hand, and about midnight we all returned home to the Black Rock mansion, and I went on with my work until the end of my job, and among other things seen in the little girl that I acknowledged as mistress of my heart, a fault which she had concealed from me of such a character, that I thought so important an item in the account, that gave me the bats and I bolted. When I had finished my job at Black Rock I went to my boss, staid with him that winter, which by the by was a dismal one, I got tired of Chester county, settled accounts with my boss, and squared off my little bills, and put out for Lancaster county,[70] lying west of Chester county, working myself into the interior of the country. When I came to the city of Lancaster,[71] I called a halt at a house kept by Mr. Daniel Whitmer, sign of the Lamb.[72] The reader may suppose that two lambs met, one inside of the house and the other on the sign; but let me inform all those whose suppositions may lead them to think so, that they are in the suds, although that of peace was exhibited on the sign, that I was not exactly as innocent as lambs are taken to be, and took boarding and lodging with Mr. Whitmer for one week. I inquired of him for a master plasterer in the city. He said he knew one, and told me that Mr. Hash was a boss at the business,[73] and supposed I could get work with him. Mr. Whitmer gave me direction, how and where to find Mr. Hash. I went and found Mr. Hash, and engaged a job of work with him; the first job I worked at was what they called the New Bank at that time.[74] I asked Mr. Hash what he would be willing to give me per day, after I had shewed him a sample of my work. He told me that he was giving his hands one dollar per day and find them their board, &c., or one dollar and twenty-five cents and they find their own

[70] Part of a very rich agricultural region, in 1810 Lancaster County had a population of 53,972.

[71] The market town for Lancaster County, with an 1810 population of 5,405, Lancaster was the largest nonport in the nation. Chartered in 1742, it served as the capital of Pennsylvania from 1799 to 1812.

[72] "Witmers Inn [was] a large brick building . . . —Witmer also has a store, a large farm, & is a man of no small consequence—in his shirt & trousers & hands rough with work he enquires the news & talks over politics of the day." Joshua Gilpin, "Journal of a Tour from Philadelphia thro the Western Counties of Pennsylvania in the Months of September and October 1809," *Pennsylvania Magazine of History and Biography* 50 (1926), 64–78, quotation p. 72.

[73] No plasterer named "Hash" or any variant of the name appears in the Tax List, 1808, Town of Lancaster, County of Lancaster, Lancaster County Historical Society, Lancaster, Pennsylvania. There is, however, a reference from 1826 to a plasterer working in Frederick County, Maryland, named William S. Hatch. William R. Quynn, ed., *The Diary of Jacob Engelbrecht, 1817–1878* (Frederick, Md., 1976), vol. 1, 26 September 1826.

[74] The "New Bank" was the Farmers' Bank that opened on North Queen Street in February 1810. Logically, therefore, this would be the summer of 1809, but Otter's account seems confused. Otter says he had been in Lancaster County for a year and a half before meeting his wife (see the text near note 79), and the 1810 census shows him married and living in Hanover. The overall chronology would seem to make more sense if the date was 1808, or even the fall of 1807. On the Farmers' Bank, see William Riddle, *The Story of Lancaster: Old and New* (Lancaster, Pa., 1917), p. 107; and John Ward Willson Loose, president, Lancaster County Historical Society, letter to Richard Stott, 19 June 1991.

board. I told him that I would not work for these wages. He said, that what he had said, was the highest wages he had been giving, and then asked me what did I ask as a fair compensation for my labor. I told him that I would not work for less than one dollar and fifty cents per day. He said that one dollar and fifty cents was more wages than he had ever given in his life to any journeyman, but allowed, that if I worked as I had commenced, and paid him two dollars for boarding per week, that he would give the wages I had asked him; to which surmise, I told him he was at liberty to discharge me any day he chosed. So according to Gunter,[75] we struck, and I worked for him three months, in that time he sent me to the house of widow H. to plaster it. I went to work, and on the third day that I worked at her house, I found out my old lady, she got right genteely boozy; she became so extremely polite, that the old lady began to be a kind of lathe hander to me, and bothered me so much with her kindness, that I could not work a bit for her, and she seated herself on the scaffold, complained very much of sick headache; I persuaded her to take bed, and between the maid and myself we got her into bed, and when she was fairly stowed away, I went to work again; this gave a kind of introduction between the maid and myself; and a familiarity necessarily followed in its train between the maid and myself, in discussing the old ladies infirmities.

I went home, and told my boss that I could not do the work I intended to do, on account of the old lady bothering me while she was in a spree; he knew what kind of a bird she was; he told me not to mind her, but to go on with my work; accordingly to his instruction I went on with my work, and the next night I staid with the maid, this is what folks in Lancaster called seeing the girls. The day after, the old lady gave the maid a hell of a lecture for sitting up with me. I overheard them, and in their confab, the maid said to the widow, that if she was not permitted to keep whose company she pleased as long as she behaved herself decently, that she would leave her house. I called the girl, and offered to her, that before she should leave the house on my account, that I would leave it. Just as I was going to dinner, I got in contact with widow H. I told her, I would leave the job, that I did not wish to have any quarreling about her house on my account. She was a little how come you so; after a few words had passed between her and myself, she to prevent my abandoning the job, at her command and to make her word

---

[75] This phrase means "In the proper manner," an Americanism derived from the seventeenth-century English mathematician Edward Gunter.

orthodox as well as the law, she took up my trowel, hawk and brush, and they being full of mortar, she took them and locked the whole of them up in her bureau among her fineries. I went to dinner and while there, I told my boss that I would not work there, at least for that afternoon, until the old lady should get better. The next day I went to widow H's house and fell to work again, and the old lady and myself made good friends, and I finished the job without the let, hindrance and molestation of the old lady; in this time, a gentleman of the name of Croutt, a resident of Columbia, a town lying on the banks of the Susquehanna, in Lancaster county, and of such notoriety that I deem a description of the place unnecessary, as every reader is well acquainted with it.[76] I settled with my boss, and had just fifty dollars in ready money, and after I had all my matters fixed, I left Lancaster and started off for Columbia. After I had came to Columbia, I agreed with Mr. Croutt to work for him at twenty-five dollars per month and found in all, for the whole of the season; in this time, he, Mr. Croutt, put me at a job in the town of Letitz, placed myself and another journeyman to board at a widow woman's house; she, good soul fed us on buckwheat cakes for breakfast and supper every day, until we were worried out with her buckwheat cakes, and we fell upon a plan to have our dish changed, in the mean time our force was enlarged by the addition of two carpenters; they asked me to devise a plan to effect a change of diet. I told them that if they would buy three or four doses of jalap, that I would mix it in her batter-pot; and to effect my purpose, I had to wait a suitable opportunity, which opportunity presented itself the next evening, for all hands in the house had an invitation to an apple butter boiling, and I mixed the jalap and batter together in the bustle going to the frolic; the hands about the house all went to the frolic, and frolicked all night, and took bed at near day break, and slept late the next morning, until we were called to breakfast. At the table a general complaining match was heard among the hands, some had violent headache, some had other ailments, and none of us touched a bite of breakfast, save the old lady and her daughter, who eat a hearty breakfast of the buckwheat cakes and jalap mixed; after a few hours the jalap as is usual in ordinary cases was determined to

[76] Columbia is a port on the Susquehanna eleven miles east of Lancaster (see Map 2). The remark about its "notoriety" refers to the riots there in 1834, the year before *History* was published. During August, September, and October, Columbia was the site of very violent attacks by white mobs on blacks and their property, events that are described and analyzed in Thomas P. Slaughter, *Bloody Dawn: The Christiana Riot and Racial Violence in the Antebellum North* (New York, 1991), pp 169–180.

find its way out, and put the female part of our family into a terrible fright, as it gave them a pretty fair scrape to get out of, they conceited that they had symptoms of aggravated cases of flux, pronounced themselves unable to cook dinner for us; they made out to provide a cold check for us, as a substitute for dinner. We began by setting up an inquiry into the probable causes of our old lady and her daughter being so violently and so suddenly attacked; and we all agreed that it was the buckwheat. I confirmed the opinion to be well founded, by asserting that I felt unwell for near a week gone by; the rest of the hands chymed in and complained in the same way that I did, and charged the whole account of flux and flux symptoms to the buckwheat bag, and by one unanimous consent of all the hands, widow and daughter included, rendered a judgment against it, and after judgment condemnation, nay, even abolition was enforced, and by these means we got a change of diet, although the means used had produced momentary flux. We worked away, at length we finished our job, it being a middling large one, and when we were done our boss removed us to within a mile of Latitz, at a tavern stand. The landlord had a very large baboon chained to the sign post;[77] after working awhile, we run out of nails; the landlord had occasion to go to Lancaster for nails. I told the lads that in the absence of the landlord, we would have some sport with the baboon, who was chained as I have already said to the sign-post, we threw pieces of apple to him to make him feel his keeping, and after we had given him enough of apples, as we thought, I concluded to change his diet, I let him have a slash of lime from my brush bip into his eyes, which burnt the poor devil equal to fire, it made him raving; he in his fit of rage laid his paws to his chain and tore the staple out of the sign-post, which was driven in about two inches, and in his fit he danced about like though he were mad, and they shut the doors upon him, and he jumped through the window attacked the landlady and tore nearly all the clothing off her back, and then he left the landlady and made an attack upon the maid, and such a rumpuss and screaming as ensued in that house among the women on one part, and the baboon on the other part, was never been witnessed any where between Dan and Beersheba; the only way we had

[77] Lititz is a small village north of Lancaster (see Map 2), which in the 1800s was predominantly Moravian. According to Dorothy V. Earhart of the Lititz Historical Foundation, two sisters of a family that had lived in Lititz since the early 1800s had heard stories about "a red-haired baboon at the Rome Hotel." Rome was a small non-Moravian settlement east of Lititz. "According to the story, an itinerant traveler left the baboon and never came back for it. The landlord kept the baboon and cared for it until it died." Earhart, letter to Richard Stott, 24 July 1991.

to conquer the baboon was, the laborer he gave him three or four knock-down licks with his hod, and we gave him the white-wash pretty free into his eyes and mouth, which at length put him so busy rubbing his eyes that we caught him, and tied a rope round the middle and then to the sign-post, until the landlord came back. The way the baboon kept us moving while he had the free use of his limbs was the right way, no time was allowed for chat. As soon as the landlord came home, the landlady related the baboon's performance to him, allowing that he was mad, and from his appearance any one who did not know the fact of the lime being thrown into his eyes and mouth, would unhesitatingly have arrived at the same conclusion that the landlady did, that he labored under hydrophobia, for he foamed at his mouth, as all animals do, laboring under canine madness. The landlord got sweet oil and anointed his mouth and eyes, allowing that he labored under great fever, which by the by was the case, produced from the lime, he chained the old fellow to the sign-post again, and as long as we were there he manifested his displeasure at us whenever he had a chance.

When we had finished that job, our boss put us to work at a job at the house of a Mr. Hartzell, in the neighborhood of Columbia and Marietta, after working there three of four days at Mr. Hartzell's we began to be somewhat acquainted with the old man, who by the by was a pretty humor-some sort of a jockey, and learning that I had a vein of fun in me, we soon found one another out, and verified the old adage, "that birds of a feather will flock together." He had a fine orchard and plenty of fine apples, which we ate just when we pleased, and had frequent conversations about it, being such fine fruit, he was aware of it, and as often as we spoke of his apples, he would regret that he had no pears to share with us. He observed, that he had a neighbor about half a mile from his habitation, who had very fine pears, but would not share them with any body. I told him by way of a slant, that if I knew where he lived that I would not ask him to share them with me, that I would find a way to get them without his consent. He said, that if I would do that, he would give us a treat of good old whiskey for one week, as much as we could drink, by way of prize, for the performance of which offer of his, I closed the bargain with Mr. Hartzell, who observed, that attempts of the kind had often been made, and every assailant had been beaten out and driven back. I told him, that on Sunday following we would take a walk past his neighbor to reconnoitre the enemy's camp, and learn how the land lay, so I was determined to show the old lad a trick or two of my own contrivance; so then we took our Sunday walk and spied how the pear trees were planted, and how things looked any how. After I had seen the local situation of the spot on which I was to display my talents, I felt satisfied that I could attain my object in getting the pears. I called for a drink of water at Mr. J's; he gave me a drink of water, and began to inquire of me, if I was a traveller; I told him not, that I was going to Marietta. I asked him to direct me the nearest road to that place; he shewed me through his lane as the nearest way, about half way down his lane I saw six head of horses in his field, among them were two colts; I said to my comrades, my lads here is the trap for the pears. One of them asked me how, and where is it, to which I said, do you see them horses over in yonder field, to which they replied, yes; I told them the plan, which they assented in a minute after I had explained it to them, would do. We then went home, and old Mr. Hartzell asked us if we got any pears at Mr. J's. I said, no indeed, we never asked for any to prevent him from forming a suspicion; then he began to quiz me, if I thought that I could get them, as the pear trees stood on each side of the gate in the front yard before the house; I told him, yes, that I had the trap set for them. I then told him that I would go for them on Monday night which was the day after, so on Monday evening I told Mr. Hartzell that he must lend me three bags. He did not like to do that, for fear we would be chased and leave the bags lay, and they would lead to a discovery, which he would not like if a bag should be left, and a discovery be made. I authorized him to say, that if a discovery should be made, I had stolen his bags away unknown to him, upon which condition he let me have the bags. My comrade and myself had a coffee bag in which we commonly carried our tools—we took it along, knowing that if the matter should go as it would, it would never leak out through our coffee bag, and on it I stayed my sole dependance to carry my designs into execution in stealing Mr. J's pears. After supper we started, Mr. Hartzell cautioned us to take care of ourselves, that Mr. J's dogs was very dangerous. I told him to make himself easy on that score, that there was no danger to be apprehended in that quarter. We went into the field where the horses were, and to give the reader an idea of the plan fixed to carry the pear stealing into execution, was in the following manner: We drove the horses down the field to the lowermost corner thereof, and we caught one of the colts and put our coffee bag over the colt's head and tied it round his neck; the dog began to bark at the house, some of our lads began to evince symptoms of cowardice, and perhaps would have fled, had I not given them the assurance that the dog would run after the horses, and not after us; and we had not much time to spare, as it is well known that there is no stop in a horse race; we started the horses, and they all took fright at the bag horse, and run as hard as old Nick could drive them through the field snorting and prancing, and the bag horse tried to follow them, and so it went round after round in the field one trying to overtake the other, the rest running to get out of his way; the dog he pursued the horses as hard as he could link, still flying, still pursuing, ever and anon, which brought Mr. J. into the field to see what the devil was the matter among the horses. He discovered that something was not right, but what it was he could not tell, and he nor twenty men could not then have stopped the horses from running, for the bag horse he always brought up the rear, and made the rest run like devils. He called to Mrs. J., she came into the field, and the daughter too, and lastly, the servant boy; after they were all in the field, and wondering as Mrs. J. did in Dutch, "was der divel fehlt do"— We put out through the cornfield for the pear trees, shook off every pear on both trees, gathered them all into our bags, which took us about half an hour, and we had what we wanted, we listened to the fun, and while we were listening, the horses jumped into the cornfield, and the bag horse after them, and the way they tore about the corn was a sin; we in the mean-time put out home to Mr. Hartzell's with our pears, leaving Mr. J. to enjoy his wonder, and that continued til near day-light; there was no stop in the horses, as long as the colt that had the bag tied over his head followed them, and the dog he liked the sport, he kept up the fun as long as it lasted, at length the colt lost Mr. J's horses, and he jumped the fence into one of his neighbor's fields and scared the neighbor's horses, they started off and broke the fence and run home as hard as they could stave, and run into the barn-yard, and the colt that was blind-folded with our coffee bag, got into the barn-yard among the horses, they began to kick the colt, which alarmed Mr. J.'s neighbor, and they got up and relieved the poor brute, and so ended that spree.

It was about one o'clock in the night when we came to Mr. Hartzell's, we found them all in bed and fast asleep; we hid our pears in the cellar in the new building in a pile of shavings, in the morning when Mr. Hartzell got up, he came to the building where we were at work, and asked us what luck; we told him we had all the pears that Mr. J. had to spare, which piece of intelligence he could not believe until I went and shewed them to him. He asked me how the deuce I had managed to get them. I told him my plan, he was very much pleased and highly gratified at my success, and allowed it was worth a barrel of whiskey. I told him a half a barrel of whiskey would do us—and Mr. Hartzell came up to his promise, for he gave us as much old rye whiskey as we chose to drink as long as we were there.

The next morning, Mr. J. came to Mr. Hartzell's and laid in a grievous complaint, first, that his pears had been all stolen, and told him the manner in which it had been effected; how his horses had acted, and how his colt had been blindfolded with a coffee bag, and that the colt was nearly killed; he brought the bag along to shew it, and try to find out a clue on the trick by a recognition of the bag. But nobody knew the coffee bag, and his inquiry failed. We all went along over to Mr. J. to see the destruction, and indeed it was wonderful, the horses had nearly run themselves to death, and the colt was skinned and nearly flayed by running against fences, posts, and the kicks it got among the horses at his neighbor's. Mr. J. had the grief to endure, and we had the pears to eat, and enjoyed ourselves most elegantly at the raps he got.

The next spree that I had, was one of somewhat more profit to myself than the horse race which we had instituted at Mr. J's without his consent, and it happened to turn out to be this: My boss placed us at work in the town of Columbia, he had taken two houses to plaster in that town, and he got boarding for his hands at the house of Mr. C. inn-keeper in said town. I worked for about the space of three week's time, I began to find out what kind of a lad Mr. C. was; David Psalm's like, he was one pretty near like myself in every respect, for he was as fond of sport as any body, with one exception, he was fond of the hardware, and I was not, although I never poured it into my shoes, neither when it was agoing, although I never was so fond of it as Mr. C. was.

On Sunday evening, Mr. C. was caught in one of his sprees, he and myself went to a Methodist meeting, when we had been there a few minutes a preacher mounted the pulpit and began to preach, and raised his voice to an excessive pitch. Mr. C. he asked me, what I thought of him, (meaning the preacher,) I told him I thought he was a tarnel fool in my judgment, he wanted to display by force of voice what he should have done in eloquence. In the middle of his sermon Mr. C. got up and interrupted the man of the gospel, and in terms not to be misunderstood; he refuted the preacher, and in conclusion told him he was a damned liar; which remark, acted in the meeting-house among the zealous members as would a firebrand in a maga- zine of powder: they began a general fight, some were for putting Mr. C. out of the meeting-house; by some friendly interference on our part, we got Mr. C. home to his house, he became so outrageous, that he began to break all his bar furniture; he played hokey among the bottles, decanters, tumblers and glasses; smashed every thing that came in his way, not even content with that, he threw the kegs out into the bargain. His wife, for such gross misdemeanor, as she held all the property in the house, and the house itself by virtue of her former marriage, had Mr. C. committed to jail; he lay in limbo three months, at the end of that time he was let out; but how he came out or by what means I never learned. Mrs. C. was under the necessity to renew her bar furniture—I still boarded on; I began to hint to Mrs. C. that I was glad the cold weather was coming on, that I should get clear of hard work. Mrs. C. asked me one day, what was I going to do that winter? I told her that I was not going to do any thing that I knew of. She asked me what I would charge her to attend to the affairs of her bar for that winter. I told her, that it would not be worth my while to think about any thing like that, remarking to her, that Mr. C. would be home shortly again. She gave me the assurance, that he would not see her house for that winter. I told her if I staid, I would not charge her any thing for my services, except my boarding, washing, and so forth. She told me she would find me in all that, and pay me besides. In one week after our confab, I quit my trade, and began to keep her bar for that winter. I lived jam, up in my new sphere till some time in the month of March. During the winter I struck a bargain with Mr. Henderson, in Marietta, to work for him during the season for twenty-four dollars per month, and to find me in every thing.

I worked in the town of Marietta about one month, in this time, as all young men will do, I sauntered about the town, I called in at a tavern kept by a Mr. J. Nichols, and happened to see a little Dutch girl, with whose appearance I was wound up pretty tight at first sight.[78] My boss was bound by our contract to find me board, I requested him to change my boarding house, to which he readily consented as the prices of boarding were all one, it made no difference to him, so I left my old boarding house and took up my board with Mr. J. N., on account of my little Dutch girl, who by the by was rather shy, owing to her youth, as she had not attained her fifteenth year,[79]

---

[78] Nowhere in *History* does Otter give the name of the "little Dutch girl" who became his wife. An 1838 sale of a small tract of land was signed by William Otter and with the mark of his wife, "Margaret Otter"; the 1850 and 1860 censuses, however, record her as "Mary Otter." (Earlier censuses list only heads of households.) Nor have I been able to discover her maiden name (see footnote 80). Liber HS 7, pp. 37–38, 22 May 1838, Land Records, Records Room, Frederick County Courthouse, Frederick, Maryland. Census Office, Seventh Census, 1850, Population, Manuscript, Ward 18, City of Baltimore, Maryland, National Archives; and Census Office, Eighth Census, 1860, Population, manuscript, Ward 16, City of Baltimore, Maryland, National Archives.

[79] The 1850 census (the first to list exact ages) gives the age of Otter's wife as 58, which would make her about 16 when these events took place, since the approximate date is 1808 (see the following footnote). 1850 manuscript census, Ward 18, Baltimore.

and not very well versed in my native language, I had a considerable difficulty to encounter to obtain an interview with her; although I had spent nearly one and an half year's among the people of Lancaster county, who are in general descendants of Germans, and was at a loss as I could not speak the language that was commonly used in that neighborhood, being of somewhat a twister. I shuffled my pack until I had worked myself into her notice. I proposed one Sunday to take a jaunt to the York county shore of the river Susquehanna; she consented, and we went to get some pears on the farm of Mr. Hoke, we got pears and cherries as many as we wanted, and on our way back our boat struck on a kind of sand bar, the male part of the boat's crew got out to shove the boat off the sand bar, and while in our exertion to get the boat afloat again, a snake bit me in the foot just below the ankle, and left a mark there which I shall carry to my grave, as the saying is; my foot swelled most prodigiously, and kept me in bed for four or five weeks in the hands of Dr. Watson. While I was convalescing, I had time and opportunity to press my suit with my little Dutch girl, and things began to go right smooth; although things began to go pretty smooth, I had two formidable rivals to contend with, insomuch as one of them had lands in the western country, which to my little girl was an obstacle for me to remove; I soon, however, fell upon a plan which counterbalanced the objection—I advanced the idea, that I held in my possession Indian lands, and that as soon as we were married we would go and take possession and enjoy our riches, which kind of blarney quieted the objection she had to me and considered me as a freeholder, however, we never yet went, and perhaps never will, to take possession of our western country farm.

The other lad, who was a tavern-keeper in Maytown, I stigmatised him as a gambler, who would lead her a life of wonders, and leave her room to rue her folly when too late, to which she lent an ear as though it were all orthodox, and so next after that I had less trouble when all her objections were removed, I perceived that I rose in her esteem daily, and I of course became more and more enamored with her, as her appearance filled my eye to a fraction. She was beautiful, in a word, she was just what I thought a wife ought to be; being chuck full of it, I proposed matrimony to her, which she refused, upon the ground that she was too young, and that her father would not be agreed to the match. I next enlisted a Mrs. Shaur, a neighbor of ours, into the service, and instructed her to help the cause all she could, and as soon as she could. She succeeded in her undertaking to a minute, she obtained all I wished, and in about two weeks we went to Maytown, and had ourselves married by an old German preacher, on the 19th day of July, 1898.[80] Her father heard that I had married his daughter, which raised his dander to such a pitch as to elicit a threat from him, that he would shoot me, which put me into a notion that he might be fool enough to carry his threat into execution, and to avert such a state of things, not willing to die then, I came to the conclusion to absent myself for a while, until his passion had cooled down to a proper temperature. So off I started, and bent my course westward, and stopped in Adams county, Pennsylvania, in the neighborhood of Oxford, and there I called a halt and commenced a job of some considerable note. I plastered a very large two story brick house for a Mr. John Steigers; the job amounted to eighty dollars. When Mr. S's house was finished, except the basement story, which was not included in our bargain, and newly married, I proposed to Mr. S. to let me have the old mansion house for that winter to live in, until I could see about me to get a house to live in, that I would pay him a rent for it during my stay, to which proposition he acquiesced in as soon as I proposed it to him. I also got him to send his team to Marietta to bring my wife and baggage from Lancaster county to Adams county, which he did. He gave me a horse to ride, to go ahead of the team to see how the land laid. I entered the town of Marietta after night, and found all was well. I loaded our affairs the next morning, and put out for Mr. S. like a man who had just been married. We arrived in safety with our cargo and remained with Mr. S. for that winter.

[80] Obviously a typographical error for either 1808 or 1809. Unfortunately, there are no existing marriage records for 1808 or 1809 for either of Maytown's two churches, the Reformed Church and Trinity Lutheran. The Reformed Church in Maytown was built in 1808, which suggests the possibility that Otter may have met the preacher, William Heister, while plastering the church and thus have been married there. "Donegal Reformed Church at Miton Grove, Maytown Reformed Church at Maytown," *Papers and Addresses of the Lancaster County Historical Society* 22 (1918), 46–47; and John Ward Willson Loose, president emeritus, Lancaster County Historical Society, letter to Richard Stott, 15 December 1992.

Hanover

I n the spring following, I changed my place of residence, by moving to M'Sherry's-town, to the house of an old Dutchman, a tailor, by the name of Overbaugh.[81] While we were in the bustle of our flitting and ready to sit down to supper, we had a coffee-pot full of hot coffee, and coffee-pot full of cold water; our landlord in the plenitude of his goodness called to pay us a visit. I asked him to help himself to a drink of whiskey, which he did by taking it in the good old way; he took the bottle and applied mouth and mouth together; the whiskey as it rolled down burnt his throat, and as our cold water was in the coffee-pot, he picked up the pot that had the hot coffee in it, and sent a swad of the hot coffee after the whiskey, which terribly scalded his throat. He screwed up his face and mouth, that it looked nine ways for Sunday. He bawled out BAH. It was fun for me, and death to Mr. Overbaugh. We lived with our good old Dutchman from April to the month of September, when I moved from M'Sherry's-town to Hanover, in York county, Pennsylvania,[82] to a Mr. F. H's house, whose wife had been

81 This was probably the spring of 1809. McSherrystown is a small village that is a western extension of Hanover, just over the Adams County line (see Map 2). A McSherrystown tailor, Peter Overbaugh was born in Alsace in 1743, dying in 1827; see John T. Reily, *Collections and Recollections, in the Life and Times of Cardinal Gibbons* (Martinsburg, W.Va , 1892), 2: 457; and Tax List, 1809, Conewago Township, Adams County, Adams County Historical Society, Gettysburg, Pennsylvania.

82 Founded in 1763, Hanover was named after the German city in honor of the large German population in the area. When was incorporated in 1815 it had a population of eight hundred. A trading center for the surrounding farming regions and a stopping place for wagons on the Baltimore-Carlisle Pike, it was also noted for the saddles made there, most of which were shipped to Baltimore. Otter is listed in the 1810 census for Hanover as heading a household of one free white male aged sixteen to twenty-six and one free white female in the same age

called, as I hope, to a better and happier than this world, and as he had been
bereaved of his better half, he concluded to sell his family provisions and
quit house-keeping, so we struck a bargain in the following articles; and
mark reader how he sowed up my eyes, he took the barrel of flour and made
it lay as loose as possible, and made me believe that two bakings only had
been used out of it, and I was to pay him five dollar for it; he had also a half
barrel of shad, and he had the meanness to sell the best of them at 18 3–4
cents per piece, and left all the small ones for me; says he, Bill, you can take
this half barrel of shad at 18 3–4 per piece, and he was to take the whole of
that out in boarding with me at the rate of $1 50 per week, for himself and
his boy. I also bought all that was in the garden, not a single thing in it was
excepted, for ten dollars. My wife, after she baked two bakings out of my five
dollar barrel, she reported that the flour was all gone. Thinks I to myself,
very well, I'll pay you for that, Mr. H., and told my wife to say nothing about
it. I in the mean time became acquainted among my neighbors, and among
the rest was a Mr. B., he asked me one day, if I had bought all Mr. H's house
ammunition, such as flour, shad, and all that was in the garden. I told him I
had; he asked me what I paid a piece for the shad; I honestly told him, that I
paid him 18 3–4 cents per piece for them. He told me, says he, that is too
bad; and continued he, why, I bought the pick of the whole barrel at that
price. I told Mr. B. that I would mind Mr. H. for that, he then told me, that I
should watch him, that he was a pretty slippery little fellow. By this time, the
fall of the year was approaching, I had a pony, and having bought the whole
garden, I put my pony called Bonaparte into the grass-patch to fill himself
on the grass that grew on that part of the lot, and when I had turned him
into the garden, I went up town; when I came home, my wife informed me
that Mr. H. had turned out my horse, and would not suffer him to run at
large in the lot—to which piece of intelligence, I told my wife, that I would
go and turn him in again. She begged of me I should not, that we certainly
would have a quarrel about it; to which I replied that I did not care, that the
lot was certainly mine till spring, and I just went and turned my pony into

category. Otter is not on the 1807–1808 Hanover tax list but appears as "William Otter,
plaisterer" on the next assessment in 1811–1812. John Gibson, ed., *History of York County,
Pennsylvania* (Chicago, 1886), pp. 574–580; George R. Prowell, *History of York County, Penn-
sylvania* (Chicago, 1907), 1: 807–813; *The Official Program of the Centennial of the Borough of
Hanover, Pennsylvania* (Hanover, Pa., 1915); Census Office, Fourth Census, 1820, Population,
manuscript, Heidelberg Township, York County, Pennsylvania, National Archives; and Tax
List, 1807–1808 and 1811–1812, Heidelberg Township, York County, Historical Society of
York County, York, Pennsylvania.

the garden again, and watched my pony to see if Mr. H. would turn him out again. Mr. H. came a second time, armed with a hoop-pole to turn out Bonaparte, and when I seen what he was up to, I observed to him, if he offered to turn out my horse, I would throw him over the garden fence; he dared me to throw him over the fence; and I dared him to turn Bonaparte out; so this was about the beginning of our quarrel. While we were in the height of our quarrel, an idea flitted over my brains, that I had bought the whole garden and nothing excepted therein; and to put him into the fidgets, I told him that I had bought the whole garden, and I would be ———— if I did not chop down every apple tree that was on the lot; and he dared me to do it; and I, to apply the action to the word, I went for the axe, which he espied, and supposed that I would realize my words, he started off full tilt down to 'Squire Hilman; he told the 'squire that I was going to cut down all his apple trees, which would ruin his garden, and he wanted a warrant for me right away. The 'squire advised him to send for me as a neighbor, and try to come to a compromise about the matter that he could do nothing with me until spring, until my lease had expired—upon which, Mr. H. came in his proper person for me, to come before the 'squire without the warrant; he acted as a kind of constable for himself in the way I have told you. I told H. if the 'squire wanted more with me than I did with the 'squire, he should come to me; and added, that I cared nothing for him nor the 'squire, or any body else. He found himself higher behind than before, as the saying is; he began to apologise to me and said, he was in a passion, and made overtures to bury the hatchet and make good friends. I told him as an offset to remember the flour and the shad, as I allowed that he could do with me as he pleased as I was a new beginner, and a little green.

I told him, however, that if he thought so, that he reckoned without his host. I consented finally to settle the hash, after he allowed me to put my pony Bonaparte into the grass-patch when I pleased, upon which we made good friends. We then for a short time had a cessation of hostilities, the truce lasted till winter.

Mr. H. was in the habit of working late at night, he had a fashion of coming every night into the kitchen to examine for himself. I asked my wife what took Mr. H. to the kitchen every night before he went to bed. She said she did not know, unless he went there to get something to eat. Said I, I'll stop him of that if I mistake not, the first cold night that comes; so one night being very cold, I took a bucket of water and hung it over the door of the kitchen, and when he opened the kitchen door, and as I went to bed, I told

my wife that she should not go to sleep until Mr. H. went into the kitchen;
she wanted to know my reason. I told her, that I had hung up a bucket of
water for him; she wanted to rise and remove it, and I would not let her; she
then said she would call to him when he came. I told her she should not, and
we laid in bed but a short time when he came and opened the kitchen door,
which gave the bucket a tilt, and the water came souse over Mr. H. and gave
him a complete shower over his head. He changed his linen and clothing
before he went to bed, muttering something all the time, and I laid snug in
my bed laughing and enjoying the fun. In the morning after his shower bath
I called him to breakfast. He asked me how I came to serve him such a nice
trick last night. I thought it was not so very nice, and asked him, if it was him
that went into the kitchen; he said, yes; and I knew very well that it was him;
I told him, yes, I know it now; he said that he might get his death of cold by
it. I told him, that I did not tell him to go there I was sure. I told him that if
he was hungry and would say so, my wife would have a piece ready for him
in the room, that he had no right to go to the kitchen. He said he went there
to see after the fire. I told him I thought my wife was old enough to take care
of them things, that was another offence which we also made up; I told him I
had merely done it for fun.

We lived in peace and harmony after the ratification of our last treaty
until spring, when spring came, and moving time which happens on all fool's
day; I moved away from Mr. H's house into the house of Mr. Swope, who
resided nearer the diamond of the town.[83] Some time after that, he asked me
what I would have to plaster the two rooms and passage I had occupied, and
which I had left; being in the fall of the year, I had not much work on hand, I
told him I would do it for twelve dollars, and he find the laborer; he said that
sum was too much, he would rather give it to me by the day, that I could do
it quicker than by the job. I told him I did not know. I asked him what he
would give a day; he told me he would give me a dollar a day and I board
myself. I told him that his offer was lower than I had ever worked in my life;
but if he would give me a half gallon of beer per day, for me and the laborer, I
would do it for him; to which proposition he agreed to, and I fell to work,
and I began to think that now it was time to get pay back for my flour and
shad. I worked until I had spun out the job for thirty-one days, and polished
my work, the walls were as smooth as glass. Mrs. Meyers, a neighbor lady,

83 The 1811–1812 tax list for Heidelberg Township, where Hanover was located, shows John
Swope, "gentleman," assessed at $3,255, a high figure. Tax List, 1811–1812, Heidelberg
Township. See also Artley Parson, *The Parson Story* (n.p., 1966, Hanover Area Historical
Society, mimeographed).

came in one day to take a look at the work, she said it was as smooth as a mirror. Mr. H. as well as the neighbors began to see that he was sucked; he began one day to throw out an insinuation, that I had caught him in our contract. I admitted I had, and observed to him, that I knew that he never would give me another chance to put it to him, and thought that now we were about even in our dealings, as he had cheated me in the flour and shad, and I had hellishly cheated him in the plastering, so I allowed it was tit for tat, the plastering was worth about twelve dollars, and I charged him thirty-one, and thirty-one half gallons of beer, so I thought I had fixed his flint pretty well.

The reader will be here informed, how I got the name of BIG BILL the plasterer; having taken up my residence in the town of Hanover, in York county, Pennsylvania, the inhabitants of the town are principally descendants of Germans, and of course have inherited from their ancestors their manners and customs; they soon found a name for me, as they were not willing to put themselves to any trouble to ascertain my name, they supplied my real name with that of "Der gross Bill der plasterer," i.e. Big Bill the plasterer, and to corroborate their ideas, suffer me to add, that in height I am six feet four inches, and my weight about that time was two hundred and fifty-two pounds; being then about thirty-one years of age; my present weight is two hundred and forty-seven pounds, and am in the forty-eighth year of my age. So after the description of Big Bill the plasterer; when I had a little leisure time, I took a tramp to Emmitsburg, and a good job of considerable value to me and my partner, Mr. Samuel Agnew. We plastered the white house for the Sisters of Charity, house of St. Joseph's, near Emmitsburg;[84] while I was in the pursuit of my labor in plastering the sisterhood house, I took sick, and laid confined to bed for two weeks. Mother Seaton was at that time superior sister,[85] their attendance on me during my sickness, was superior to any

[84] In 1809 the White House became the first house occupied by the Sisters of Charity (see Figure 4). It is still standing and is on the National Register of Historic Places. The following is from Mother Rose White's Journal, 16 March 1810: "Men began to plaster the first story; we moved from one room to another, and at one time lived in the hall" (typescript, St. Joseph's Provincial House Archives, Emmitsburg). The archives also contain the record of a payment of seventy dollars to "S. Agnew, plasterer," dated 28 August 1810. I thank Sister Aloysia Dugan, archivist, St. Joseph's Provincial House, for this information.

[85] Elizabeth Ann Bayley Seton, 1774–1821, was a native of New York City. While teaching at a Catholic girls' school, in 1809 she and four companions formed the religious community that was to become the Sisters of Charity, the first American Catholic religious order. In the summer of 1809 she moved the community to Emmitsburg, Maryland. Considered the founder of Catholic education in America, she was made a saint in 1975, the only American to be so honored. Annabelle M. Melville, *Elizabeth Bayley Seton, 1774–1821* (New York, 1951).

Fɪɢ. 4. Edward Augustus Seton, *The White House,* (detail), Emmitsburg, Maryland, 1810. Courtesy, St. Joseph's Provincial House Archives.

attendance I got in my life. I can scarcely refrain from passing an eulogy upon the association incorporated by the name and style as above stated, and am only restrained by the feeling that might be awakened as they wish to be styled only what they de facto practice, CHARITY; for which I here present them my warmest and most cordial thanks for their kindness towards me, as a mark of esteem and respect for them as a body politic. After I had recovered my health, Mr. Agnew and myself finished our job, and after we were done we started for our home, and between the town of Gettysburg and Oxford, Mr. Agnew and myself, we were attacked a little after dark by a set of very cross dogs at the farm of Mr. J. Witter;[86] we were in the main road leading towards Hanover, the rascals were so fierce that we could scarce defend ourselves; I at length made use of my hatchet,[87] I threw it at one of

[86] Jacob Witter (also spelled Witters and Withers) was a farmer who lived in Mount Pleasant Township to the east of Gettysburg in Adams County. In 1810 his farmland, two horses, and two cattle were valued at $5,050, an above-average assessment. Tax List, 1810, Mount Pleasant Township, Adams County, Adams County Historical Society, Gettysburg, Pennsylvania.

[87] Used to cut the laths, a hatchet is a standard plasterers' tool.

them, and it being dark, I could not find it again, Mr. Witter came out and asked us what we were doing there, I told him I had lost my hatchet, he said if you do not clear out you Irish Rascals I'le hatchet you with the devil to you. I began to think that poor comfort was about for us.

I told him that I'd go just where I pleased, and I scarcely had the word uttered until he hit me a pelt and knocked me down, my partner he had a stick in his hand and he up and knocked Witter down, and when he was down I crawled on top of him and began to hammer him, when he began to sing out murder, at his cries his mother came out armed with a pair of tongs in her one hand and a candle in the other hand, and she saw that I was on top of her son beating him, she hit me a lick across my back with her tongs, my partner he gave the auld lady a kick and sent her heels over head, and then she sung out murder, the lick the old witch gave me on the back gave me a very severe bruise and unstrung my nerves, I let go my hold and Witter he crawled on his porch with a broken skin, and head fractured, he called to his hireling, Yunt by name, to bring him his gun to shoot the rascals, as he called us, at which we picked up our tacklings and put to our scrapers as speedy as we could move, they followed us to Upbolt's tavern near Oxford, we told Mr. Upbolt the circumstance, he told us to hide up stairs, we were scarcely there ten minutes when Mr. Witter came along inquiring after us, the tavernkeeper said he heard us go past the bridge towards Oxford, they then renewed their pursuit after us, the landlord told us we might now come down they were gone, so I called for a gill of Brandy to wash my face and neck which were pretty much scratched and cut from our rencontre. I washed my wounds with the Brandy, we then made the best of our way home through the country. When we came home on the following day we started off for Baltimore, to draw our pay for finishing the white house at the Sisters of Charity, our order was drawn on the Reverend Mr. Balchster at Baltimore. When we presented the order it was promptly reduced at sight; we returned home, and on our return found out a trick or two. Witter he found the hatchet I threw at his dog, and sent his man Yunt to Gettysburgh to ferret out whose hatchet it was, and in his inquiries he met John Agnew, the Brother to my partner, he told Yunt that his Brother Samuel and myself had passed through Gettysburgh that day. Witter having a clue upon the matter he got out a states warrant for us; when Samuel Agnew learned that a states warrant was out for us he put out and left me to make of it the best I could. One day I rode to M'Sherry's-town on my poney Bonaparte, to a kind of a shop kept by a certain man by the name of Oaster. Mr. Witter's Brother, who was a constable and held in his possession the state's warrant I have already

spoken of he inquired of Oaster if I was Big Bill the plasterer, to which
Oaster replied I was. So then he arrested me and began to call for assistance,
I told him he need not call for any help that I would go with him to Oxford
to Squire Slagle's. So when we came to Oxford we stopped at the house of
George Hirne, and sent for Squire Slagle, I had not been there fifteen
minutes until all the men, women and children in the town were there to see
me and some called me the big Irish Murderer, they made a great many
remarks about me and all unfavorable, I began to feel the lads a little for I got
some idea of the German language by this time, the constable as usual in
those cases had the Squire brought to the town, and they told him that they
had got this big Irishman; the Squire asked me if I was the man, I told him
yes I was one of them, he asked if I was prepared with security for my
appearance at court, I told him I was not acquainted with any body in that
county, he said that it was a very hard case that such a young man as I should
go to jail and lay in jail until court time, he then asked where I lived, I told
him that I resided in Hanover. Well said he have you no acquaintances about
here said he to me, I told him I knew no body except his Father, who was
Judge of the court, he asked me how I came to know his father, I told him I
became acquainted with him when I plastered Mr. Steiger's house, he asked
me if I was the man who had plastered Mr. S.'s house, I told him I was, he
then said that if I would ask the old man, meaning Judge Slagle, that he
perhaps, would go my security for my appearance at court, I told him I could
not ask the Judge, or any other person about here, meaning the neighborhood of Oxford, and gave Justice Slagle an idea that I would have to go to
jail, inasmuch as I could not furnish the security that he as a conservator of
the peace would require of me to fulfil the office which he filled, he observed
it would be a pity if I should lay in jail until court and he took his Magisterial
Chair and began to discharge the duties imposed upon him by virtue of his
office and wrote a Mittimus,[88] and when he had written it he gave it into the
hands of the official officer who had arrested me. When the constable had
the commitment in his possession he asked Mr. Hirnes, the landlord, for a
pair of pistols in the German Language. Mr. Hirnes in the same language
replied to the constable to make me drunk and after I was drunk he could
take me along just as he pleased, that he had no occasion at all for a brace of

---

[88] "A warrant under the hand and seal of a justice of the peace or other proper officer, directed
to the keeper of the prison, ordering him to receive in custody and hold in safe-keeping, until
delivered in due course of law, the person sent and specified in the warrant" (*Oxford English
Dictionary*).

pistols. He took Mr. landlord's advice, he called for a large glass of brandy sling mixed with other liquors, called stone-fence; we drank the brandy sling amongst us and in the meantime I called for a gallon of oats for my pony Bonaparte, the Squire asked the constable if he was going to take me to Gettysburgh that night, he told him no, that he was going to take me to his brother's, which was about half way between Oxford and Gettysburgh that night, that he would there tie me and remain at his brother's for the night, and take me to Gettysburgh the next day. Thinks I to myself boy you have not got me there yet, he called for another glass of brandy sling, the first being drank, we drank that, and he called for another glass. Hirnes, the landlord observed to him after the third glass was drank, that he thought that now I had enough; by this time he had our horses ordered to the door, I mounted my pony, the crowd of folks being gathered around us to witness the scene, off we started, and rode about one and a half miles to a Mr. Knight's tavern, near the tavern was a fine piece of woods, I began to think that those chances which there presented themselves to me to make my escape ought not to be neglected. I addressed my Mr. constable in plain words (which he did not expect, I knew he was not armed with any kind of weapons more than the one nature supplies all men with, the fists) by saying to him I believe I shall go no farther with you tonight, he asked my reasons for my wish, I told him I never was tied in my life, and did not intend to be tied by him that night, I laid my hand on my pony's neck and turned his head into the woods, gave him the whip, and off he ran into the woods as hard as he could lay legs to the ground, and the constable he after me and he raised the cry of stop thief and I hollowed stop thief, we run as I thought about half a mile, until my pony ran bolt up to a high fence, I jumped off, pulled down a few rails and jumped my poney over, thinking that if the constable came up to the fence I would knock him down, at length I heard him give tongue about one hundred yards from me, I made answer to him, he came to where I was, he asked me where the devil I was going to, I told him I did not know yet, where I was going to he began to expostulate with me and advised me to come back and go with him; to which I told him I would not, and said I would sooner die than go with him, he tried to persuade me, I told him it was useless, that go with him I would not upon no account, he then made an attempt to get on the fence to which manouvre I gave him a caution to stand off, if he made the attempt to get on the fence I certainly would knock his brains out for him; we then maintained our position as we were with a fence between us, we had a long argument on the state of our affairs. At length he offered to go my security upon condition that I would not run away, I told him I could not depend upon that kind of mush, and observed to him that I believed that I would rather depend upon my own course. I got on my pony and made a move to be off, he did not like to see me go as he said to me when I was on the point of riding off, to which I said if he would swear that he would go my security that I would go with him, to which he swore a very heavy plantation oath that he would, and told him to ride a head to Squire Slagle's and I would follow him. So we rode to Squire Slagle's, and when we came there he was in bed, we roused him up, the Squire asked who is there, to which interrogation he answered that it was Mr. Otter and himself, saying he believed he would bail me, that he pitied me, the Squire he thought it was right, he thought there was no danger in it. I staid on my horse until the Squire said it was all fixed, we then went to George Hirne's tavern and took a drink in friendship, and then I mounted horse and rode home. My wife knew nothing of this performance until court time came on. When the time of Oyer and Terminer and General Jail Delivery came up on the court rolls, amongst the rest my case made its appearance, I called upon an attorney, Mr. George Mitzgar, a practised Barrister, to defend my case.[89] Mr. Witter, the State's evidence, he produced the bloody shirt as an evidence against me, as also the hatchet, and swore point blank that I had struck him with the hatchet, which was as point blank a falsehood as ever fell from the lips of man, for I threw the hatchet at the dog before we came into contact with each other. In the course of the trial while Mr. Witter was on the stand, Judge Hamilton, presiding Judge of the court,[90] asked the witness pointedly this question, did you see the defendant or his partner distinctly strike you with the hatchet, to which he answered that he could not distinctly and positively say that he did for it was dark and could not discriminate which of the two had struck the blow, the absence of proof of my guilt in striking the blow, my attorney impressed the idea upon the Jury, who without ever leaving the box pronounced a verdict of not guilty for me—upon my acquittal one of the witness made information upon oath

---

[89] *Commonwealth v Samuel Agnew and William Otter,* "Jacob Witter the prosecutor," came before the Adams County court on 23 August 1810. Although Agnew was listed as a codefendant, only Otter was tried for assault and battery. George Metzgar was a well-known Adams County attorney, admitted to the bar in 1805. Sessions Docket, 23 August 1810, Clerk of Courts, Adams County Courthouse, Gettysburg, Pennsylvania. On Metzgar, see *History of Cumberland and Adams Counties, Pennsylvania* (Chicago, 1886), 3:98.

[90] James Hamilton, judge of the Adams County Court from 1805 to 1819. *History of Cumberland and Adams Counties,* 3:92.

against Mr. Witter for keeping a set of dogs so ferocious in their nature as to constitute them a public nuisance, and proved them such to the satisfaction of the court and Jury, and Mr. Witter was fined ninety dollars, and he had the court charges to pay in both suits, and I came off with flying colors and glad of it.[91] Mr. Metzgar my attorney, told me to go to Witter and ask him for my hatchet, and if he refused to deliver it up to me to sue him on the spot for it, and to prosecute him for false imprisonment into the bargain. I went to Witter and demanded my hatchet, he asked me if it was mine, and I asked him if it was his, he said it was not, I said then give it to me or else I'le sue you for it upon the spot, as for the false imprisonment I care nothing for that, I was glad I was clear of the scrape, and so ended this spree.

The next spree was one of rather more force than fighting dogs and men, it arose as the reader will learn in the sequel. I got a job of plastering to do in Gettysburgh for a Mr. Davis, a chair maker, he had a journeyman of the name of James Doogan,[92] in a few days after I had commenced work at Mr. Davis's, James Doogan and myself became acquainted. I found that James had got himself in the habit of running after night, and was determined to watch the lad; I watched him, one night he took away the shop ladder down to the lower end of the garden to a small house that stood near a vacant lot, he put up the ladder against the gable end window of the house, it was a one story house. I laid concealed about a quarter of an hour, I then went and took away the ladder and alarmed the old people, who occupied the house, the Daddy of the family was somewhat a rough sort of a christian, he in short order raised a hell of a rumpus, James he slipped his understanding out of the window to catch with his feet the top of the ladder, but no ladder was there, being hard pressed he had to let go his hold and down he came sock on the ground. I had laid myself into a fence corner watching the lad, and to see the performance, poor Jim who by the way had a very hard fall, he came crawling on his hands and knees towards me, making his way homewards as well as he could, every yard or two he would mutter the words O Lord, which tickled me most prodigiously, I almost killed myself laughing at him—he crawled over the fence into Mr. Davis's lot, and I ran round by an

[91] "Twelve good and lawful men . . . Do Say the Defendant William Otter is not Guilty and that Jacob Witter the prosecutor pay costs of Prosecution," Sessions Docket, 23 August 1810

[92] The 1811 Gettysburg tax list, under single men, records a "James Dugan, chairmaker." No Davis is listed in 1811, but the 1810 tax list shows an "Edward Davis, wheelwright," the same occupation Dugan is listed as following that year. Tax Lists, 1810 and 1811, Gettysburg Borough, Adams County, Adams County Historical Society, Gettysburg, Pennsylvania.

ally and got into bed before him, and by and by my Jim he came crawling up
stairs upon his hands and knees, when he came into the room he called for
me thus, oh Otter, and I pretended not to hear him, then he called to me O
Bill, I responded who is there, he said for God sake get up, and go for the
Doctor for me, I told him to go the devil and not bother me, he by this time
crawled up to the bed side and insisted on me going for the Doctor for him, I
then asked him what was the matter, he had a good lie made up bad as he was
hurt, he said he was coming up the back alley, that two dogs attacked him
and in trying to get out of their way he fell over the fence, and believed that
he had broke some of his ribs. To which speech I remarked that he was only
making fun—he declared to God that he did not, I then said he should come
to bed that I would go for the Doctor for him, he said he could not that he
had crawled from the lower end of the lot up to the bed on his hands and
knees. I then went for the Doctor for him, the Doctor came and I got a
candle, the Doctor examined him and found his ribs black and blue all on
one side of his body, from his shoulder to the hip. The Doctor after the
examination pronounced his ribs very much jarred but not broke; he asked
him how he fell, Jim told him that he was so much in a hurry he could not
tell him how he fell, which in part was the truth, for the old fellow was so
wrothy that there was no time to think either before or after he fell from the
gable end window. I asked Jim, to humor the joke, if he knew whose dogs
they were, he said he did not, and added if he knew whose they were he
would be switched if he wouldn't shoot them. I added and so would I if I
were him. The Doctor said it was well that the dogs had not caught him, I
allowed they had caught him, the Doctor he tapped Jim's claret and took a
good deal of blood, and told him that he would call to see him the next
morning. After that he put out, and as he went out he enjoined it on Jim to
lay as still as he could for that night. —Jim he obeyed the Doctor's directions, he lay as quiet as he could during that night until morning. Agreeably
to the Doctor's promise to call and see Jim in the morning, Doctor Wells[93]
came as he had promised and gave him some medicine. I inquired of the
Doctor how he was, the Doctor said that he must certainly have got a higher
fall than off of the fence as he was bruised too severe for a fall of the size
described by Jim, and allowed that he was not dangerously ill, he the Doctor
asked me if I was with him when he fell, or did I know any thing about it, I

---

[93] Probably Gettysburg doctor Roger Wales, recorded in the 1810 Gettysburg tax list as owning
$550 worth of property. Tax List, 1810, Gettysburg Borough.

told him I was not with him when he fell and that I knew nothing about it. Mrs. Davis she came in the morning to pay Jim a visit, as he was an inmate of the house, and had some toast to refresh him, with that she set up an inquiry about his misventures, he told her the made up story of his falling over the fence. Jim lay quiet as a mouse until about the middle of the afternoon when a circumstance occurred which led to a discovery of the true cause of Jim's caper and mine. Mr. Davis the boss had occasion to go aloft for some stuff to make chairs, he could not find the ladder which they had to ascend with to get their chair stuff off the garret, he asked the boy if he knew where the ladder was; the boy said no, Mr. Davis sent the boy to enquire of Jim if he knew where the ladder was, Jim answered him no, he then asked me if I knew where the ladder was, and I answered him no. So there was all no, and no ladder amongst us as we did not want it then, the boss told the boy that he must go and hunt the ladder, and the boy had some idea for what purpose it had been used on former and similar occasions, for he went down to the end of his master's lot and found it like a daizy. Davis and his wife arrived at the true conclusion of Jim's scrape, they allowed that in visiting a certain house which stood at the end of their lot that Jim must have fallen from that window in the gable end, and asked me if I knew any thing about it, to frustrate their surmise as all their ideas on the subject was conjecture, I replied to them that I knew nothing about it, and told them that I would ask that night when I went to bed. I told Jim when I came to bed how I had been chatechised about the ladder by the boss and how and where he found it, and his suspicions about it. Jim he confessed to me that all was true, and that he would give ten dollars if he knew who took away the ladder, yet enjoined it on me not to say any thing to the boss about it. I told him I certainly would conceal it from him, and told Jim that if any body was to serve me so, that I would give him a hell of a thumping if I would find him out. Poor Jim had to keep his bed for about two weeks, until he was able to work again—so ended that scrape, and Jim he paid for the roast, and when I was done with my work, I put out and left all hands about the house, as the military phrase is, "as you were."

The next job that I done was a house for a Mr. Joseph Walker, near Monococy, where I once got dinner while the old man was saying grace at the table; he had been in the habit of saying grace before meals, and one day we had apple-dumplings for dinner, and my work admitted of no delay; when the old man began to say grace, he closed his eyes, and kept them closed until he was done with his prayer, and as he began to pray, I began to play away at the apple-dumplings, and as he finished his prayer I finished my dinner; and when he opened his eye, he invited me to help myself to which invitation, which was a very cordial one, as they treated me very well all the time I was there, I thanked the old gentleman, and informed him, that I had just finished my dinner. This I thought was doing business on a middling short scale.

One Sunday, I had a notion to take a ride to myself, I kept dodging about the stable till about two o'clock, P.M. when I thought dinner should be ready, and no sign of dinner, I asked one of the little girls how soon will dinner be ready; she said not until-the-cows-come-home. I told the little girl to go for the cows that I was very hungry; her mother saw us talking together; she inquired of the little girl what I had said; she told her mother that I had said, that she must go for the cows, that I wanted my dinner. The old lady told the little girl to call me to the house, that she would give me pye and milk. I went to the house and eat pye and drank milk as much as I wanted, and then got my horse and took a ride to myself, and that was one way of taking dinner when the cows-come-home. When I was done with Mr. Walker's, I went to Hanover to see my family; and when I had got home, the fair at the town of Berlin came round, at a fair estimate, I thought I should be there to see the sport. I started off for the Berlin fair myself, and went as far as Abbotstown, and was there joined by a certain Mr. Caleb Bailes, who was one of the wonders of the world,[94] we went from Abbotstown to Berlin together, and sported about all day, and another man in company with Bailes and myself, who was the owner of a small pony; he was solicitous to know if Bailes and myself were going home that evening. Bailes, he asked me if we would go. I told him I would rather stay than go home—and I asked Bailes where the fellow lived; he told me he lived near Abbotstown; I asked Bailes what kind of lad he was; to which Bailes said, that he was a kind of a green chap. I said to Caleb, let us keep him with us for the night, and let us have a spree. Bailes asked how would we keep him; I said to Bailes, I would hide the fellow's pony; Bailes told me, that if I would hide his pony for him, that he would give me a handsome treat. I told Bailes to keep the fellow in the dancing room, I would soon fix that matter. Bailes kept the fellow, and I went to the

---

[94] Caleb Bailes, 1784–1850, was an Abbottstown mason. In 1815 his property was assessed at $1,095, about average for the community Pennsylvania State Septennial Census, 1821, Berwick Township, Adams County, Adams County Historical Society, Gettysburg, Pennsylvania; Tax List, 1815, Berwick Township, Adams County, Adams County Historical Society; Cemetary Inscription File, Adams County Historical Society.

stable and looked about the stable, and found near to the stable a corn crib, wherein they had stowed some barrels filled with rye, and some empty barrels, and a door to the corn crib. I told the hostler to take my horse and Mr. Baile's horse down to the creek and wash their legs well, that we would be there all night, while the hostler took our horses to the creek to wash their legs as I directed him, I took the fellow's pony out of the shed and put him into the corn crib, and shut the door on him. I went to the hostler when he came back from the creek with our horses, and ordered a peck of oats a piece, telling him we would not go away until morning—next after that I went into the tavern, and went into the room where they were dancing; Caleb Bailes when he seen me, he asked me if I had fixed him, I told him I had; this young man was dancing at that time, the owner of the pony which I had hid in the corn crib. Bailes, he asked me where I had hid the pony, I told him he was in the crib; Caleb, he allowed that the pony was in a very good place. After the young man had his dance out, we all went up to the bar and took a drink; while we were drinking, Mr. Bailes asked me if I was going to stay all night, I told him I would, as the day had worn away too far now to think of going home, that I should stay in town now for that night. He then addressed himself to the young man whose pony was hid in the corn crib, if he was going to stay for the night; he said he believed not, that he was going home. We all three agreed that we would go and take supper, it was about supper time; after supper we all went down to the stable; Mr. Bailes asked the hostler if he had fed our horses; he told Mr. B. that he had, that I had been there and had ordered him to give them a peck of oats a piece. Mr. B. looked about for the young man's pony; the hostler said he was hitched in the shed; he told the hostler to bridle him, and he took the lantern and went into the shed, and when he came there, no pony was there; we went into the shed ourselves and looked all about the yard and could see nothing of the pony; the young man began to feel for himself in the absence of his pony, and said that he would look to the hostler for him. The hostler said, that he never gave him to him to keep him for him; he said it was a very nice piece of business. We began to persuade him to stay all night, that perhaps he would find him in the morning; he consented, and we cruized about until midnight, we all called for beds; the landlord, Mr. Swartz,[95] he put us into a bed-room, that he had at least one dozen of beds in it. The beds were

---

[95] Adam Swartz kept in Berlin between 1814 and 1827 a tavern that was known at various times as the Indian King or the Indian Queen. "Adams County Tavern Licenses to 1850: A Source Book," Adams County Historical Society, Gettysburg, Pennsylvania.

arranged in a row on one side of the room in which they were placed, with a sufficient room to get into them. Two young men lay in a bed next to the one Caleb Bailes and myself occupied for the night, and they were both fast asleep when Bailes and myself retired to rest. Bailes observed to me, if I could and would keep from laughing, that he would have them two fellows a fighting in about five minutes, and I was all my life fond of sport; to see how he would manage the fellows who were soundly asleep at the time to get them fighting; I made him a faithful promise, that I under all and every circumstance would refrain from laughing; he lay on the far side of the bed; he reached over me and uncovered the lads and exposed their legs, and when he had that done, he had an extraordinary knack to pinch with his toes, and to heighten the scene for fun, his subjects had a dram or two ahead; he reached with his toes over our bed and got a hold of the lads hams and gave him a hell of a pinch; he sung out to his bed-fellow, "HAR UFF DU," i.e. behave yourself; this performance of Bailes made me feel the force of it so sensibly, that I was forced to take my pillow to my mouth to smother the laugh which was welling within, and which I was apprehensive I could not stifle, as I measurably had anticipated, the fun which had in part then been realized; he let the lads lay a little while, and then he gave the fellow another nip; the lad who received the pinch, addressed himself to his bed-fellow in the German, saying, "ich will verdamnt sey, wan du noch a mohl mich petz'st ich schlagt deir ains he das dich der deifel hohld." The fellow whom he addressed in such rough and uncouth language, all the while lay snoring and unconscious of what was going on. Caleb let him lay a little while longer, and presently he reached over a third time and gave the Dutchman a rouser of a pinch with his toes, upon the receipt of which he hastily set himself up in bed and addressed himself to his comrade who all the while was asleep with "By God ich will dish Schaarckzes," and whap he let the fellow have a hell of a blow with his fist right between his eyes, the fellow who was asleep jumped out of bed and began to sing out murder, the other fellow who had been pinched by Bailes he out of bed after him, and the two Dutchmen had a very hard fight for about five minutes, when we began to feign ourselves awake, we jumped out of bed and begged them not to fight. We as well as the fellows who fought were all in undress, the one he asked his comrade, after we had parted them for what he had struck him, he asserted that he had pinched him, that it was all black and blue, the other he called him a verdaumter ligner, conscious of his innocence, and at the exchange of the lie, they got at fighting the second time and did beat one another most unmerciful. After they raised the second row, the landlord and the landlady came into our dormitory to see and learn what was the matter and they had a candle or two, to throw light upon the subject, and as luck would have it they caught the whole of us in an undress, and the combatants stark naked, for they had torn one another's shirts off of their backs.

We got the boys parted a second time and begged them to drop it and make friends, and after keeping them apart for a considerable time they at last agreed to make it up; they did so. After it was all made up the landlady inquired into the cause of their rumpus, the one whom Bailes pinched asserted that the other one had pinched him, and to confirm his assertion he turned his bum to the landlady's inspection to corroborate what he had said was the truth by producing the marks which he said were black and blue. Next he drew her attention to his ham, and there showed the marks which were then visible of the fellow's pinching him. The landlady having before her the evidence of the facts and by her declared as such—the other fellow who by this time stood convict in the landlady's estimation, said that if he had pinched him he must have done it in his sleep and was unconscious of it, and our pony man he lay in the bed next to our's trembling, and half scared to death, all the while the fellows were fighting; and to close the scene they got a drink and we joined and got the pony man to participate in it. When we had all drank friends, we went to bed and slept soundly for the balance of the night, and the blackest pair of eyes I ever seen was exhibited by the fellow who got the first blow the morning after the affray, and so ended the scrape, and the pony man the next morning he paid for the fun until he got his pony, which was about all the sport I enjoyed at the Berlin fair. And the way the pony business wound up was, we all fell to searching after his pony, and all to no purpose, he at last told the hostler that if he would find his pony he would give him a dollar; and after a reward of a dollar had been put upon the pony I told the hostler if he would keep dark I would tell him where the pony was, the hostler he said he would not divulge it for the sake of getting the reward, I then told him that he was hid by us in the corn crib adjoining the shed, he went there and seen that the pony was there as I had told him, and after some time he came in and told him that he had found him, we asked him where he was, he said that if we would come out he would show us, we all followed the hostler to see where the pony was; he took us to the corn crib, and sure enough there Mr. pony was, the owner he said that he was the biggest rascal of the horse kind he ever knew.

I told him that all that kind of ponies were like him, and he believed me as

he had been so wofully tricked by his, as he thought by the pony, and he
happened to be tricked by me all the time, the hostler he got the pony out of
his place of concealment and the pony man paid him the reward. We all took
a horn and mounted horse and started off from the Berlin fair for Abbotstown, when we came to Abbotstown, we all three Bailes, the pony man and
myself, we stopped at the tavern kept by Mr. Gardner, the pony man he put
out for his home, and Bailes he lived next door to the tavern, and opposite a
Mr. Ickes also a tavern-keeper in Abbotstown,[96] and a very inquisitive kind
of an old root; Bailes knew exactly what kind of game we had before us, he
told me that he, Ickes, would certainly call over to see and learn who I was
and where I was from and where I was going, and fifty idle questions besides,
which he was in the habit of asking strangers, and Bailes knew Ickes's
propensities and told them to me, and said that he would introduce me to
him, under a fictitious name, and that I then must humor the joke; I seen the
web laid by Bailes to hoax old Ickes, and I began to prepare accordingly. In
about five minutes, sure enough who came across the street but old Mr.
Ickes, leaning on his walking cane, he came into the bar-room, the place
where I was, and began his interrogatory as Bailes had anticipated by asking
me how I did, are you, continued he, travelling; by this time, being at a
happy juncture of our affairs, Bailes he came in, I addressed myself to Bailes
if he would take a drink of something; he said he did not care, I called for
some brandy and Bailes and myself we took a drink of brandy. Mr. Ickes he
called Caleb to one end of the bar-room and asked him in Dutch who I was,
Mr. Bailes told him that I was a gentleman from Buffalo. Mr. Ickes began on
Bailes just as he, Bailes, wished it, by signifying a wish to be introduced to
me so that he could learn from me if I knew his son or not, who was captain
of a company of Militia men, in the service of the United States, stationed at
Buffalo,[97] Mr. Bailes he brought Mr. Ickes up before me and said to me Mr.
IRVINE, I'll make you acquainted with Mr. Ickes. Mr. Ickes, said how do you
do. He waived all farther ceremony being extremely anxious to hear from
Buffalo, he asked me in nearly half Dutch and half English, if I came from
Buffalo, I told him I was just from it, he then asked how times was at Buffalo,
I told him to excite him the more that times there was very hard—he asked
me in what respect—I told him that a great many of the men were dying
with the camp-fever, and my object was to go on to the city of Washington to
give the intelligence to the heads of Department to get our quarter changed

---

[96] Peter Ickes kept a tavern called the Sign of the White Horse in Abbottstown between 1807
and 1814. "Adams County Tavern Licenses to 1850."
[97] This was during the War of 1812.

for a healthier place, he said he supposed that I scarcely ever was along with the army, I told him I was very seldom with them, that my business principally was buying cattle, that sometimes I went as far as a hundred miles from the army to procure a sufficient quantity of cattle for them—he said he supposed I got good wages for my office—I told him I got eighty dollars a month, and found in a horse, &c., he allowed that I had reason to be glad that the war should last a good while, I told him I should not be grieved if it would last my life time. He then asked me if I had ever been in any of the battles, to which I answered him that I had not, my not having any occasion to fight, my whole business was to procure provisions. He asked me if I had any acquaintance with any of the captains who were out at the lines, this was the hoax, I told him I had, and was the bearer of a list of all the names of those who were wounded—he then asked me if I knew a certain captain Ickes, I told him I did, and added that captain Ickes had either a leg or an arm shot off, and did not recollect which of the two limbs he had lost.— This piece of intelligence brought the old man to shedding tears, and his sympathy was aroused, he pitied him, and yet allowed with all that he knew that captain Ickes was a soldier; he allowed that the rascally English ought all to be killed. He began to inquire if there was any danger of death among the officers who were wounded, I told him it was thought not, that if care was taken, that they were all convalescing. He asked me when I was coming back again I allowed myself a month's time, when should be able to transact my business, I should then return, he wished me on my return to call, saying he wanted to write by me to his son, I told him that I dare not carry any letter for any person as I was doing business for government. He asked Bailes and myself to take some brandy. After a while I mounted horse and put out for Hanover, and when I came to Hanover, being then at home for a day or two, a gentleman from Liberty, in Frederick County, Maryland, came to my house and told me he had lost a negro man, who had ran away from him, and he had been informed that I had the knack of apprehending fugitives of that class,[98] he gave me a handbill describing his black man, and a reward of fifty

[98] Pennsylvania had passed a gradual emancipation law in 1780—the first state to do so— providing that all children of slaves born after that date would become free at the age of twenty-eight. Later amendments speeded up the process. By 1810 there were only twenty-two slaves among York County's 31,958 inhabitants. All fugitive slaves from other states, however, had to be returned. Gary B. Nash and Jean Soderland, *Freedom by Degrees: Emancipation in Pennsylvania and Its Aftermath* (New York, 1991); Edward Raymond Turner, *The Negro in Pennsylvania: Slavery—Servitude—Freedom, 1639–1861* (1911; rpt., New York, 1969), pp. 64–68. Treasury Department, *Aggregate Amount of Each Description of Persons within the United States of America* (Washington, 1811)

dollars to any person who would apprehend him and lodge him in a jail, or deliver him to the boss so that he would get his negro again. He wished me to take horse and immediately pursue him, I told him if he would give me five dollars I would pursue him two days, and if I overtook him and apprehend him I should then charge him the reward, and if I did not succeed in overtaking him, that the five dollars should be my fee for my two days service; he acquiesced in my proposition, he gave me the five dollars, and the next morning I got on my horse and went in pursuit after the runaway, and rode that day until about the middle of the afternoon in the direction of York in Paradise township, I became very hungry, I called at a house and asked the man if I could get something to eat and my horse fed, and added that I would pay him for it, he said yes, that he could feed me and my horse. I dismounted and we took my horse to the barn to feed him, and as we were to wait awhile until my dinner should be ready, he said he was making mortar, and to suit the action to the word he went to the mortar bed and I went along with him, and while he was at work at the mortar I asked him if he was building, he said that he had a chimney to build and a room to plaster. I then went into the house and the plasterers were at work to see how things were, after I came out I asked mine host how long the plasterers had been at work at the room, they were at the first coating, he told me they were at it two weeks, I then asked him what he gave them for doing it, he said he paid them a dollar a day. I then told him that I knew a man that could finish it in two hours, yes said he, I would give him five dollars if he were there to do it, as he was quite sick and tired out with the hands he had at work, and added that he also knew a big Irishman who lived in the town of Hanover that could do the whole job in one day, to which I observed that I did not know any thing of him, I then told him if he would give me five dollars, provided the plasterers were agreed that I would do it in two hours, he said that I could not possibly do it in that time, by way of surprise I told him if the men would give me their tools, and if I did not finish it in the time by me limited that I would do the work free from charge, but if I done it in the two hours he was to pay me the stipulated sum, he said that he would give me the five dollars, if I done it I told him I would upon condition, if he would keep me in stuff, he also agreed to do that, he allowed that they all hands could keep me a going. I then asked the men if they would allow me to put on the ceiling in that room, they said yes, with a great deal of cheer, and confessed that they did not understand the business. So then all things being fairly understood amongst us and the hands, I then hauled off my coat and began to get ready to work, and the two plasterers and mine host were kept very busy in carrying and tempering mortar for me during the time I was putting on the ceiling, as no time was allowed for chat, and in one and a half hours I was done with the whole, gimbang. One of the plasterers said he had often heard of that Irishman at Hanover, who was such a celebrated plasterer, but he allowed that the Irishman was no touch to me. The owner of the house asked me where I resided, I told him I lived in Baltimore some time, well knowing that they alluded to me all the while, but they did not know that I was the Big Irishman all the while, and I did not wish them to know that fact, one of them said that if he could work like me that he would not work at it long. We all washed ourselves and went into the mansion house, the man of the house paid me the five dollars, I asked him how much he charged me for my dinner and for feeding my horse, he said that he would charge me nothing for that. He told his men that Appleman talked so much about the big Irishman in Hanover, he allowed that I could plaster round him. I then asked the two plasterers how long they allowed it would take them to finish their job, they said that they did not know, and being ashamed of their work they allowed that they would have nothing more to do with it; they in turn asked me how long it would take me to finish such a job, I told them that I could do it in about half a day. I told them that it was time for me to be moving, as I was in pursuit of a black man who had run away from his master, I asked them if they had seen or heard of any black man passing through that part of the country, they said they had neither seen or heard of any. I then mounted my horse, bade them a good bye, and went on to Little York that evening, and put up at a tavern in York, kept by Harry Shafer, it was at the time of the last war, the militia of York County that had been called into the service were encamped on the commons, waiting for marching orders; the next morning I went to see the troops and when inside of the guards, I seen an old man inside of the lines who had a waggon load of onions, cabbage and potatoes, the onions were strung on long bunches; by this time I got along side of the wagon, and while there, four or five soldiers came along that way, one of the soldiers asked the old man how he sold his onions, he said twenty-five cents a bunch, the soldier allowed them to be too dear at that price, and offered the old man a dollar for five bunches, the old man he picked him out five bunches, and the soldier he took them from him and laid them on the ground and turned himself towards the old man in the act of getting out the money to pay for the onions the old man observed to him, that one of the hands that was with him had taken the onions and was running away with them as hard as he could, and the one that was to pay for them he ran after the thief to overtake him, as hard as he could, and the pursuer did not overtake the pursued, and the old man laughed at the performance ready to split his sides, and by the bye the soldiers forgot to come back to pay for the onions, which was a complete bite, and he only seen the hoax when it was too late, and no doubt the soldiers in their turn laughed as hearty at the old man as he did at them while they were carrying away his onions. After I had witnessed the above related performance I went to the town of my host, Mr. Harry Shafer, I asked after a man of the name of Stoutzenberger, an officer of the peace, and when I found Stoutzenberger I told him that I was after a runaway, I showed him my handbill he said he seen nothing of him, and added that he had in his possession some handbills from Baltimore, and believed that they were in Columbia, and said that if I would go along with him we would go there and see.

I told him I did not care, and off we started for Columbia, and put up with Mr. Livergood's for that night; we asked the hostler if he knew of any negro houses about there; he told us that there was one in one of the back alleys in which the negroes danced almost every night, and said that he could find out in a few minutes if they would have a dance there that night; we told him he should find out for us that fact; and we went into the house and called for supper, and when we had supped, over we went into the stable again; he, the hostler told us, that there was a negro dance down the river, a short distance from town. We told the hostler that we would give him a half a dollar if he would go along with us to the house: he said he would, if we would say nothing to the landlord; we agreed we would keep dark. We went there and took a look at them dancing, and Stoutzenberger, he seen one of the lads he was in pursuit of; then came the rub how to get him out. We were looking out, and asked the hostler, if he knew a certain negro whom we pointed out to him; he said he knew him very well, that he lived at Mr. Wright's, cutting wood for him on the bank of the river. After we had received this piece of intelligence, we went home to our lodgings, and came to a definite conclusion, how we would take the lad in the morning. We got up and ordered the hostler to give our horses a gallon of oats a piece, we then got our breakfast; then we told the landlord our business, and requested him to let the hostler take our horses about a half a mile from town. He said that he would, if we would keep it a secret. We promised we would, and enjoined on him to keep our business a secret; he assured us that there was no danger of his divulging our business. We told the hostler to take our horses and ride them as far as the old road, and wait for us there until we came. We went up the river, and at length we heard our lad chopping wood. I staid behind, and in concealment, and Stoutzenberger he went to where he, the negro, was chopping wood; and he told him that he would give a half a dollar if he would come down to the river and help him off with his boat, that it was fast. The negro he came to help us off with our boat, and we took him into our special custody, and told him that he was our prisoner, and told him that if he said one word, that we would blow him through. We took him up the river a piece, and thence through the country to the old road, and we took him on to the city of Lancaster before a justice of the peace, and had him committed to jail. We were called upon to give security for four days. We entered the required security, and went to the stage office and wrote on to the fellow's master in Baltimore immediately, informing him of the apprehension of his negro man, and to come on immediately to prove and identify the black man whom we had arrested to be his property.

He came on the third night and released us and our security, by entering the jail with his proof required of him, and identified the lad to be his slave, and took him out of jail, and from the jail he took him to Mr. Slaymaker's tavern, and put on him a pair of hand-cuffs; paid us the reward and all our expenses, and hoisted off the lad for Baltimore.

After the man had gone, we also started off, and put out for home, each of us having in our pockets an equal share of the reward, which was one hundred dollars—so there ended that performance, and I then put out for Hanover, and did not hear or see any thing of the negro who I had started especially for, when I left Hanover. In the mean time I undertook a very large job of plastering for the next season near Maytown.

I laid on my oars, having no particular employ for several days, and one night while I had nothing to do, I in the evening got into company with several jolly fellows. We sat down at the tavern of Mr. John Amich in Hanover, to take a few games at cards for a little sport. While I was indulging myself in the dissolute amusement, Mr. Jacob Eichelberger[99] sent his man Friday down to tell me, that a gentleman had called at his house who had a

---

[99] Jacob Eichelberger, 1743–1832, was a well-known resident of Hanover. He was a sheriff of York County and four times chief burgess of Hanover between 1816 and 1825. According to an 1887 reminiscence, "He was a merchant, a farmer and for many years owned a tavern. . . . He was quite an influential man in his day in local affairs. He was tall, well-formed, walked very erect and was a true representative of the gentlemen of olden times," wearing his hair in a queue "Old Time Hanover—Its Incorporation in 1815," *Hanover Herald*, 15 January 1887. The article is based on the recollections of Judge William Young.

wish to see me. I told his man as soon as our game was up, I would call up and see the gentleman; and, when our game was finished according to promise, I called up at Mr. Jacob Eichelberger's tavern, to wait upon the gentleman who had sent for me. He told me, that he had lost his negro man, Congo, and said, that if I would get him, the negro for him, that he would give me fifty dollars; he gave me a hand-bill describing his man Congo; and after a moments reflection, I knew where Congo was harbored. I then went back to Mr. John Amich's tavern to see a comrade of mine, in whom I had a great deal of confidence, a certain Mr. Wm. Albright,[100] to whom I shewed the hand-bill I had got, and told Mr. Albright that I knew where the negro was, and got his consent to assist me in apprehending negro Congo, and off we started for Mr. Jacob Hoffman's tavern on the road leading to Abbots-town, at the foot of the Pigeon Hills,[101] where negro Congo had been hired to haul stones for a barn that Mr. Hoffman was about building. It was about ten o'clock at night, when Mr. Albright and myself came to Mr. Hoffman's, and they had all retired to rest for the night. We rapped at the door loud and strong, at length Mr. Hoffman got up, and I pretended to be warmed with a little steam. Mr. Hoffman, inquired where we had been; we told him, we were at Abbotstown, and our horses had broken loose and here we were, and on our way home. He advised us to take bed and stay all night, and go home in the morning. I told my landlord, that if my comrade was agreed to stay, that I did not care to stay myself. Mr. Hoffman gave us a candle, and told us to go into the ball-room, and take bed in that room, the carpenters and all hands were quartered that were employed about the building. We went up into the ball-room as Mr. Hoffman had directed us. The boss carpenter was awake when we entered the room; he asked us WHAT'S BROKE, said he. I told him that we were on a sort of a Jerry,[102] and wished to get a bed for that night if we could. He said there was a vacant bed in the far end of the room;

---

[100]William Albright (or Albricht) was a Hanover bricklayer who, as Otter was later to do, kept a tavern. The 1818–1819 tax list shows him assessed at only $95, not owning a house. Tax List, 1818–1819, Borough of Hanover, York County, microfilm in the Hanover Public Library, Hanover, Pennsylvania. John T. Reily, *History and Directory of the Boroughs of Gettysburg, Oxford, Littlestown* (Gettysburg, 1880), p. 143.

[101] Low hills north of Hanover on the border of Adams County and York County (see Map 2). Otter's account suggests that it was not exactly a center of genteel society in this period.

[102] "Jerry" means spree, from Pierce Egan's enormously popular book *Life in London; or, the Day and Night Scenes of Jerry Hawthorne, Esq., and his elegant friend Corinthian Tom, accompanied by Bob Logic, the Oxonian, in their Rambles and Sprees throughout the Metropolis* (London, 1821).

and I pretended to carry my cantico[103] so far as to induce the hands to believe that I was really in a spree. I said, I must see all hands first, and by this time they were all awake, and I took the candle in my hand and began a general inspection of the hands, and got to the lower end of the room, in a bed, and under the feather bed lay snug and comfortable negro Congo. I said, ho ho my lad to Congo, are you here. The boss carpenter said to me, the negro was very tired, that he had worked hard that day, I should let him rest. I said he is the very lad that I wanted. He told me that I had no business with the negro, and if I did not go to bed he would call Hoffman up. I told him that I did not care how soon he would call up Hoffman, that the negro I must have. I pulled the bed from off the negro and ordered him to get up, and if he did not rise I would exercise him with a club, to which he bluntly replied, that he would not get up. By this time Mr. Hoffman was amongst us, and asked me what the devil I wanted with the negro. I told Hoffman that he belonged to me, and I shewed Hoffman the hand-bill describing Congo. After he had read it, he being satisfied that Congo was the very fellow who was described in the hand-bill, he told me that I might do with him just as I pleased, that he had nothing more to say to him, or for him. Mr. Hoffman went down stairs and went to his bed. I then peremptorily ordered the negro to get up the second time, and he again refused to obey my mandate; I laid hands on him and hauled him out of bed, and the boss carpenter begged me not to abuse the negro. I told him, that I was not quite so tipsey as he imagined I was, I would use him just as I pleased. In putting on his pantaloons, the black rascal drew upon me a jack-knife; at the exhibition of his knife, I up fist and knocked him down, and took his knife from him, for fear of small accidents, and tied him with a rope. The boss carpenter swore, that if he knew that, that I should not have had the negro. I told him, I knew that. I then made the negro go down stairs into the bar-room; he asked me to give him a dram before we started. I told Mr. Hoffman to let me have a half pint of whiskey; he told me to go to the bar and get it. I got the whiskey, and told the negro to lean back his head and I poured it down his throat. I paid Hoffman for the whiskey, and started Congo for Hanover. On the road, he

---

[103] "A dance or dancing party, a social gathering or jollification," apparently derived from the Algonquian word for dancing. The word was "'in great use among the Dutch and English colonists in the region between New York and Virginia from the latter part of the 17th to the 19th century.'" See Mitford A. Mathews, ed., *A Dictionary of Americanisms on Historical Principles* (Chicago, 1951).

asked me if it was his old or his young master that was at Hanover. I told him he was a young man; he then said he did not care, as he did not fear his young master as much as he would the old man. I then asked him from what reasons he ran away; he began his reason, that he used to drive the team, and that they charged him with stealing salt.

We arrived in the town of Hanover about two o'clock in the morning with negro Congo. Just before we came to Mr. Eichelberger's, the house where his master was, he begged me to untie him, that he did not like to meet his master tied. I told him, that made no odds that it was night, and nobody seen him; I roused Mr. Eichelberger up, and requested him to awaken his guest, and inform him that I had his negro. Mr. Eichelberger who is a perfect gentleman in every respect, and one of the laziest men in York county, he was too lazy to rise and let his guest know that I had his negro; and told me to take him to my house and keep him till the next morning; thinking no doubt to shab me off in that way. But the owner of the negro heard us, and he demanded a candle, and Mr. Eichelberger at last was forced to get up, contrary to his wishes. I took the negro into the bar-room, and by this time the master was there. I told him that I believed I had got him his man. He held the candle close to the negro's face, and interrogated him saying, "Well, Congo, is this you," to which Congo answered, yes, sir. He asked the negro how he had been; he told him very well. He then asked him if he had got all his business arranged in Pennsylvania; Congo allowed he had—to which the master expressed a satisfaction; saying to me, I wish you to secure him until morning, that he was a smart, keen, shrewd fellow, that for his part he could do nothing with him. I then took a chain and chained him to the stove, made a good fire into the stove, and left him, and I went home—when morning came, I went up to Mr. Eichelberger's tavern, about seven o'clock in the morning and found master and servant in the bar-room. His master bade me good morning, and asked me if I would take some bitters. I told him I had no objections, so we took a horn together, and he asked me where he could get a pair of hand-cuffs made. I told him he could get a pair of hand-cuffs made at Hensy Mauser's blacksmith shop. We started off together to the shop, and on the road to the shop, I asked him where he lived. He told me he lived in Frederick county, Maryland, near Liberty-town; so we got our irons made, and fixed them on him, went back to Mr. Eichelberger's tavern; he paid me the fifty dollars, and I shared the reward with my comrade Wm. Albright, and put out home, and the Frederick county man and Congo they put out for their home.

FIG. 5. John Lewis Krimmel, *Village Tavern*, 1813–1814. The Toledo Museum of Art; purchased with funds from the Florence Scott Libbey Bequest in memory of her father, Maurice A. Scott.

The time of year was arrived when mechanics of my profession are obliged to lay upon their oars. I was spending my time in all sorts of fashions. One evening I happened to go to the house of Henry Bear who kept a public house in Hanover;[104] and while there, an old collier of the name of Fetzer, he was in the tavern pretty well how-come-you-so. Fetzer had a spang new coat on, what folks now a days at a fair estimate would term, a long tail'd blue, and had in his coat pockets a parcel of ginger-cakes. I got some beer, and got the landlord to enter into a conversation with the old collier, and while the collier and Mr. Bear were in the height of their conversation, I took up the beer and poured it into old Fetzer's pockets among his ginger-cakes, and began to chafe the pockets pretty well; and it

[104] Henry Baer, Hanover innkeeper, assessed at $1,660 in Tax List, 1818–1819, Borough of Hanover. (See Figure 5 for an illustration of such a village tavern.)

may be as easily imagined, as described, what the cakes looked like without much strain of imagination. Fetzer he let go the landlord, and he began on me, by asking if I was the big plasterer. I told him I was; he then said that he knew me dis long while ago. I told him, inasmuch as we knew one another so well, that we ought to drink together; that I would buy a quart of beer, if he would buy one too; to my proposition he was agreed on the spot; so he called for a quart of beer, we drank that; and I called for another, and drank that too; and I observed, that I smelled somewhat a sort of a disagreeable smell; the rest of the company they chimed in with me to heighten the sport, that they smelled it too; and the landlord said, that something was not right amongst us. I made a proposition that all hands should be inspected, and the guilty one should pay a gallon of beer for his misconduct, to which Fetzer was also agreed. A general search was then instituted, and nothing was found—we all agreed that it was too delicate a subject for one man to feel every man's pockets in the company, that every man should have the freedom to search his own pockets, and by that, every man in company put his hand into his pocket, and old Fetzer he had forgot his ginger-cakes, and not knowing that I had poured beer into his pocket and chafed them well together; and it is well known to every body the nature and tenacity of ginger-bread and its general appearance. When all hands were drawn out of the respective pockets into which they had been thrust, the ginger-bread hung to Fitzer's hand like wax, his fingers were stiff full of the stuff, and his feelings were very much hurt at his dilemma. The whole company burst out in a roar of laughter, that lasted at least fifteen minutes without any kind of abatement, and as loud as any I ever heard, which terribly mortified our old collier. After the burst of laughter was over, we washed his hand and cut out the pockets out of his coat; he immediately attached all the blame to me, and the more I tried to convince him he was in a mistake, the closer he laid the charge to my door. I then by way of offset threatened to have the pocket brought in and examined to see WHAT was in it. I told the hostler to go and bring in the pockets, and that if I was guilty, that I would pay the beer. I then asked the old collier, if any thing was in his pocket before he came into the house. He said, that he had nothing in them before he came into the house. I said if that was true, that I would pay for the beer; so then the pockets were produced and examined, and their contents were declared to be ginger-cakes; when the ginger-cakes were named to him, he recollected that he had bought six and a fourth cents worth before he came to the tavern. He was convinced in his own mind that he had lost the bet, and was agreed to pay for the gallon of beer; to which I objected, and told him that he should pay only for the one half, that I would pay the other half, by way of making good friends with the old lad. He, after the beer was drank, he set awhile talking, and at last he called for his horse to go home. The horse was brought out and hitched to the sign-post; the night was very dark; I slipped out while he was talking to Mr. Bear, and turned the saddle hindside foremost, and slipped the bridle-bit out of the horse's mouth, and then went into the house again and sat down by the stove. He in the conversation with Mr. Bear, his landlord, forgot to pay his bill which occurred to him; he hauled out his money purse, paid his bill to Mr. Bear, and said, "Well, I must go home," and out he went, got hold of the bridle reins, threw them over the horses head and mounted his old bay horse. The lamp that hung at the sign-post threw light on the subject, and the saddle being turned, the old fellow pretty well cocked, he thought that things were not in their proper fixture—he addressed himself to the landlord, "Bear, des is net my saddle, er is zu verdamtd braed forne," i.e. Bear this is not my saddle, it is too d——d broad before. The landlord responded, O yes, I think it is YOUR saddle; the old collier swore he would b——d if it was his saddle, and dismounted his rosinante.[105] I placed the saddle as it ought to be, and we allowed that the hostler had made a mistake about the saddle—after the saddle had been planted right, the old fellow got a straddle of his pony the second time; he generally had a large cane with him; he with his cane gave his old horse a clue into his ribs, bade us all good night.

The bit being out of the horses mouth, as he gave him the clue with his cane he reined him up by the bridle, gave a good smart pull with the bridle, and off started the old pony, took round the corner of Mr. Bear's house and run into the shed, the place where he had been hitched, as hard as he could lick, the old fellow, when he found himself safely moored in the shed, and felt sensible where he was, he addressed himself in the German language to his horse thus "du bist ein Narr, und bleibast ein narr, so langed as du lebest, die verdamter narr (i.e. You are a fool, and you will remain a fool as long as you live, you damned fool) and at the last sentence he raised up his cane and hit the old pony a hell of a pelt across his head, we all followed the old man and heard and seen the performance which afforded us a good deal of

[105] Old, worn-out horse.

amazement, I approached him and asked him what was the matter, he said he did not know WHAT THE DEVIL had got into the horse, that he could not get him out of the shed, I then proffered my services to him to lead out his horse for him, I took the pony and led him into the street and gave him a fair start, the horse he started off up street, and ran toward the Diamond of the town and in the Diamond or rather on the opposite side of it was a Brewery, and the road which led to it was through a gate which was open, the pony made for the Brewery yard and run in among a parcel of beer barrels, the dogs in the yard got after him, he hallowed murder in Dutch, the brewer, he came out and asked who was there, the old collier he answered him by saying it is me; by this time the brewer he had got his lantern to see who it was, as he could not learn from his answer he had given him; after he seen that it was old Fetzer, he then knew him, he got a hold of his horse and led him out on the street to give him a fresh and a fair start, then I made my appearance (being concealed all the while till then) I said to him well Fetzer, are you not out of town yet; he said no, he was not out of town yet, and he did not know when he would get out, that his damned horse was fairly crazy, I felt the horse to see if the bit was yet out of his mouth and found it was, I let him go again, and told him to take another start, he did so and thought he was fairly started for home, and instead of going down York street in Hanover, the road leading to Fetzer's home, the pony he ran out the Abbotstown road to a tavern kept in the suburbs of the town, by a Mr. Henry Michael, and there he run into the shed, the old fellow found himself once more in a shed which terribly offended the old collier, he began to exercise his pony with his cane, and in raising up his cane he disturbed a parcel of chickens that had roosted there, they began to flutter and caw-caw, and the old fellow swearing at his horse at a round rate; by this time we were all there to see and hear the sport. Mr. Henry Michael he was awakened by the fuss the chickens kept, he got up and heard the rumpus in the shed, he asked what was the matter; old Fetzer said to him to go to hell, as he was very much enraged at his pony's performance. Mr. Michael told him if he did not tell him his name that he would shoot him, he told him he might shoot and be damned, that his name was Fetzer, he then got his lantern, got old Fetzer out of the shed, put up his horse, took the old fellow into the house to tarry there for the balance of the night, as he could not get his horse home, and it 'was nearly day when we brought the spree to a close, we put out home.

The next matter that presented itself to me worth relating was, one day I was in the tavern of Mr. John Bart, an old fellow who lived at or near the

Pigeon Hills,[106] accompanied by his daughter, and her intended husband came into the tavern for the purpose of a matrimonial spree, he addressed himself to me and asked me if I was the big plasterer, I told him I was the man, he said that he had often seen me, and invited me to take a drink with him, I went up to the bar and took a drink with him, he then began to tell me that they came to town for the purpose of getting Suse married to that man, pointing to her intended husband, and he was a sweet looking lark, the old fellow he made no secret of its being a case of necessity, as Suse had been fixed for slow travelling. The old fellow he led me farther into his secrets, he told me that a dollar and a quarter was all the money the trio had in the world, he inquired of me where I thought that they could get them married the cheapest, I told him O yes I could tell them that, and then told the old fellow by way of sport how I fixed the Minister when I got married, and told him that if he would come back to Bart's tavern and spend the balance of the money they would have left, I would let him into the secret, he as well as the balance of the trio was a soapstick,[107] he said that he would spend the remainder of the money cheerfully if I would put him on a way to save some, so then the bargain was struck, and I got a new half cent enveloped in two pieces of paper and directed the old fellow to go to Parson Meltzheimer[108] and ask him to marry them, and when the whole ceremony was over, and not before, he should give him the money wrapped up, which direction the old fellow kept tally agreeable to promise and direction, the Hymenial knot was tied and the Parson when his fee was handed to him he thanked him for it, and he came back to the tavern chuck full of it, and a dollar and a quarter in pocket, so then came the rub, the dollar and a quarter was all spent in wine, brandy and cakes, while that lasted we lived jam, and never gave it up until the money was all spent, and all hands pretty glad. In a day or two after the wedding was over Parson Meltzheimer had turned his horse out into his lot to let the horse exercise himself, he was at the head of his lot, I went up

106 John Bart, innkeeper, assessed at $1,885 in the 1818–1819 Hanover tax list. In 1815 he was elected high constable of Hanover. Tax List, 1818–1819, Borough of Hanover, *Hanover Borough Digest of Special and General Acts of Assembly, Officers, Contracts, Leases, Etc.* (Hanover, 1910); and Prowell, *History of York County,* 1:811, 846.

107 A slang term for a rifle, "so called for its length and slimness, suggestive of a stirring stick used in making soap" (Mathews, *Dictionary of Americanisms*).

108 Probably John F. Melsheimer. F. Valentine Melsheimer was minister of St. Matthew's Lutheran Church in Hanover from 1790 to 1815 and was succeeded by his son, who was pastor from 1815 to 1827. Because Otter includes this episode in his narrative after the War of 1812, it seems likely that it was to the son that he refers. In 1806 Valentine Melsheimer published *Insects of Pennsylvania* and is considered the father of American entomology. Gibson, p. 582.

through my lot which was adjoining Parson Meltzheimer's lot, and asked him if he had married a couple a few days ago, he said he had, with a small laugh on his countenance, he asked me if I knew them, I told his reverence I did not, that I only had seen them. I made a supposition to him that he had been well paid by them for his service, he replied that he had not been paid so very well, and allowed that I had the regulating of the fee, I told him I had been asked where I allowed that they could get the job done the cheapest and I allowed that it could not be done cheaper any where, he allowed in conclusion of our confab that the poor creature wanted all the money he had, and I allowed so too. The next was a hoggish cast of performance as it was in my hog killing time, our hero went the whole hog, tail and all, John Barts was my place of general rendezvous for sport, I was setting in his tavern one afternoon, there was from the Pigeon Hill country a man who had about three sheets in the wind, he had a wonderful gift of the gab, and I thought I had been peculiarly blest in that way, I soon found by experience that I was far behind the lad in that particular and to make up on my part, when he got too fast for me I held in my hand a small switch which I occasionally drew across his mouth when it ran too fast for me, and he then would try to catch it, we kept on that piece of sport until at length the end of my switch took my old fellow in his eye, the eye began to weep water pretty freely, being smartly wounded, some of the wags that were in the room, full of fun and presuming that they could work upon the fellow's feelings, they asserted that I had jobbed the fellow's eye out, and kept up the delusion so well, that the fellow began to believe it himself that his eye was really knocked out, they to heighten the sport with the fellow began to express vindictive feelings towards me for the injury done him, saying if they were him that they would have me taken up, I told them they need not apprehend me that I was willing to do any thing that was right, and added that I would send for a Doctor and hear what he would say, by this time they had worked so far upon the poor devil's feelings that he cried, and the water trickled down his cheeks as fast as rain, and they allowed that I should be very quick in my sending for the Doctor, that the aqueous humor of the eye would all be destroyed; I then told my companions and feigned competitors that here was the Doctor, and we took him and stretched him out on the barroom table, and the examination then commenced, the Doctor declared the eye defunct, and said that he must put in a new one, and John Bart was butchering hog's that day, I went into his yard and got a hog's eye, went into the house and gave it to the Doctor, and he fitted the hog's eye and placed it right to the place where an eye ought to be and tied it up with a handkerchief; after they had been matched by the Doctor he expressed a good deal of self complaisant satisfaction at the idea that the eyes matched so well as it was the only one that he now had left, he began to feel for his wife and children, he allowed that it would afford him a world of pleasure if he could only see them once again. They then told him that I was in the habit of fooling with every body, and at last had the misfortune to put his eye out for him, that if they were him that they would go down to Squire Shultz and they would sue me, the Doctor (Lauman) told him he would give him the bill for fixing a new eye into his head, which he allowed should be fifty dollars in case he would sue me, and I had to pay for it, and if he had to pay for it himself he would charge him twenty dollars only. So then the pretended Doctor furnished the bill, and got him started to go to Squire Shultz, before we got him to the Squire's shop, he had got the whole town into an uproar, every man, woman and child within the hearing of his voice were at their doors and windows to see and hear him for he kept on incessantly hallowing and bawling out "Herr Jesus my aug" i——e oh Lord Jesus, my eye, it took the jockey nearly one hour to get from Mr. Bart's tavern to the Squire's shop, for by turns he would forget himself and he would shut the wrong eye, and then he would fix himself in the attitude of some awkward clown, playing BLIND MAN'S BUFF, groping his way and getting the help of some mischievous boys to help him along on the road to der Schultz, as he said, at length he came to the Squire's shop, surrounded by a mob of boys, the appearance of which made the Squire's dander raise, he addressed our hero pretty gruffly what he wanted, he told Squire Schultz[109] in as pitiful a manner as he possibly could that "der gross plasterer hat mir my aug heraus geschlagne" and was going to show the Squire, that what he said was stubborn facts; he raised up the handkerchief and bandaging, and as he disturbed them, out fell the hog's eye on the pavement; that performance satisfied the Squire, that the whole mess was a hoax; he shut the door on the fellow and went into the house, and the mob of boys that were around him, they got alarmed at the dropping of the hog's eye on the pavement, they all put out, and our hero stood on the pavement all alone. He cried most bitterly when he seen the cold charity of the world showered on him so profusely, he picked up his hog's eye and went back again to John Bart's tavern. When he came to the tavern, we put his eye to its

[109] Henry Schultz, assessed at $1,320 in the 1818–1819 Hanover tax list; Tax List, 1818–1819, Borough of Hanover. (See Figure 6.)

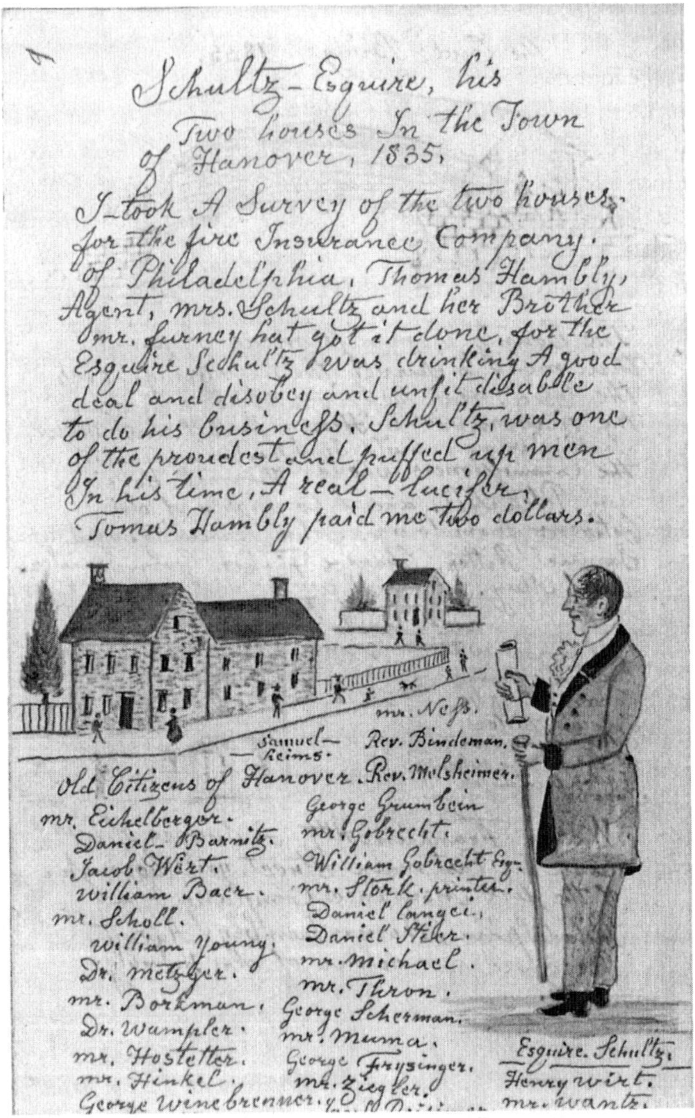

FIG. 6. Lewis Miller, *Schultz-Esquire, his Two houses In the Town of Hanover, 1835*. Miller was a York carpenter; he made a sketchbook in the 1850s of interesting people and events he had seen. Courtesy of The Historical Society of York County, Pennsylvania.

place a second time, and suggested to him, the idea of his going to bed; he consented to go to bed and we landed him safely in bed; the next morning his eyes were well enough, he put out home, and the whole of it was hoggish, and so ended the hog eye spree.

The next affair was a rouger which happened in Gettysburg, between Dr. Vanpike and myself, in company of several of the most worthy and respectable citizens of that borough, amongst which were Messrs. Barney Gilbert, Lewis Shaver, and Mr. Welsh and others.[110] This Dr. Vanpike was a dandy in the fullest sense of the word;[111] his manners, together with his habits rendered him a complete nuisance in every decent man's opinion; as he was fond of gin, he kept a supply of that article constantly in a flask about him, to use it when he wanted a horn. The landlord, Mr. B. Gilbert gave me an introduction to Dr. Vanpike, and after the usual ceremonies of an introduction were over, the doctor, who wanted to blow off some of the exquisite—he asked me if I understood the science of fencing with the broad sword. He blowed a puff or two as to his acquirements in the science. Barney Gilbert told me, that the doctor kept his gin bottle in his coatee pocket, that I should accept his challenge and break the bottle of the doctor; he said that if I succeeded in breaking it, he would treat me to a bottle of wine. So then after the doctor had blown off the steam for his broad sword acquirements, I told him I understood the broad-sword exercise myself, and thought that I was no slouch at it; the doctor understood that the challenge was accepted; he was provided with a cane and ready for action. I asked B. Gilbert if he could supply me with a cane. He said there was canes in the bar, that I should go into the bar and pick a suitable one for myself; so I stepped into the bar and got a common walking cane, and came back to the room in which our doctor and the rest of the company was. The spectators made room for us two combatants at the broad sword. The doctor he gave me a word of command, "make ready"—to which I answered, "ready." He then said, cut figure one;

---

[110] Bernhardt Gilbert kept the Spread Eagle Tavern in Gettysburg between 1814 and 1821. One of the town's wealthiest citizens (assessed at $8,507 in 1818), he gave up control of the Spread Eagle after he was elected sheriff of Adams County in 1821, as required by law. There was no Lewis Shaver in Gettysburg in this period, but the tax list does show a Thomas Shavers worth $1,200 in 1818. The list also shows a George Welsh, no occupation given, assessed at $1,266. "Adams County Tavern Licenses to 1850"; Parson, *The Parson Story; History of Cumberland and Adams Counties*, pp. 93, 145; and Tax List, 1818, Gettysburg Borough, Adams County, Adams County Historical Society, Gettysburg, Pennsylvania.

[111] There was no Dr. Vanpike in the Gettysburg area. Otter is either using a pseudonym because of the embarrassing nature of the story or spinning a tall tale.

at the word cut figure one, I up cane and hit my doctor a pelt souse on the gin bottle, and smashed the concern for him; when he found his gin bottle was broke, he said that I knew nothing at all of the broad-sword exercise. I told him I thought I did know a good deal about it, that I drew blood the very first cut; which remark raised a tremendous laughter at the expense of the doctor's feelings. He allowed that I knew nothing at all about it, or I would not have struck so low; to which I answered, that I knew that his heart laid pretty low, and concluded that I had bursted his boiler for him; here ended the broad-sword business; he got the bar-keeper to pick out the pieces of the bottle out of his pocket; we however drank friends, and the whole company were delighted at my dexterity at the business, and at my peculiar success and skill of management to get the whole victory so triumphantly.

We then went to bed and slept soundly for that night on our broad-sword business and the next morning then came the tug of war. Our doctor he arose and displayed as much foppery as would have done the folks in the borough of Gettysburg for a month. He came out cap-a-pee with his ruffle shirt, parading about the house, like a peacock in the spring of the year; he, when I came into the bar-room to get my boots, was walking to and fro in the room; when he seen me and I seen him, he had a glass of wine or gin standing on the stocks ready to devour it, and an egg laying along side of it; he bade me a good morning, I responded; said he to me, I'll bet you a glass of bitters that you cannot tell what that is, pointing to the egg; I told him I'll bet you; I then went and laid hold of the egg, broke it, and let it fall into his glass of liquor, and drank it off, and then said to him—I believed it was an egg. He looked at me, and asked me, if I did not intend to retaliate, which expression tickled me so much, that I could hardly contain myself as he was guilty of murdering the king's English. I thanked him, and said that I did not wish another drop; he looked at me, and said to me, that from what he yet had seen of me, that I must be a very impudent man; I asked him, before I answered, if I had not the common right to think too; he said, certainly; then I answered him and said, I thought he was a very big fool, which caused another big laugh at my doctor's expense. To give the whole business the finishing blow, I began to complain of being very unwell; after I had made my complaint as long as I could, he, as a doctor, asked me the nature of my complaint. I pretended to be totally unacquainted with the technical phraseology of complaints. I gave him to understand that I was laboring under venery, and he made very light of it, and said that he could and would cure me for ten dollars. I told my doctor if he would cure me, that I would cheerfully pay him twenty dollars; so then he asked me to walk with him into his room for the purpose of seeing how the land laid, to which I objected upon the modest principles of human nature. He made very light of the matter, and allowed it was nothing at all; still I refused to go with him into his room, and suggested the idea to him to go with him to the stable to stand his examination, so down me and my doctor went into the stable for the purpose aforesaid, and he wished to see, and I cautioned him that I could not control the water by any means, so down he stooped to take a look, and I let him have a squirt pop into the eyes, into his face over his ruffle shirt, and bepissed him all over, that he could not see a single stiver; after this dreadful accident had occurred to me, or say rather to the doctor; he allowed that I might be —————— before he would do any thing for me again; and it offended Dr. Vanpike so much, that he was determined to see himself righted at common law; he went to one of the Judges of the Court, which then was in session, and complained of my mal-treatment towards him. The Judge told him that he knew nothing of the affair, and could not take cognizance thereof, that he should apply to an attorney who would conduct the affairs for him; when he had received at the hands of the Judge the poor consolation above stated, he allowed that there was no balm in Gilead for him, so he just bundled up his duds and left the house. Whenever Barney Gilbert sees me, this spree occurs to him, and has a hearty laugh at it.

The next was a spree of a character with a friend of mine of much serious interest; it happened in the town of Hanover. My readers will come to the same conclusion with myself, when I shall have related to them the circumstances:—My friend he had the misfortune to get tipsey, and did not wish to expose himself in the condition in which he was in; he wished me to take him to a certain lady's house, in which he would be countenanced and allowed to get sober again, without any apprehension of being exposed; so we went to the house, it was late in the night, she had been in bed and soundly asleep. We went to the back door and found our way into the house and took possession of one of the back rooms of the house, and in grouping about in the dark for a chair, I got my hand on a flax-hackle and hurt my fingers. I told my comrade that I had found a chair, that he should sit down until I should have found a bed, so down he soused plump upon the hackle, when he got in contact with the flax-hackle and the parts I need not name; he sung out murder most horridly, which frightened our old lady; she got up to see who we were; to allay her fears, I told her who we were, and for what we came there; she then came into the room we had taken possession of with a candle—and my friend who had a light colored pair of pantaloons on, he was all over blood from his heels up to the false seat of honor, and with an addition of at least sixty holes pierced in his behind, and indeed I cannot say, that I felt the least compunction at heart for playing such a painful trick upon my crony.

Cincinnati, the Eastern Shore, and Baltimore

I n the spring of the year, I took a notion to take a look at the Western Country, entertaining a remote idea, if the country pleased me, that upon my return I would sell off and remove my family. In the month of March I started off from Hanover,[112] and bent my course for the West, and never came to a halt until I had arrived in the emporium of the West (the city of Cincinnati,)[113] when I arrived there, I spent about six days in taking a good look out through the city, to see how things went on—during that short space of time, I became acquainted with the firm of T. and E. Graham, merchants of that city;[114] they were in the act of building a handsome country seat, which in part was ready for plastering when I became ac-

[112] The date was 1819 (see footnote 117). The York County Sessions Docket, 19 May 1819, records a judgment against Otter for $850 on a loan from Peter Winebrenner, due 1 April 1820. The docket does not explain what the bond was for, but Otter's comments on pages 138–139 suggest that it involved Otter's purchase of a house from Winebrenner. Filing a loan agreement with the court seems to have been a fairly common practice. Otter's journey west may have been motivated by the desire to earn money fast to repay his debt to Winebrenner. *Peter Winebrenner v William Otter*, York County Sessions Docket, 19 May 1819, Archives Room, York County Courthouse, York, Pennsylvania.

[113] Cincinnati was one of the fastest growing cities in the United States. An 1818 city census showed the population as 9,120; the 1820 population census, 9,642 residents. Incorporated as a city in 1819, the year Otter arrived, it had the reputation of being something of a paradise for artisans, especially those in the construction trades, with a scarcity of labor and very high wages. Unfortunately, Otter arrived in the spring, just as the 1819 panic was starting in the West. *The Cincinnati Directory*, "by a Citizen" (Cincinnati, 1819), p. 32; Richard C. Wade, *The Urban Frontier: Pioneer Life in Early Pittsburgh, Cincinnati, Lexington, Louisville, and St. Louis* (1959; rpt., Chicago, 1972); and Steven J. Ross, *Workers on the Edge: Work, Leisure, and Politics in Industrializing Cincinnati, 1788–1890* (New York, 1985), pp. 7–24.

[114] "Graham, Thomas, merchant, 38 c. L. Market & Sycamore," in the 1819 *Cincinnati Directory*.

quainted with them. I made an engagement with them to work for them at
the house for two dollars per day—I then had to undertake two rooms and
finish them, which was to be the sample pattern of my professional abilities,
and if he approved of my performance, I then was to have the balance of the
whole house, and if he did not like my performance, he was to have the
privilege of discharging me after the two rooms were done—before my two
rooms were done, Mr. Graham boasted of my facility in working; he allowed
that I could do as much in one day at plastering as any man he had as yet
seen at the business could do in two; and expressed himself, that he had a
very cheap hand at his house, which I learned as I have already stated. This
piece of intelligence coming from so high and responsible source as the firm
of T. and E. Graham, spread itself among the hands pursuing the same trade
with myself in the city; they called out at Mr. Graham's country seat to see
me at work, and every one of the craft made themselves acquainted with me,
and told me that I done the work too cheap for Mr. Graham. I told them that
I had popped on the job at a haphazard not knowing any thing about the
prices of labour in or about the city, the first man that made himself acquainted was a Mr. Thorb, a boss plasterer,[115] he offered me two dollars and
fifty cents per day if I would come and work for him, I as a stranger naturally
felt a strong disposition to get into business.

I told him that I could not then make an immediate engagement not until
I had finished the one I then had on hand, and when the two rooms which I
had engaged to finish were done and my boss did not raise the wind I then
would come to him. So I finished my two rooms, I then asked him how he
liked my work as he had a sample then before him to judge for himself, he
said that he was very well satisfied with my work, and that I now should go
on with the balance of the house without delay, I intimated to him that I
could not work for him any longer for the wages he was giving me, that the
plasterers had informed me that I was working at prices which were lower
than was the usual rates in the city; he wanted to know from me who those
plasterers were, my informants, I frankly told him that Mr. Thorb offered
me two dollars and fifty cents per day, or twenty cents per yard if I rather
chosed to work by measurement, he then asked me how many yards I could
plaster in a day, I told him I could plaster fifty yards in a day, he told me that
he was very much pleased with my work, and I should go on to finish his
house for him, that he would double my wages, so when he offered me the

---

[115] "Thorp, John, plasterer, 158 Sycamore," in the 1819 *Cincinnati Directory*.

four dollars per day as wages I went on to finish the house, and added that he could get me into better business than Mr. Thorb could if I would finish his house as I had commenced it, I told him that the balance of the work to be done in his house should be equally as well done as the part I had then finished, I assured him and did the firm of T. and E. Graham equal justice with myself, in regard to my work, I done the work well, and in a work-manlike manner, and speedily too; when his house was entirely finished, as a mark of satisfaction entertained by them as to the discharge of my duty, he told me that he would get me a good job, that would last me the whole summer, he recommended me as a superior plasterer, to a Mr. John H. Pyatt,[116] who is a gentleman so well known to every body in or about Cincinnati that to attempt to describe him would be spending time and words uselessly, though I am not now writing for a community that exactly is in the latitude of Cincinnati, and shall content myself to tell my readers who are residents of the Lord knows where, that Mr. John H. Pyatt was in them days the only enterprising man in the city of Cincinnati, who built first rate houses, and who is the man who had the City Hotel built, he kept about one hundred hands employed of various professions, in putting up the most splendid buildings that were erected in the city, he was very rich indeed, he had a banking establishment of his own, to him I got a letter of recommendation from the firm of T. and E. Graham. Mr. Pyatt engaged me to do some buildings for him right straight away, upon the strength of Messrs. T. and E. Graham's recommendation at two hundred dollars per house, and the only condition was that I was to do them as well I had done Mr. Graham's. So then, gentle reader, you may suppose I had my hands full, and to work I went right merrily at Mr. Pyatt's houses, and worked away till I had finished five houses, I drew as much money from him nearly every week or two as paid off all my hands and kept my teeth clear; while I was engaged at the sixth house, which I had about half finished, a report was circulated that his bank had stopped payment, and it was only too true for joke; the hands in his employ all went up to his banking house to see, and it was confirmed what

---

[116] John Hooper Piatt (1781–1822), a merchant and a financier, was one of Cincinnati's most distinguished men in this period. His Cincinnati bank, incorporated in 1818, was one of the first in Ohio. He was also extensively involved in real estate and, according to Richard C. Wade, Cincinnati's "most important landlord," owning thirty-one houses in 1818. C. C. Huntington, "A History of Banking and Currency in Ohio before the Civil War," *Ohio Archeological and Historical Publications* 25 (1951), esp. pp. 294–311; John J. Rowe Collection, Box 1, Folder 2, Cincinnati Historical Society, Cincinnati, Ohio; and Wade, *Urban Frontier*, p. 109.

FIG. 7. Piatt bank note, 1818. Cincinnati Historical Society.

had been reported; at the time the bank was broke,[117] I owed my hands about ten dollars, and I had fifty dollars of Mr. John H. Pyatt's bank paper in my trunk, I paid off my hands with it, and then I came off as independent as a wood sawyer. In a day or two after the breaking of the bank, when the bustle was over, and the excitement was a little cooled down, I went to Mr. Pyatt to see if I could squeeze some of the necessary out of him to carry me home; I intimated to him my intention of returning home, and having sold my horse, when I came into the city wished to purchase another to carry me home, and such like things, which were indispensably necessary on a journey, he heard me, and when I had done with what I had to say he asked me where my place of residence was, I told him that I lived about five hundred miles eastward of Cincinnati, near the city of Baltimore, he told me that if he gave one, that he

---

[117] Piatt had gone into debt provisioning western forts during the War of 1812 when inflation forced him to pay higher prices than his government contracts called for. Piatt sued the government but did not receive a favorable decision until after his death in 1822. At first, Piatt's bank seemed to be weathering his personal financial problems—in October 1818, despite the worsening banking crisis in the West, Piatt's bank notes were being discounted at only 4½ percent. By April 1819, however, the *Ohio Watchman* was reporting that Piatt's paper was "touched with a trembling hand," being shaved 12½ percent. I have been unable to discover exactly when the bank failed, but by November, Piatt's bank notes were worthless. Huntington, "History of Banking and Currency in Ohio," in which the author, on page 309, presents a March 1819 statement of the financial condition of Piatt's bank which clearly shows its precarious position; Rowe Collection, Box 1, Folder 2; and Walter Lowrie and Walter S. Franklin, eds., *American State Papers, Class IX—Claims* (Washington, D.C., 1834), pp. 734–736, 780–791, 894–909. (See Figure 7 for an example of a Piatt bank note.)

would be bound to give to all the hands upon equitable principles; I told him my case was an exception, that the rest were inhabitants of the city, and I was a stranger—he told me if I would go to the State of Kentucky to keep his conduct towards me a secret he would give me one hundred dollars to buy a horse for me; he lent me one of his carriage horses, and off I started for Kentucky and purchased a horse for myself, the money I had was not counterfeit as he had only stopped payment, I did not know its solvency, nor did Mr. Pyatt know that fact, it turned out upon inquiry into the solvency of his banking establishment that it was bursted all to flinders.

I brought my horse over to Ohio, he looked at the horse and allowed that I had made a very judicious purchase, I then put at him again for another additional lot of money to carry me home, he rather was for baffling me; his wife asked me if I had a family, I answered her I had a wife and five children, and that I had no way of supporting them only by my daily exertions and earnings,[118] she then addressed herself to her husband and said under those circumstances that he might give me some assistance, he asked me if I was indebted much in the city, I answered his question that I owed about fifty dollars, he told me as I was going away and would keep it a secret he would pay me a hundred dollars in Eastern money, and the farther sum of fifty dollars of the Miami Exporting Company, if I would give him a receipt in full. I made the best of a bad bargain I could, took him up at his offer, took the cash, executed the receipt by him required of me. From there I went to my boarding house and began to make arrangements in settling up my little affairs to take my final adieu, the day before I started for my home I called to see my worthy friends T. and E. Graham, to give them my good bye, he sympathized with me and regretted very much that I had such bad luck with Mr. Pyatt, by whom I lost the sum of nearly four hundred dollars. In our conversation an elderly gentleman stepped into the store-room of E. and T. Graham, a merchant, by the name of Taylor, from Baltimore, he inquired if he knew of any gentleman that was going Eastward, Mr. Graham observed to him that I was going Eastward, Mr. Taylor asked me when I was going to start, I told him I was ready to go the next day, he said he would be glad if I

---

[118] Otter says very little about his children, who were Edward, b. 9 March 1811; William, Jr., b. 10 December 1812; Amelia, b. 20 September 1814; and Eliza Ann, b. 11 November 1816. The 1820 census shows his wife had had another daughter. "Church Records of Emanuel's Reformed Church, Hanover, York County, Pennsylvania," copied by William J. Hinke, Historical Society of York County, York, Pennsylvania; Census Office, Fourth Census, 1820, Population, manuscript, Borough of Hanover, York County, Pennsylvania.

could delay another day that he would like to have company, I told him that I
should start in the afternoon of the next day, and I then would travel slowly,
so then I bade Mr. Graham a cordial farewell, and on the following afternoon
I put out for the East and overtook a young man from St. Louis, travelling
towards the city of Philadelphia, we lodged together for that night and
discovered to one another our pursuits; I observed to him that a gentleman
was coming on from Cincinnati for Baltimore, that he was a half day's ride
behind us; he observed that we would jog on our own gait, if he overtook us
well and good, and if he did not overtake us was no matter. We were
travelling in the month of August, the weather was very hot and sultry, we
took advantage of early starting in the mornings; one morning we made a
start earlier than usual, we had before us a very steep hill, a very narrow
road, and a long uphill, when we came to the summit of the hill, it was a
complete thicket of Laurel, we were a talking, I espied ahead a large bundle
lying in the road, to which I invited my travelling companion's attention
thereto, he asked me what I thought was the meaning of it, my apprehensions were awakened, and indeed roused to a considerable pitch, and sur-
mises began to present themselves to me of an unfavorable character, which
multiplied themselves with the rapidity of thought, I observed that I was
apprehensive that robbers were about, and had lain a bait for travellers, or
that a murder had been committed; after the remark had been made by me I
found that my companion changed colour, from a rosey red to pale, if I did
not look as I have described his looks they betrayed my feelings; as we
approached the bundle a good looking young man emerged from the laurels
with a large club in his hands, he bade us a good morning, he picked up the
bundle, and at the distance of eight or ten yards out came another young
man and he too armed with a club in his hands, we had not gone five yards
further until the third one arrived as the two former ones were, made his
appearance, and they kept company with us, they inquired of us how far we
were going along this road, we told them we were going on to Pittsburgh,
one of them asked us, if we were mechanics, I told him yes, he asked how far
we intended to go for breakfast, we told him we intended to go about eight
miles, he asked me how far we had been out west, I told him we had been as
far as Cincinnati, he asked us if we had been to work, I said we had not, that
we could get no work there, they then began a confab amongst themselves,
and I began to urge my horse ahead, one of them observed that we should
not be in a hurry, I told him I wanted to get on to my breakfast, we rode on
pretty smartly for a few miles, until we were sure we were freed from their

company, which we by no means desired; when we thought that we had cleared the skirts of harm's way we then jogged on as usual, many strange sensations pervaded my breast, and many schemes of defence presented themselves to me.

While we were annoyed with their company we rode ten miles before we could get breakfast, which we succeeded in getting at a tavern, we dismounted and got our horses some hay while our breakfast was getting ready, and after we had attended to our horses we then went into the house, and called for something to drink, we were at ease resting for about three quarters of an hour until our breakfast should be ready, during this time we made our landlord acquainted with our adventure with the three sturdy fellows who we had met; as I have already described; the landlord he then told us that he had often heard that there was a band of robbers about Cadiz; we asked how far it was to Cadiz,[119] he said it was thirty miles, I told him that perhaps they were going over there, and I said that I was very glad that we had got clear of them; he said that we had reason to be glad, for there was no knowing what folks of such depraved manners would do as they were as ready as willing to do any thing; in this time we were called into a room to take our breakfast, and before I sat down I took off my brace of pistols and laid them on the mantlepiece, and while we were eating our breakfast, our unwelcome companions came into the tavern, they called for some bitters, the landlord waited on them, and while they were drinking one of them asked the rest if they would stop and take breakfast, the rest said no that they would go on, one of them he espied my brace of pistols laying on the chimney piece, he drew one of them out of the holsters, he observed to his comrades here is a nice pair of pistols, his comrade he came up and took a look at the pistol, and the initials of my name was engraved on the barrel W. O., for William Otter; said he to the one that first invited his attention to the pistol, W. O. what does that stand for, the other said it stood for wo, and by this time me and my comrade came out of the room we were eating breakfast, in the bar-room, they were a set of tremendous impudent fellows, one of them said to us that they had caught up with us again, I answered him yes, they picked up the bundle and took up a line of march ahead of us again; as soon as I seen the manouvre I observed to my comrade that we were just

---

[119] Cadiz, founded in 1804, was located in Harrison County about twenty miles west of the Pennsylvania line. Otter was on the main road from Cincinnati east, going through Chillicothe and Zanesville. US 22 follows this route today. William Utter, *The Frontier State, 1803–1825,* vol 2 of *The History of the State of Ohio,* ed. Carl Wittke (Columbus, Ohio, 1942), p. 201.

in as bad a box as we had been in early in the morning with the lad; the landlord's impressions of the fellows was unfavorable, he allowed that they were after no good from what he could deduct from their conduct; he cautioned me to examine my pistols and keep my shooting irons in ample order, that I should reload them, and if they manifested any of the slightest disposition to attack us just to crack away and pop them down; I thought the landlord's council very good, I drew the loads, reloaded my pistols and put them in serviceable order, I asked the landlord how far it was to the next tavern, he said fifteen miles. We at last got on our horses and started, and travelled about four or five miles; when we were at the foot of another hill, we espied the lads sitting on a rock at a small branch close to the road side, we came up to them, one held a bottle in his hand, he asked us if we would not stop to drink; I thanked him and said I believed not, he in his vulgar way of expression said that we had as well, as wish we had not, by this time my companion he put spur to his horse and put out and I after him, and they hollowed after us as far as we could hear them; we rode on to Mr. Moore's tavern. About the middle of the afternoon I told my comrade that we would stop here and feed our horses, the day was exceedingly warm, I ordered the hostler to take my horse to the fountain pump and wash him; we went in and called for a gin-sling a piece, and Mr. Moore invited us into the parlor; I laid myself down on the settee and took a nap to myself, my comrade he wakened me and said to me that we had better be travelling on. I got up, expressed my willingness to go ahead, I then told him to order out our horses and I would pay the bill, I asked Mr. Moore what our bill was, he said 37 1-2 cents, I paid him, and asked him how far it was to the next good house, he answered me the question, and said it was about five miles, we then got on our horses, bade him good bye and started. We rode on until we came to the five mile house, we there inquired if we could be accommodated with lodgings for that night, the landlord told us we could, we had our horses put away, called for supper, we ate supper, after that office had been performed we signified our wish to the landlord to retire to rest, a good many travellers had stopped there for quarters for the night, the landlord he put us into a small room right over the passage, the room had but one window and one door, there had been at one time a lock to the door, but at this time nothing was there but a latch, I told my comrade that I would stick my knife over the latch, for fear our three unwelcome guests might come there that night, I stuck my knife over the latch, laid my pistols under my pillow, my comrade he laid his dirk under his pillow, being weary and fatigued we fell asleep, we slept about two hours or thereabouts, I awoke and heard a tapping at a room door, and I seen a candle through the key hole of our door, I wakened my comrade slyly, I told him that I believed that them fellows was in the house; we both sat up in bed, I grasped my pistols and he laid hold on his dirk, we presently heard a tapping at another room door and still seen the candle, said I to him you may depend they are here, said he I believe they are.

I felt my comrade trembling in bed, a mark of confessed fear. We both got up out of bed, hauled on our pantaloons, and we watched the key hole very sharp; we then seen two men come out of the room, the one had a candle in his hand, and the other had a club in his hand. I then told my comrade, that there was two of them; they retired for a short time into a distant apartment, at least I judged so from the disappearance of the light of the candle. I whispered to my partner, if they made the attempt to beset our room with a view of forcing their way in it, that then I felt convinced that evil was their intention, that he should take a pistol, he should shoot the one, and I would take the other and shoot one also, that we would make sure work of our game. We sat down on our bed listening, and coolly waiting for the attack which we apprehended; at length sure enough they came to our door; they wrapped at our door twice; when he wrapped a second time, I asked him, who is there; he answered, the landlord and another gentleman who wished to see us, that we should not be alarmed. I told them, that I thought that nobody had any business in our room this time of the night; by this he tried to raise the latch of the door; and I cautioned them, if they would force their way into our room, the first man that would dare set his foot into it I would blow his brains out; and my comrade he caught the word, and said that he would blow out any man's brains that would dare set his foot into our room. The landlord, he said to us, that was all right enough, and said he wanted to reason the case with us. We said that we wanted an explanation from him. He began to tell us, that Mr. Moore, his neighbor was along with him, that a gentleman had put up at his house who had been robbed, and he wished to know if any of the robbers had taken refuge in his house;—at this piece of intelligence we opened the door, and let them in; as soon as Mr. Moore entered our room, he said he knew those two gentlemen, that we had stopped at his house that afternoon; we all sat down on the bed, and he related the circumstance of a certain Mr. Taylor from Cincinnati to Baltimore, who had been attacked about one and a half mile from his house by three robbers, who took him off the road about one hundred yards, blindfolded him, and cut off his bridle-reins, and tied his arms behind him on his back and robbed him of sixteen hundred dollar; when they attacked him, it was about two o'clock, P.M., and they let his horse run in the thickets, and kept Mr. Taylor tied and blind-folded until sun down; two of them had resolved to kill him, the third one however was not agreed to destroy Mr. Taylor's life, as he was an old man. After the resolution had carried that they would spare him his life, he began to get a little heart to speak to the robbers, and expostulated with them to let him have as much money as would carry him home; one of them then asked of Mr. Taylor where he lived; he told them that he resided in the city of Baltimore, that he hoped that they would give him as much money as would take him home. They said yes, that they would act honorable with him —so then they gave him back eleven dollars of his money. After they had given back the money, they then gave him company until the sun was down, they then loosened his arms, and enjoined it on Mr. Taylor on pain of being shot, that he should not untie the hand-kerchief which they had tied over his eyes, until they were out of sight.

The old gentleman he kept it on until he heard no more of them, he then took it off. The next thing Mr. Taylor done, was to go in quest of his horse, which he at last found in the laurel bushes—he made his way out of the thicket to the big road to Mr. Moore's tavern, the best way he could, and then gave the alarm.

Mr. Moore had several mechanics at work, he gave them horses and sent them out in every direction in pursuit of the robbers, as well as himself; he made every exertion in his power which brought him to our lodgings, and from whom we got the first piece of intelligence of Mr. Taylor being robbed.

I then told him what we had seen in the morning, gave him a fair description of the men, and of their performance, and added that I believed that they were the robbers. When we ate our breakfast, I deducted a fact from an expression made use of by the landlord, which made me believe that those fellows were from Cadiz, as he said there was a band of robbers in that neighborhood. Mr. Moore he came to the conclusion, that he would get one of his neighbors to accompany him, and that he would push for Cadiz instantly. Mr. Moore thanked me for the information I had imparted to him, bade us good night, and started for Cadiz. The next news I then heard was, that Mr. Moore had overtaken the very three fellows who had annoyed us so much, just as they were going into the town of Cadiz. On the second day after they had committed the robbery, Mr. Moore recovered Mr. Taylor's money from them all, except sixteen dollars which they had spent. After the apprehension and the confession of the robbery, the replacing of the stolen property, it followed as a matter of course, that they smoked for their impudence in the penitentiary.

On my road home, I undertook a job of work to plaster in the town of Waynesburg, of some considerable extent, the Catholic Church in that town.[120] After I had made the bargain, I then left Waynesburg and moved off for Hanover, my place of residence. I rested myself a few days on my return; after the fatigue of the journey had worn off a little, I went back to Waynesburg to finish what I had engaged to complete. When I came there, I began work and finished the job, and when I was done there I did not get the money for doing it. The fall of the year was at hand, and I had no money. I had beef and pork to provide for myself and family, and no money to pay for it. To raise the wind, I went to the city of Baltimore and sold my horse to a Mr. Sullivan, a master tailor, for a new suit of clothes and eighty dollars in ready rhino.[121] I then came home and laid in my provisions for my family, and laid on my oars for that winter. Some time during that winter, my brother Edward wrote a letter to me, to come on the Eastern Shore of Maryland, assuring me the sum of two dollars per day during the summer. I laid the matter before my wife, and we came to the conclusion that we move to the neighborhood of my brother on the Eastern Shore; having in my possession a house and lot in the town of Hanover, which I had purchased, and on which I owed the sum of six hundred dollars,[122] and wished to get rid of it at any rate, as times was dull in Hanover;[123] I thought that by those means I would be able to effect a sale of my house. I went to the man whom I owed the money to, and told him my intention, and offered him my house in the liquidation of the debt. He as much as called my proposition a fudge; I assured him that I was in real earnest about it; and to convince him in a few days after I got ready, went on to the city of Baltimore to get a vessel that would carry me and my family to the place where my brother resided in

[120] The town's present name is Waynesboro (see Map 2). The name of the town was changed in 1831 to avoid confusion with another Pennsylvania town named after Gen. Anthony Wayne. St. Andrew's Catholic Church in Waynesboro was built in 1819 at a cost of four hundred dollars. Terry Mitchell, *Around Waynesboro with Pen and Ink* (Waynesboro, 1947), p. 21, and *History of Franklin County, Pennsylvania* (Chicago, 1887), p. 536.

[121] Money on hand. See Francis Grose, *A Classical Dictionary of the Vulgar Tongue* (1785; rpt., Menston, England, 1968).

[122] This house is presumably the one Otter purchased from Peter Winebrenner and the subject of the 1819 court judgment. See footnote 112.

[123] According to George R. Prowell, Hanover saw a "steady increase in buildings and population . . . until the period of the War of 1812, after which the town remained nearly stationary until 1840." Prowell, *History of York County, Pennsylvania* (Chicago, 1907), 2:812.

Somerset county, Maryland;[124] and I waited in the city of Baltimore until my wife came on to join me with the family—in three days I was joined by my wife and the rest of the family. The old fellow who had thought all was a joke, until I had left Hanover for good,[125] he seen that I was in earnest—he accompanied my wife to the city, and there bought the house; in that time I had rented the house for one year, at sixty dollars rent. We agreed that I was to give him an order to draw the rent when it should have expired. I gave him at the advice of the Squire in the city, instead of an order, a note for the rent; if Mr. Hays paid the rent, the note should be null and void; and if Hays did not pay the rent, in that event Mr. Peter Winebrenner[126] would have my note, which he held in his possession for ten years, and at the end of that time he sent the note to an attorney in Fredericktown, who brought suit thereon, and he obtained a judgment in Frederick County Court against me for the whole sum, principal and interest; it amounted to one hundred and twenty-five dollars, including the costs.[127] So now I returned to Baltimore, as I had to make a short digression from the even tenor of my Eastern Shore

[124] As noted earlier, Edward had to leave New York City after marrying Jacques Delacroix's daughter. The 1820 manuscript census shows the Edward Otter household in Somerset County, Maryland, containing an unnaturalized adult male and female (presumably Edward and his wife), another adult male, and six children all under sixteen years of age. Edward is listed as being engaged in agriculture. The tax records show Edward Otter having a house, land, and personal property worth $440, more than Big Bill ever owned. On William's taxable property, see footnote 156 and page 201 in the commentary. Census Office, Fourth Census, 1820, Population, Manuscript, Election District No. 2, Somerset County, Maryland, National Archives; Assessment Ledger, 1817–1822, Election District No. 2, Somerset County, Maryland, Hall of Records, Annapolis, Maryland.

[125] Otter is last listed in the Hanover assessments in 1821–1822.

[126] Peter Winebrenner, Otter's nemesis, "was a saddler and understood his trade well. He prospered in life. . . . Like all the other tradesmen of Hanover in his day [he] took much of the products of his industry to Baltimore to dispose of them. He was an able man and was prominent in the affairs of the church. For many years he engaged in the lumber business." "Old Time Hanover—Its Incorporation in 1815," *Hanover Herald,* 15 January 1887; see also Prowell, *History of York County,* 1: 846.

[127] This suit was Winebrenner's second against Otter with respect to the house in Hanover (see footnote 112). Peter Winebrenner filed suit against William Otter in Frederick County Court—Otter was by then living in Emmitsburg—on 4 December 1830. After numerous filings of interrogatories and the taking of testimony, the suit came to trial on 28 February 1833. The court minute book recorded the result: "Verdict for plff + find due $60 . . . and assess damages to $135.80. . . . Jury did not leave the box." The York County Court records show that the 1819 suit was finally satisfied on 5 December 1834. Court Docket, Frederick County Court, January Term 1833, Hall of Records, Annapolis, Maryland; *Peter Winebrenner v William Otter,* Minute Book, Frederick County Court, February Term 1833, Hall of Records; York County Sessions Docket, 19 May 1819.

trip, as I then thought I went clip and clear, but in ten years I learned better than all that, I paid for the roast, particularly if Mr. Hays paid the rent to Mr. Winebrenner; so here we go to the Eastern Shore, the whole crew of us, and in three days we got safe to the end of my journey, and arrived in safety at my brother's. He appeared very glad to see me: he took a walk with me the next day to shew me the place;—every man, woman and child were touched with chills and fevers—as far as they came under my observation; at the sight of these poor fellows I began to get the horrors. I frankly told my brother that I never would stay in that country. He asked me my reasons why, I told him I had too good a wife to bring there to die, as all the folks I had seen were candidates for the bone-yard. He asked me, if I would not do General Wilson's house while I did stay there. I told him I would not strike a single stroke for any body, that if I did once begin work that perhaps I could not quit when I wanted, and while I was clear I would stay so. I stayed with my brother four weeks, and then a chance presented itself to me to go up to the city.

I took my wife and family along, and we set sail for the City of Washington; I arrived in the City after a voyage of three weeks and three days. The first man I met in the city who I knew, and who was a gentleman of character, was Mr. Jas. M'Sherry, a member of Congress of the United States,[128] which was then in session. He gave me a recommendation to a boss as a first rate hand at my business. The boss who had undertaken to do the Capitol, told me that I was too early, that if I would stay till May, that he would give me work. I had my family with me, my expenses were heavy, and my money began to run short, I could not stay until May. I made a stay of three weeks in the city—in these three weeks I seen Mr. M'Sherry again; he asked me how I had succeeded. I told him that I was too early to get any employ at the Capitol. He asked me to be patient, that he knew that Mr. John Nelson, also a member of Congress[129] was then about building a house in Frederick City, perhaps he could get me into business there. He then spoke to Mr. Nelson about it in my presence. Mr. Nelson made his reply to me, that his house was partly engaged, yet, when he came home he would get me to assist in the finishing of it. I told Mr. John Nelson that I resided in

[128] James McSherry, 1776–1849, was a merchant from Littlestown, Adams County, Pennsylvania. He served only in the Seventeenth Congress, 1821–1823. See *Biographical Directory of the United States Congress, 1774–1989* (Washington, D.C., 1989).

[129] John Nelson, 1794–1860. A Frederick County lawyer, he also served in the Seventeenth Congress (*Biographical Directory of the United States Congress*).

Baltimore: when the building was ready, he sent his boss plasterer down to see me. I went to Frederick-town and helped to finish his house—when that job was done, I got the house of Mr. John Schly, Esq. to do on my own contract, and when I had finished his house which amounted to three hundred and eighteen dollars I went back to Baltimore again;[130] by this time it was in the autumn of the year, I opened an oyster shop for that season, when I also attended to the selling of horses,[131] among the rest of my purchases of horses I bought one that was stone blind, which he got by a water founder. I rode the blind horse and led two others down to the horse market, a gentleman by the name of Ellicott[132] he asked me if the horse I rode was for sale, I told him he was, he asked me what I would take for him, I told him that I would take one hundred and ten dollars for him, he asked me to move him, I did so, I found he had a notion for him, I gave the two horses I led to a boy to take care of them until Mr. Ellicott examined him, and after he had examined him all over excepting his eyes, which I held up so high that he could not see them, he asked me if the horse worked, I told him I would insure him to work any place, he would hitch him, he then said, I will give thee eighty dollars for him, I thought if I had the money, he might have the horse, but to keep trade agoing I observed that I was offered more money for him at home, I did not like to make such a big fall, I offered him the horse at ninety-five dollars, he told me if he would work as I said, he would give me eighty-five dollars for him, I insured him to work as well as any other horse in Baltimore, I told him he should have him for $90, he said no, that he would give me $85, and not a bit more, I told him to take the horse, he took the horse and paid me the eighty-five dollars, I took the saddle off him and

---

130 Otter most likely returned in the fall of 1822 but does not appear in the Baltimore City directory in this period.

131 In Emmitsburg in the late 1820s and the 1830s, Otter owned a livery stable, presumably connected to the tavern he owned there, and engaged in selling horses. The Frederick County Land Records, 26 March 1832, lists Otter's sale to Joseph Danner of "one grey horse, one white horse, one Sorel mare, one dark bay horse, two gigs, one carriage," and miscellaneous furniture for $570.06; Liber JS 41, p. 609, 26 March 1832, Records Room, Frederick County Courthouse, Frederick, Maryland; see also Liber JS 48, pp. 219 and 220, 18 May 1835. (Additional evidence on Otter's stable is found in footnote 26 in the commentary.) It should be noted, however, that stories about canny horse traders were a minor genre of American literature, from Augustus B. Longstreet, *Georgia Scenes* (New York, 1840), to Edward Noyes Wescott, *David Harum· A Story of American Life* (New York, 1898).

132 The Ellicots were a prominent Quaker family in Baltimore, whose members included a bank president, an iron merchant, and a flour merchant. In *The Baltimore Directory for 1822 and '23*, "compiled by C. Keenan" (Baltimore, 1822), Andrew Ellicot is listed as a "gentleman," but there is no way to know if he was the member of the family with whom Otter was dealing.

the bridle, put the saddle on one of my other horses, and as soon as convenient I put out from the horse market, to Mr. King's tavern, Howard street;[133] I had been there scarcely half an hour until Mr. Ellicot came there in quest of me, the first words he said was, "Thee is here is thee," I said yes as we were all personally present, he said that horse of thine is blind, and thee knowest it, I told him if the horse was blind, that I hoped he was not; he requested Mr. King to keep me in his custody until he should be ready to procure a constable to apprehend me. Mr. King told him that I paid my way and he had no control over me; he started off in quest of an officer, and while he was searching for a constable I submitted the case to Mr. King for his opinion about the business, when Mr. King learned that I had insured no farther than that the horse would work; he allowed that I should stand the rubs, that Mr. Ellicott had no proof, and no great matter would arise out of it, so I staid to buffet the storm; presently he met on the street an officer, of the name of William Rosensteel, a man whom I knew very well at Hanover,[134] they came in, and Mr. Ellicott pointed me out to Mr. Rosensteel as his man, when Mr. Rosensteel seen me, he addressed me in the familiar phraseology, well namesake how are you, I said to him in turn well William how are you, Mr. Ellicot he said to Mr. Rosensteel to take me to the Squire—Mr. Rosensteel refused him that office, upon the grounds that he had no authority to arrest me; he then called Mr. Rosensteel out, and I ordered my horses out, in a few minutes he sent Mr. Rosensteel into the tavern with authority to make an overture to me to take back my horse, he would give me ten dollars, I seen in his overture a ketch, and got Mr. Rosensteel to tell the story before Mr. King, he told it again, and I told Mr. Rosensteel to tell Mr. Ellicott if he would add a bottle of wine to his proposition that I would take back the horse, he then came in and asked Mr. King if he would be so good, and let his black boy go down to the horse market for the horse, Mr. King answered yes, I offered him one of my horses to ride down, that he could do it in less time—while he was gone (the boy) Mr. E. observed that he would sooner lose ten dollars than go to law about it; Mr. Rosensteel said it was best when men could settle things among themselves. So we drank wine and talked until the black boy came back from the horse market with the horse; I went out and told the boy to put him up in

---

[133] The *Baltimore Directory* lists only a "King, Samuel, proprietor of the Cross Keys tavern, 116 High [Street]"; there was no King with a tavern on Howard Street.

[134] The only Rosensteel listed in the *Baltimore Directory* is George Rosensteel, "grocery and liquor."

the stable, and returned to the house, went into the parlor to my company
and set down, Mr. E. observed to my friend I should like to go if thee art
ready, I told him that I was ready and wished also to go, thee has to give me
back seventy-five dollars, said he to me, oh no, said I, you are to give me ten
dollars, or I would not have taken the horse back again; oh no, said he, that is
not at all our contract, I appealed to Mr. King and Rosensteel; that what I
had said was our contract, so then we were completely at issue as to the
construction of our bargain; Mr. King and Mr. Rosensteel were called upon
to define our contract and what they understood, and how they understood
the contract, when they definitely decided that I was to take back the horse,
and Mr. E. was to pay me ten dollars. He got up from his seat and addressed
himself to me in these words, does thee think that I am a fool, which
question I popped directly at him, and said to him does thee think that I am
a fool, he got into a passion, paid for the wine and put out, I got on my horse
and went to the horse market to sell the rest of my horses, so ended this
quaker horse business.

The next spree was a comical performance, it arose on an order that was
given to me for five dollars, which said order I gave to J. M. of Emmitsburgh
for goods, the drawer of the order refused to pay it when it was presented to
him for payment, and Mr. J. M. came to the city to lay in a stock of spring
goods, he met me on the street, and after the usual salutations were over, he
told me that the order which he had taken for the goods he had sold me was
unredeemed, and claimed the amount from me; I told him that the drawer
was bound to pay him, that I certainly owed him nothing; he in plain terms
told me that he would coerse payment, and asked me where I lived, I told
him I lived near Irishtown, so he got a warrant to carry his promise into
execution, gave it into the hands of a constable, and I was a newcomer, the
officer did not know me, but having from description an idea of me and my
place of residence, just as I was eating dinner, the constable, he wrapped at
the door, I asked him to walk in, when he had come in, he inquired does Mr.
Otter live here, I said no sir, he moved away from here yesterday, over to Old
Town; at this piece of intelligence the constable shabbed off, and as he was in
the act of stepping out I inquired of him if he had any business with him, he
told me that a gentleman from the country had placed a warrant into his
hands for him; I told the constable that it was not worth his while to go after
Mr. Otter, that he was worth nothing, at any rate, he told me he did not
intend to bother his head about it, that he had been paid the cost. After I had
palavered the constable in the manner I have already related, he put out, and

I finished my dinner, and went to my work; in about a week after I made myself acquainted with this self same officer, I inquired of him if he had seen Mr. Otter yet, he told me he had not, I asked him if he would know him if he did see him, he said he would not, but from the description he had from the gentleman from Emmitsburgh, that he must be a man of my size; I thought the performance of the prank so well played off on my part, too good for any man to consume by himself; I imparted to the constable the secret, that I was the man, he appeared well pleased, he asked me into a tavern, and called for something to drink to top it off. While I was doing the plastering at the house of Mr. John Grabill[135] near Emmitsburgh, we had a charming spree with a certain John Brown, whom Mr. Grabill had employed to dig a well for him, inasmuch as he had good *livin* and *malin* as the Scotchman would term it, at Mr. Grabill's he made shift some how or other to make a long job of it; he was often-times taken sick from no apparent causes; led Mr. Grabill to suspect him, for not being as temperate, as Mr. Brown endeavored to make himself appear in the estimation of Mr. Grabill. Mr. Grabill one day suggested to me the idea, with a view to detect Mr. Brown, to take a bottle of whiskey over to Brown's to see if he would take the bait; Brown he lived in one of Mr. Grabill's houses, I took a bottle of whiskey one evening, which Mr. Grabill gave me to try Brown on, as he had been sick for a few days as per report, and went to Brown's; when I had talked a while I asked them if they had any thing to drink in the house, Mrs. Brown observed that they had not at that time, I said to her, I supposed it was no harm to drink, if a body had any thing to drink; I then drew my bottle on them and said that I had got a bottle full out of the still-house, which we would drink if they would keep it a secret and not inform on me, they made solemn protestations of eternal secrecy, produced two bowls, Mr. Brown and myself drank whiskey punch to ruin Bessy, as John Brown used to call his wife, produced sugar, and drank in turn her bowl like a man; she, dear soul, made the time fly fast, with the

---

[135] John Grabill (also spelled Graybill and Greybill) was a prominent citizen of Emmitsburg, near which on Middle Creek he owned a mill and distillery assessed at $1,431, the second highest total in the Fifth Election District. According to the 1820 Census of Manufactures, his still produced $3,040 worth of rye whiskey. Grabill described demand for whiskey as "not great," but it should be noted that Otter did not arrive in Emmitsburg until 1823. James A. Helman, *History of Emmitsburg, Maryland* (Frederick, 1906), p. 57; T.J. Williams and Folger McKinsey, *History of Frederick County* (1910; rpt., Baltimore 1967), p. 183; Commissioners of the Tax, Assessment Record, Real Property, 1825, Election District No 5, Frederick County, Maryland, Hall of Records, Annapolis, Maryland; Census Office, Fourth Census, 1820, Manufactures, manuscript, Election District No. 5, Frederick County, Maryland, microfilm, National Archives.

charms of her melodious voice; she sung songs for us like a nightingale; the
higher we raised the steam the nicer the thing went. When I came home
from my first whiskey mission, to Mr. Grabill's, they were all in bed; the
next morning Mr. Grabill came into the building where I was at work, he
asked me how Mr. B. was, I told him he was a great deal better, he asked me
how the whiskey business took, why said I, they took it all; said he, does she
drink too, yes said I, she drank her share, well said he, William you must take
another bottle full of whiskey over to them to night again, and then I'll talk
to them. When evening came, he filled the bottle, gave it to me, and away I
started for Brown's, with the second jorum; when I came to the house I said
that I had another bottle full of stingo, and as soon as I had that out Bessy
paraded the sugar bowl, and we made whiskey punch just in the same way
we had done the evening before; we went through all the wheelings and
facings, and when the fountain was dried up, I took my bottle and started off
for Mr. Grabill's, went to bed; the next morning Mr. Grabill came to get the
morning report, which was the same as the day before, none missing at the
bottle, Mr. Brown still on the sick list, and would certainly remain sick or
convalescing for a month if I had appeared every evening with a whiskey
bottle. Mr. Grabill he said that now he would go and talk to them himself, I
said yes that he now could learn himself what ailed them. Mr. Grabill he
went in a day or two after to Mr. Brown's, and when he came back he told me
that he met Bessy near the house, he inquired of her how Mr. Brown was,
she said to Mr. Grabill that he was getting something better, he said that if
he was able to work that he did not like to be disappointed, he would like that
he would come and work; he then popped the question at her if he ever drank
any whiskey, she said no indeed; he said he wanted to ask her one question, and prefaced it with a hope that she would tell him the truth, she said
well what is it, he asked her did my plasterer ever bring any whiskey here,
Bessy denied it most manfully, saying in reply to Mr. Grabill's inquiry, no
indeed, he never did, God knows; he then let her into the secret as she
thought; he, Mr. Grabill, gave her to understand that he had heard that I had
carried away some of his whiskey, she still denied that I had ever been there
with whiskey; he then asked for Mr. Brown, she told him he was in the
house, he rode up to the house, dismounted, and walked in the house, and
asked Brown how he came on, he told him that he was getting better, that he
would soon be able to go to work; he asked Brown if Otter, his plasterer, ever
came over to see him, Brown told Mr. Grabill that I did some times, he then
put the same question to Brown he had put to Brown's wife, and prefaced it

with, that it was not for the sake of the whiskey, only the satisfaction of knowing the truth about it, and said that he hoped he would tell him the truth about it as such he had been informed was my conduct in smuggling away his whiskey unbeknowns to him; Brown allowed that the question which was popped at him was a pretty hard one, Grabill told him that it did not hurt him, and all the satisfaction he wanted was that I should own it to him, he only wanted to know if I was guilty of it or not; Brown, he was so closely pressed and such strong convictions pervaded his breast and Mr. Grabill seen the workings of the fellow's inward monitor, and a hard look of Mr. Grabill at Brown, he was conscious that Grabill seen in his countenance the guilt, he then told Mr. Grabill that I had carried to his house one bottle full, and alleged that one bottle full was all he knew of. Now all I want is that the plasterer will acknowledge the truth said Grabill to Brown, and if he denies it I'll put him out of harm's way for one while. At this juncture Mr. Grabill came home, he told me that he got Brown to own to it, that I had carried whiskey to his house. He gave me to understand that when Brown came over that I should humor the joke, I told Mr. Grabill that I would; Brown had no rest, he came over the next day, he came to the building to inform me that Grabill had been at him to inform whether I had carried whiskey to his house, and he pressed him so hard that he had imparted to him the fact, and he labored under an apparent fear for me that a serious affair might grow out of it between Grabill and myself; when I seen the consternation Brown was in, I told him that he had betrayed me, that he should have told Grabill by no means; I added, to excite the fellow the more when we had him on the fence, that I would not for one hundred dollars that Grabill should know it, he said that Grabill had said to him that if I would own to it that was all he would ask; I told him that as he had told it that I would be forced to own to it now, and said that I sooner than own to it, I would go one hundred miles, and took my hawk and trowel and threw them on the mortar board violently, as a mark of sovereign contempt for his infidelity in betraying me, and continued, that was the first whiskey I ever took to any place, and it should be the last; Brown began to make apology by saying that Grabill had pressed him so hard that he was forced in a manner to tell; and by way of an offset to smooth the affair he had said that I had brought one bottle. I told him he might as well have told him that I had carried the two as the one, that I would have to own to it any how. The next morning Brown came to work, and the dinner table was the theatre to finish our sport with Brown, Grabill he began on me in this manner, I have a question to ask you and hope you will tell me the truth; said he, did you ever carry any of my whiskey over to Mr. Brown's house, I told him yes that I had, he asked me where I got it, I told him where every body else got it, at the still house, he asked me how much I had carried over to Brown's; Brown answered for me and said one bottle, to make valid the lie he had told about it; why said I Brown you certainly must know that I brought to your house two bottles full, you and I and Bessy, we drank it; well, he said, there might have been two, I told him why to be sure there was two, I said it was not worth while to say a word of a lie about it, for I cared nothing at all about the whiskey. Grabill to humor the joke asked me in rather a sarcastic tone and manner if I had paid for the whiskey, I told him no, but could pay for it, he said that was against his rule to carry away whiskey without his order, or paying for it, I told him I did not know his rules, I thought that I might take that liberty, allowing myself the privilege to pay for it at any time, as I was working there. Brown, when we came out from dinner, allowed that I had come off devilish well. Grabill then unveiled the joke and told Brown that he had acted a very bad part in the play; he gave him a lecture about his intemperance, and added that he must do better hereafter, or else he would give him the sack, that he had acted the worst of the two in the whiskey business. Brown he took care in future of No. one, and when he came home his dear wife, Bessy, abused him outrageously for his treachery. In the affair between the two he formed a resolution of becoming a sober man, which he pretty strictly adheard to for the space of one year. Brown he had a large dog who accompanied his master faithful. Mr. Benjamin Yingling, the boss painter, and myself, we came to a conclusion that by some means or other we would work the dog's death for a piece of sport; one day after dinner, Mr. Brown descended his ladder and was at the bottom of the well, the dog laid on his clothes near the well, Ben and myself we seized on the opportunity, we got some spirits of turpentine, caught Brown's dog and gave him a touch of the stuff[136] and then went up stairs in the new building to see the performance which was shortly to take place; the spirits of turpentine had its desired effect, the dog began to manifest symptoms of uneasiness, and at length he began to run round the house like all nature, and occasionally would take a sleigh ride to himself, which happened at or near the same spot, every rounds he ran round the house we called to Brown, and imparted to

136 "Turpentining" a dog or cat was a common prank in this period. Gerald Carson, *The Old Country Store* (New York, 1954), pp 225, 330.

him our ideas that we believed that his dog was mad, that he was dancing waltz's and cutting all sorts of fandango's. Brown he hastened up ladder with all reasonable speed, as he had a deep interest at stake with his faithful dog; we cautioned Brown to take care of himself, as we seen his desire to catch the dog, not to catch him, that he assuredly would bite him. Brown said he knew better, that his dog would not bite him if he labored under hydrophobia; he after two or three attempts caught him, and the turpentine tickled the alfactory organs in Mr. Brown's nose, he smelled the rat; he took the dog down to the creek and held him into it to cool the parts that had been annointed with the turpentine. The distiller seen Brown at such an unusual occupation as that of holding his dog in the manner aforesaid, he asked him the cause, Brown said somebody had turpentined his dog; the distiller told him to oil it, that oil would kill the effects of the turpentine. After he had poured oil out on the poor dog he came back, we asked him if his dog had got well he said yes; we asked what was the matter with him, he said somebody had turpentined him, we disowned and disclaimed any knowledge about it, as we thought the dog was mad, we kept out of his way for fear he would bite us. This trick which had afforded us a good deal of amusement led me on to another, which led to the destruction of the animal's life, as we were bent on it never to give him up until his existence had a period put to, which happened in the following manner: Yingling and myself went to our respective homes on Saturday noon, we returned on the following Monday by dinner. When we quit work at night, supper on the table and all hands around the table I asked Ben Yingling if he had seen any handbills in the country where he came from, Ben said he had; this ambiguous question excited Brown's curiosity about the handbills, what handbills said he, I told him of a gentleman who resided in Baltimore, advertised for a dog that could dive in the water to the depth of six feet, and bring up twenty-five pounds weight; that for a dog that could render such a performance, he would give fifty dollars for, Ben he allowed that there was a dog in their town that could do it; Brown said that his dog could do it "like a shot." We told him if his dog could do it that we would insure him the fifty dollars for him; we came to an understanding and agreement the next day at dinner to try him. The next day after dinner we took the dog to Mr. Grabill's mill dam, tied a stone about 8 or 9 lb. around his neck and threw him in the water, at the edge of the dam, he paddled to shore with the stone round his neck pretty well, we all admired his performance. We then took a stone a few pound heavier, tied that round his neck and got into the flat, Brown, Ben, and myself.

Mr. Grabill he staid on shore; we threw the dog overboard and to our surprise he paddled to the shore the second time; we admired that performance also, which tickled Brown's fancy to the "nines." We rowed our boat to shore, and I picked out a nice stone about twenty pounds weight, allowing that if he would bring that to the shore, that we would insure him the fifty dollars, (knowing that that was the last time his dog was to see day light,) he insured it, so we tied the stone round his neck, rowed the boat into the middle of the dam; I took a look to see that all was well secured, and we hoisted the lad overboard in the middle of the dam. I told Ben, that I thought that he would come out up stream. Brown he allowed, that he would come out down stream. Ben allowed, that he would come out at the side of the dam. We all had our peculiar notions as to his coming out—I, of course, looked up stream; Brown he looked down the stream, and Ben he looked across the dam; and we looked for the movings of the waters to see him come out—the dog in the mean time was safely moored at the bottom of the mill dam, with a stone round his neck, dead enough; when a sufficient time had expired to convince all hands on board that the dog must be assuredly drowned, Brown began to cry, and whether he cried at the fate the dog met, or for the fifty dollars, we never could learn, and under either circumstance we made him up the sum of two dollars as a recompense for the loss of his dog. The donations were given by the following persons, and the respective sums, Mr. Grabill gave one dollar; Benj'n Yingling and myself spliced, and gave the other dollar, and so ended that performance.

Another small fracas happened at the same place, the boss he happened to take sick, he gave me his negro man Frank to carry the hod, who had a knack of his own to finish every bottle of whiskey that came into his way; one day, Ben Yingling and myself, we took about a gill of turpentine and poured it into the whiskey bottle, and as we went to our breakfast, Frank he attended to the bottle as usual, and downed the whole mess, whiskey and turpentine;[137] presently it began to operate on him; he came into the kitchen crying, and asked his mistress how his master was. She said that he was very low, Frank expressed a great desire to see his master, that he allowed himself to die before his master, that he had such dreadful burning in his belly, and

---

[137] Substituting turpentine for whiskey and enjoying the subsequent effects is a commonly recounted prank in the régional literature of the period. See, for example, George Washington Harris's popular tale "Snake-Bit Irishman," in *Sut Lovingood's Yarns* (New York, 1867); and Carolyn S. Brown, *The Tall Tale in American Folklore and Literature* (Knoxville, Tenn., 1987), p. 81.

still a crying to such an extent as to alarm Mrs. Grabill, who was afraid to tell Mr. Grabill; she told us of it; we told her to let him alone, we knew what was the matter with the lad, and when breakfast was over, we went to Frank, who was in the kitchen; we asked him what was the matter; he said he was burning up alive. We took Frank and gave him a bottle of oil, which in short time allayed the fever in his intestines, the oil in the course of some time produced a rumbling in his guts, but in fine, relieved him. Frank let bottles alone, he never minded them after that. In the course of all my sprees, I have one to tell, that I shall call the story, "Dance to me, Miss Betsey." This Dance to me Miss Betsey, happened near Berlin, and in the following manner: I was plastering a house for a gentleman in that neighborhood, who had two negro boys, who were in the habit of stealing the old man's bacon. We watched the boys after they had stolen a parcel of bacon, they carried it to a widow woman's house, a tenant of his, who had a daughter whose name was Elizabeth; the two negro boys and Betsey they took a three-handed reel, and of course Betsey was the Jack for both sides; she was in the middle dancing to one, and then presently the other would say, dance to me Miss Betsey, and she would turn herself around to her sooty companion and dance to him awhile; and as they danced, the other would call and say, dance to me Miss Betsey, and so they kept up the sport in this way. The old widow was sitting in the chimney corner singing away for life, to whose music the negroes and Miss Betsey kept time. Me and my employer were all the while looking on through the cracks of the house. In the morning after breakfast; they were farmers, the principle part of their work was in the barn; the old fellow he armed himself with a "cow hide," and called one of the boys down from the barn-floor to the stable, and then he told him, he intended to flog him for stealing his bacon, and he began to lay on, and every cut or two he would say to him, "dance to me Miss Betsey;" and when he was done with him he sent him aloft, and told him to send the other boy down. He came and was lambasted in the same way the other one was, and every once and awhile the old fellow would say to him, "dance to me Miss Betsey." They know bravely what was intended, by dance to me Miss Betsey, as they had taken the dance only the evening before, and I think they would rather have repeated it than the dance they had in the stable with their master, and him to say to them, dance to me Miss Betsey.

While in the neighborhood of Dillstown, I was plastering a house for Mr. Mullen, and while there, the evening of a singing school came round, we all agreed we would go to the singing school, to hear and see Mr. Thomas

Essom, who was the teacher, whose name and fame is spread far and wide as a musical performer.[138] I was delighted with his performance, he sang beautiful, his manly voice with deep swelling tones, full and round, sounded solemnly sublime in my ears. I think, as far as I am able to judge, that he is really a master of his profession; he is a master at music in every sense of the word, and my opinion is supported by men whom I have since heard talk of him, say that he is the only man, whom they know that is a master of music in every sense of the word. Well, then we had three or four other capers which we played off, going to and from the singing school, they will be related in the order they happened—the first one was, we stopped at the house of Mr. Kindig, got our horses fed and we took supper; we then drew about one dozen of suphoena's, and I served every one of them as we went along on the folks, to attend an arbitration on Saturday, in Dillstown.— Well, then we must leave this arbitration business as it did not end till Saturday, which will be related as it occured. The next was a spree we had with an old horse farrier; we agreed to rouse him up, so I rode up to the door and hallooed—the old fellow he answered. I told him to get up, that there was a gentleman at Mr. Kindig's tavern, had a horse that was taken very sick with the cholic, he should get up and go there; that the man said that if he would cure him, he would give him five dollars; Very well, said he, I'll be there directly, and up he got, lit his lanthorn, went to his stable, got out his horse; and we were in the road watching him to see him start; so on he got and rode to Mr. Kindig's tavern; when he was started, we then jogged on: when he came to Mr. Kindig's, every body was in bed, and our old horse farrier had to ride about two miles back again to his home, and he never found out that I had tricked him; he knew that he was tricked, but not by whom. We laughed at his errand, and no doubt he gave us a plantations blessing, about it; by the time he got to Kindig's tavern we were in Dillstown, there we took a little parting drink, and every man went to his respective home. On Saturday then the arbitration business came on in the afternoon, I went to Dillstown to Mr. Howard's tavern, and there was about one dozen of fellows in attendance on the arbitration, and none of them knew who was plaintiff or

138 Otter is referring to Dills*burg*, Pennsylvania, in northwestern York County (see Map 2). In the 1820s Thomas Essom resided in Mount Pleasant Township in Adams County; the 1820 tax list gives his occupation as "Teacher of Musick." I can discover no evidence that Essom achieved renown as a singer; he is not mentioned in local histories or histories of music and was a poor man, owning no real property. Tax Lists, 1820–1825, Mount Pleasant Township, Adams County, Adams County Historical Society, Gettysburg, Pennsylvania.

who was defendant, and as I started for the town to see the witness whom I suphoened, Mr. Mullen; he went along to give me an idea of them, he knew them, being his neighbors, the whole twelve were in attendance, and were wondering what they were summoned for—some of them inquired of Mr. Mullen if he knew; he said he did not. I then observed, that the parties who had them summoned, might have compromised their dispute. One of them asked me who was to pay their expenses. I allowed that the county would have to pay them. They observed, if they knew that, they would not have been caught there that day—some got restive, and signified, that if the fellows did not soon come, that they would go home; and we kept them in talk, and at last they got into a kind of a caper and staid till evening, and at last when it was night we all put out and the arbitration business ended all in smoke.

I plastered a house near Baughman's mill, in Frederick county, and had with me a man who made the mortar for me, he was what is usually termed "near sighted;" when we had done our job, we had about twelve miles to walk to get to our homes. I was riding and the rest of the hands were on foot; near the house of General Sherman there was a parcel of large white stones laying in the road, and it was after day-light by the light of the moon, and my man Friday had a dram ahead, by this time we were in the middle of this pile of stones. Said I to him, Bunty take care of the goslings, and he could not for his soul suppress his feelings at the caution I gave him; he up with his foot and gave one of the stones a tremendous kick, and with an oath said,—the goslings; he bruised his foot at such a rate, that we were obliged to tarry all night with General Sherman; we bathed his foot with vinegar and camphor and put him to bed; we made an early start the next morning, I had to give him my horse and I had to foot it; I took him home to his wife—his wife she asked what was the matter; I told her a gosling had bit him in the foot; she said yes, and supposed he had whiskey too. I said no, that he had not much, it was all my fault, and I had to pay the bill at Sherman's, and Bunty paid the balance by being disabled from work for about three weeks, and so ended that business.

Near to the town of Hanover, the Carlisle and Hanover Turnpike Company erected a gate to take toll within the precincts of the town, the turnpike company had a very saucy Irishman as their gate-keeper, through his impertinance he got into the ill graces of every one of his neighbors who resided in town. I, as one, who was determined to lead my Irishman such a life as to make his berth a burden to him, to tease him out of his life, and until he

should put out—it was in the dead of winter, a snow fell, and in a day or two
after the snow had fallen, it blew bitter cold, I thought that would be the
time to let a prank or two fly at our son of the Emerald Isle, I made all the
exertion I could to let him have it, by getting all the hands I could to join in
the spree. We got about eight or ten sleighs hitched up, and we had one of
the sleighs drove up to the gate from town, and turned the sleigh towards the
town, and then roused up the gate-keeper; when he got up, we started off
and drove into town; this performance was played off on him by every
sleigh—we had at intervals sufficiently to make him rise out of his bed, and
time enough to let him get to his bed and get warm in it. After this
manoeuvre we drove up all the sleighs we had to the gate, and demanded of
him to rise and let us pass the gate. He refused to rise; we told him that if he
did not get up and let us through, that we would hitch our horses to the gate
and tear it into splinters. At which menace of ours, he got up and let us
through; he seen what kind of a gang we were, and the force we could
muster—he said he thought the devil was in the people that night, he could
hardly tell how often he had been roused. We told him by way of a taunt, that
we would make him rise just when we pleased, and cracked whips over our
horses and away we went for M'Sherry's town at a merry gait; when we came
to M'Sherry's town we stopped at old Oaster's and took a drink; we then
came to the conclusion to go to Reinecker's tavern, and there we would feed
our horses and take our suppers. We started off and drove up to Mr.
Reinecker's door, they were just in the act of going to bed when we arrived—
we went in and signified our wish to have supper and our cattle fed. He said
it was too late; we insisted on it, saying we were going to Gettysburg. His
wife said she could get supper. We unhitched all our cattle and got them into
stables and sheds; we had them all well fed; after we had taken great care of
our horses, we went to the house and asked for some brandy, not to forget
ourselves in the sleighing time. The old woman she came in and asked what
we wanted for supper. I told her we wanted sausage and pudding, and
nothing else—she then went to work to prepare our supper. The old man he
walked into the kitchen and seen the preparations going on for our supper—
he, the old man, was a poor narrow-hearted, miserly, niggardly fellow; he
began on his old woman, and threw out insinuation that she had prepared
too much for us; whilst he was, as he thought, learning his little wife to cook
and to save, I took it into my head to make him lose on another point as
much as he could save, so I filled the stove chuck full of wood, and it became
outrageous hot. The landlord had an old monkey chained to a box in the

house, which was kept for the purpose of keeping their stove wood in—this box served for a kind of a place or kennel for the monkey. I took the monkey and removed him from his place of retirement, and brought him to a more conspicuous part of the bar room, I chained him as short as the chain would allow, and around the stove pipe, the stove was very hot, some of the plates were red, and the monkey within one foot of it; the heat of the stove seemed very oppressive to the old fellow; he sat on his haunches, rolled his eyes about in his head at a frightful gait, lolled out his tongue, and spread out his fore-paws as if to screen him from the heat of the stove; and while the landlord and landlady were frying puddings and sausages for us, I was roasting the monkey—at last his situation was intolerable, he screamed most horribly; the old man he came running in to see what was the matter, he seen the fix the monkey was in; he ran to unchain him; he had the bad luck to burn his fingers at the monkey's chain. We then all agreed that he must be cut loose, and at it we went and cut the strap, and as soon as he found himself at liberty he ran out of the room into the kitchen, and jumped on the old woman's back; the old woman knew nothing of the monkey being let loose until he jumped on her back, and it frightened her. The old man he could not catch him, and for fear he would run over our puddings and sausages we opened the kitchen door that led to the back yard, and there we almost froze him by the time we were done with him, at last we caught him and tied him in his box, the place from whence he came. After the monkey business was over, our supper was ready, we all sat down to supper, we ate all the puddings and sausages that was prepared for us in short order. We called for an additional supply; she fried more and brought them to us; we cleared the board the second time and called for more; the old woman she brought us a third supply, and we also called for brandy, and no brandy was to be had; we had drank his brandy bottle dry, he would give us no more drink, and said, that if we would quit eating and drinking, that if we would only clear out, he did not care if he would get pay for what we had or not; we assured the old man that we wanted to pay, and would pay all we already had, and would pay for all we would call for; he should only get for us what we called for, we would pay for all; and we called for another mess of puddings and sausages, she cooked what she had, and we called for more—she said she had no more to cook, that we had ate all she had in the house. While we were paying our bills, some of the company went and took old Reinecker's sign down, and hung it up at a weaver's shop, about three hundred yards from the tavern, and wrote on it, "Nothing at all for sale here"—this was done as a mark of humorist's, from the facts that they were ate and drank dry by us. We asked him, how much our bill was, the old fellow was so wrothy at us, which confused his ideas so much that he could not tell what it was in the gross.

We then took it per single man, and asked him if 50 cents per man would satisfy him, he said yes, so we paid him twelve dollars and fifty cents, we drove home, one by one, at intervals sufficiently long between to make our Irish gate-keeper rise and go to bed again between our arrivals. That provoked him so much that the next morning he went to the board of directors and complained that the devil might keep the gate among the Dutch there, they kept him up day and night, and he resigned to them the trust they had reposed in him. He left the town and what became of him no body knows, and no body cared what became of him, all we cared for was to get him away.

Once upon a time, I went to Westminster to do a job of work; one day a gentleman and his lady, who are by law acknowledged vagabonds, came there to amuse the citizens of Westminster with their performance, the lady was to perform on the slack wire. She went through the manual exercise and a great many little capers; he performed on the violin while she was performing, and he had the camera obscura or the magic lamp, and other hocus pocus, &c.

On the evening of their performance, me and sundry other lads we went to this performance, we took along with us a bucket full of water, and a large horse syringe, accompanied by the beau monde of the town. Well, when all was in the room, the actress at length got on the slack wire, and began by playing off some of her exploits; at length she came to the military part of the performance, when the word "fire" was given, I had prepared myself with the horse syringe full of water, I let her have it right on the false seat of honour; being somewhat of a practioner at the art I made sure work, and brought my game to the floor. She gave tongue by screaming and hollowing, her dear half he dropped the violin, on which he was scratching to fill up the interludes of her performance, and took the lady behind the curtain and came back and told the spectators that the wire performance was over, and expressed a sorrow that such an undecent liberty had been taken with the performer, and hoped that the like would not be done again. We spoke out and said we hoped not, and said that such people ought not to be in the room. He then prepared his magic lamp, and the landlady sat opposite to us, and somewhat of a loquacious disposition; she could not get done talking about the syringe business. I observed to my comrades as soon as the lights were extinguished to give the magic lamp more splendor I would let her have a blast. And when the lights were put out for the purpose aforesaid I charged the syringe chuck full, and let drive at the landlady, and took her bip into her face and mouth, and it came with such a force that it nearly took her breath from her. As soon as she had fairly recovered from her squirting match she sung out for the landlord, when he come into the room he inquired of her what the matter was, she told him and he asked where it came from, some said it came from one corner, and others alledged it came from another quarter. While the landlord was looking about to find out where it really came from, the candle was blown out, which was in the neighborhood of the room where the landlord was, and he being somewhat in a quandary about the squirting business, and for the sake of gratifying his curosity about it, how it felt, I let him have a squirt full butt on the ear. When he had received his portion of it he got in a passion, left the room abruptly, went down stairs to get a club to set things to right. While the landlord was below trying to procure a cudgel, the showman, luckless wight, he came out from behind the curtain and began to make his comments on the impropriety of such conduct at such a place; and in the midst of his exordium I made a charge at him with my squirt, and squirted him right well, and the candles were all extinguished as though it were done by magic, and in this juncture the landlord he was in the act of coming up stairs armed with a club, I let him have a second dab on the stairs. We then all rushed down stairs, drove him before us, and I made the showman play the violin for us till nearly day, to satisfy us for our money which he had fobbed for the show, which we expressed a full dissatisfaction at the performance of his show, and to satisfy us by playing the fiddle for us, and we danced stag dances till nearly day light, so ended this spree.

Shortly after the above performance I had a job to do in Hanover for a grass widow, of the name of Koogler,[139] she was building a house, the plastering of which I done, and while I was there I learned something of the traits in her character. She was one of the most ill natured creatures in the creation, crabbed, cross, ill contrived and stingy as the deuce. The old lady she had in her garden a very fine apricot tree, which had a very fine parcel of apricots on, it leaned about half over the fence into an adjoining lot, the apricots were about ripening, she observed to me that she was afraid that the boys would steal her apricots for her; she was, as her fears run so high,

---

[139] Mary Kugler, assessed at $300 in 1818–1819. "Grass widow" refers to a woman who is separated or divorced. Tax List, 1818–1819, Borough of Hanover, York County, microfilm in the Hanover Public Library, Hanover, Pennsylvania.

that lest they might be stolen she was watching them every night. She took me into the garden one day to show me the apricots, and gave me one to taste, I advised her to go to her next neighbor, a Mr. Nace, and borrow from him one of his large dogs, and chain the dog fast to the tree to prevent the boys from stealing the apricots; knowing that if she would get the dog which I had advised her to get that I would be likely to get a share of them myself. She succeeded in getting the dog from Mr. Nace, she chained him to the tree as I had directed her, and I seen the whole fun; about midnight I went into the adjoining lot with a stick, and would job it at the dog, and he was vicious and cross, he would fly at me with all the force in his body, and down he would shake the apricots, and the old woman she laid in a room next the garden, she heard the whole performance, and would hiss the dog and he would repeat his effort with all his might, and down a parcel of apricots would come again; the more he forced the chain the more he would shake the tree, and the more apricots he made fall; I picked up all the apricots and stowed them away for my own special use and benefit. In the morning I went to work at her house, she told me that some good for nothing fellow was at the tree and made the dog shake off all the apricots, and took them away. I observed that it was a pity that the dog did not catch him, she was so full of it that I had to go with her into the garden to see the destruction; and showed me the apricots the dog shook off for her; I did not treat the lady quite as courteous as she treated me, for I did not show her the apricots I had. She lamented over her loss, and asked me what she should do with them, I advised her to share them among her neighbors, which she did, she gave me a few, and I am sure that the neighbors never before nor since ever got a single taste of her apricots.

After that I went to Emmitsburgh to plaster a house for Dr. Annan, and while I was at that job one day, I observed a man of the name of Jacob Trenkle,[140] he was in the habit of getting tipsey; he just had a skin full, and he went into a wheat patch of Mr. George Wirter's, he rolled about and spoiled a good deal of wheat. I took a large horse syringe that the doctor had, and went into the lot and hunted up the lad; at last I found him, and I had the syringe charged in the dung yard; I gave him a shot; he got up and was blinded that he could not see; he also labored under the intoxicating influence of the liquor he had drank; he laid down again in the wheat patch, and I

---

[140] The 1825 Emmitsburg tax assessment records a Jacob Troxell, valued at $160. Commissioners of the Tax, Assessment Record, Real Property, 1825, Emmitsburg, Frederick County, Hall of Records, Annapolis, Maryland.

went back, got another charge and let him have it the second time; he got up and got two stones, one in each hand, and I run for it for the dung yard; and after I had charged again, I went to meet him, and asked him what he intended to do with the stones he had in his hands; he said, that he would knock my brains out; and I said if he made any such attempt, that I would shoot him; he threw at me with one of the stones, and I up syringe and took him into the mouth, and the force of it whirled him about so much, that the stone flew another direction. I run again and went into the building; he went home to get his gun for the purpose of shooting me; he came with his gun, and inquired where I was. Robert Annan, he persuaded him not to mind it until evening—when evening came, he came to the tavern up town, which was then kept by Mr. Jacob Bohn, and I repaired to it and got into contact with him and made good friends with Mr. Trenkle—After we had healed up our old sore, we sat down and began to play dominoes, and I beat him out, and quit him with a view to play another prank upon him. Another man took my place, and I got behind the chair of "come across by Durney," as the folks used to call old Trinkle, and shook a shower of cow itch down the back of his neck. After a while the cow itch began to operate, and in the meantime I undertook to show him how to play, and dropped some cow itch on his hands, and such another scratching match as old Trinkle had was nobody's business but his own. Somebody told the old fellow that it was cow itch, and it was pinned to my sleeve, which was the cause of another rumpus, which we put over in a way honorable on all sides. I once played sein in my life time, in which I lost all my money, and ten dollars worth of honor, and then I quit, and never played since. The way it began was, Mr. B., of Hanover, H.R., H.W., M.D., and myself set down at the tavern of John Amich, in Hanover, and played, as I have already stated, for money, until I was bursted. I then told them that my money was all gone, and I now would play upon honor; the company were all agreed that my honor was quite good enough; so I played away upon honor until I had lost nine or ten dollars. Said I to them, gentlemen I think my honor is gone far enough; I shall play no more, and I am determined to pay no more. Mr. B. said to me that he would play no more with me in the world. I told him I was very glad, that I was sure I never would play with him again, and so ended the sein playing for money and on honor.

Sometime after I got a house to plaster for Mr. B., who had, in the meantime, moved to the town of Westminster. I had a journeyman working with me, and a laborer from Baltimore of the name of Donahoe. It was very warm weather, and we slept in the brewhouse. My journeyman thought he was a very smart sort of fellow; he played off some pranks on the laborer by hanging a bucket full of water over the brewhouse which would spill over him as he opened the door. The next day the laborer told me of it. I comforted him not to mind it, that I would match him for it the next night; so I went the next day to an apothecary shop and bought 6¼ worth of cow itch, and let my lads go to bed a little while before I went. It was on a very fine warm moon-light night; one could easily lay without cover. Our bed stood along side of a window, my journeyman lay fast and soundly asleep. I souzed my bundle of cow itch over him right genteely. I laid down easily beside him, pretending to be asleep, and in the course of about five minutes he began to roll and to scratch, and wakened me by his fuss as he thought. I asked him what was the matter with him? He said somebody had put horse hair into our bed; that it was killing him. This wakened the laborer; he asked what was the matter? I told him I thought George was crazy. He got up and began to scratch and tear, and the brewer had a large bed of sand in the room, for the purpose of keeping the ale cool, which he kept in bottles; he laid himself on the bed of sand, and finally buried himself in it, and rubbing himself with it. Some of the bottles had bursted in the sand, and the pieces were sharp. George cut himself with the glass while he was rubbing himself with it, and he kept on rubbing until day-light, and abused himself so much that he could not work for two days. We examined the bed in the morning for horse hair, and could find none. I went to work, and in the course of the day I imparted to the laborer the fact that I had put cow itch on George. That piece of intelligence pleased him very much. I told the laborer I would give him a touch of something else in the course of a few days. George came to work after two days had elapsed from the cow itch spree. In two or three days after he had begun work, one night there came up a very heavy gust. I was at Bohn's tavern, at least five hundred yards from the brewery. I buffeted the whole storm; George and the laborer laid in bed laughing at me for being caught in the rain. I told them that they would not laugh if they had seen what I had seen. George was curious to know what I could have seen that was an equivalent for the shock I endured in fronting the storm? I told him that I saw an Indian dance, which has gratified me so much that I thought I would come up to let them know it. Said he, I never seen an Indian in my life. He said he would like to see it. I told him if he would hurry and go down to Bohn's tavern that they were dancing yet.

I found his curiosity aroused, and he asked me how many Indians were there. I told him there were four in number, two men and two squaws. I have, said he, a great notion to get up and go to see them, and he asked the laborer if he would go along. The laborer said he had often seen them in Baltimore. Well, said George, I will go any how. Up he jumps, and put out for Bohn's tavern, and it was as dark as pitch, and raining as hard as it could pour, to see the Indian dance. Now Philip, said I, lock the door on him, and Philip Donohoo locked the door. By-and-bye George came tearing through the rain, dripping wet, and puffing and blowing, and we pretended, when he wrapped at the door, to be fast asleep, and let him stand in the rain about fifteen minutes, until he was completely soaked. At last Philip got up and let him. I asked him if he had seen the Indians. He said not, that Bohn's were gone to bed. Then we had a good laugh at him, and he was too drunk to see that he was sucked in. He was not satisfied. He went the next morning to see the Indians. He got up before sun-rise, went down to Bohn's and asked him where those Indians were. What Indians, said Mr. Bohn. Why, said George to Bohn, Otter said that there were Indians there at his house. There were no Indians here you fool, said Bohn to him, and so ended the Indian business.

The next affair was a lottery which I had a hand in. A certain old Dutchman, a cabinet maker, made a first rate bureau, and put it off by lottery. The bureau was put up at 40 dollars, and the lottery was drawn after all the chances had been disposed of by Pickle. Well a day was appointed to draw the lottery, and Mr. George Frankhauser was the holder of the fortunate number that drew the bureau. Then came the tug to deliver the bureau to the winner. Mr. Pickle asked me to haul the bureau down to the neighborhood of Westminster to the winner. I hired a horse and sled, and off Pickle and myself started with the bureau. On the road I began to feel old Pickle's pulse about the propriety of sucking in the winner for a few dollars. The old fellow was agreed to any thing that would bring him a few dollars into his pocket. So I told him that I would make Frankhauser believe that Dr. Byrenheit had won the bureau. At length we came to Frankhauser's house. We stopped in the middle of the turnpike. Frankhauser came out and asked who had won the bureau, and we told him Dr. Byrenheit. My God, said he, I was sure of winning it myself. He admired it very much, and his wife came out to see it also, she allowed it was very pretty. I told Frankhauser the road was so bad, that I did not like to go on to Westminster to Byrenheit, that if he would give me my day's wages, pay Pickle five dollars, and keep it a secret, that we would unload it at his door. Agreed, said he, and down he planked the money to us, gave us a very good dinner, and some fine bounce,[141] and then we started off for home.

[141] A mixed alcoholic drink to which sugar and fruit—often cherries—had been added.

Emmitsburg

I n eighteen hundred and twenty four I removed from the city of Baltimore to the country, and fixed myself and family in the town of Emmetsburg, in Frederick county.[142] At which place I am still residing, and very probably shall finish my days here.

The very first job I done in my line of business was to plaster the Seminary of Learning near the town,[143] then under the Superintendance of the Rev'd. John Dubois, the present Bishop of New York.[144] While that work was going on, I had many good hands at work under my charge, and one day one of my journeymen happened to take a seat at the breakfast table which did not exactly suit the views of an Irishman of the name of McHenry, who thought that he was the rightful owner of the place at the table, which my journeyman had by mere accident taken possession of; McHenry he

[142] One mile south of the Mason-Dixon line, Emmitsburg, Maryland, was on the main road between Baltimore and Pittsburgh. Emmitsburg's local economy was based on its function as a stopping place on the road west and its emergence during this period as a center of American Catholicism, with a seminary and a convent. According to Fr. Simon Bruté, Emmitsburg's population in 1823 was seven hundred, about half Catholic and half Protestant, including twenty-six slaves and seventeen free blacks. Fr. Simon Bruté, "Emmitsburg, 1823," manuscript, Box 7-3-1-1, St. Joseph's Provincial House Archives, Emmitsburg, Maryland. (See Figure 9.)
[143] The Seminary of Learning had been started in 1807 (see the following note). The contract between Otter and the president of Mount St. Mary's, John DuBois, is printed in the Appendix. The "new building" at the seminary cost sixteen thousand dollars and burned down immediately after completion. *Frederick-Town Herald*, 12 June 1824.
[144] John DuBois (1765–1842) founded Mount St. Mary's College when the instruction at the seminary was broadened to include lay students. A French priest who came to the United States during the French Revolution, he became bishop of New York in 1826. Mary M. Meline and Edward F.X. McSweeny, *The Story of the Mountain: Mount St. Mary's College and Seminary, Emmitsburg, Maryland* (Emmitsburg, 1911), 2 vols. (See Figure 8.)

Fig. 8. Mira Vizzala, *Bishop John DuBois*, 1830. The original in The Founder's Room, Mount Saint Mary's College and Seminary, Emmitsburg, Maryland.

began to jaw about his place, as he called it, and threatened that he would turn any body out of the room that in future would trespass upon his right in enjoying his place at the table: this menace raised my blood and I began to let him have a squall, and as my journeyman was a man who had not been by nature an athletic and robust made man, on the contrary he was delicate made and very modest, I saw the necessity of taking his part; and I walked up to McHenry and to quiet the matter, just now to put me out instead of my journeyman, and he without any further ceremony up with a bowl full of hot coffee and throwed it into my face; this I considered as a war of defence on my part, and as soon as I could see, I seized a hold of McHenry and hoisted him up and threw him lengthways upon the table, after two or three ups and downs I landed him among the fish, plates, and bowls, on the table, just the right way, and the way they were mashed and ground to pieces was a caution. This all happened in the absence of the Rev. Mr. Dubois. On his return home, a complaint was lodged against us as disturbers of the peace and quiet of the institution; the Rev. Mr. Dubois he held an enquiry into the matter, found McHenry guilty; gave me an honorable discharge, and enjoined it on McHenry on fine of forfeiting his birth, if ever he said another word to me or any of my hands while I was there.

The next thing that happened, that had music in it, to me was, I plastered a house for a Mr. J.S. in Adams County; the way it happened was—one Sunday morning Mr. J.S. started to go to church, I was laying on the porch reading, and amusing myself. The madam had put over the fire (which was a very fine one) the dinner-pot; when she had the dinner on she laid herself down on the bed to take a nap: the chimney caught fire, at this juncture; J.S. happened to look behind him and seen that the house was on fire, he wheeled about and came running back as hard as he could, he run past me into the house and run into the bedroom to secure his valuable papers;—the noise he made in the haste wakened his better half, she rose up and in her raising herself up she asked him in these words, "why Johnny are the humblebees after you" bumble bees, said he to her, the house is on fire. She got out; and at the remark he made, I jumped up and ran out to see how the matter was. And I saw that it was confined to the chimney; I told her the chimney only was on fire; she went to the kitchen and got the salt box and landed the box and the salt into the fire; and the steam put the fire out in the chimney. After the danger was all over Mr. J.S. told me that he never had experienced a severer fright in his life.

I once was called upon by the Reverend Louis De Barth, superior of

Conewago, to do a job of plastering for him in his room;[145] it was in the winter, and he considered it a particular job: he told me he would give me one dollar and fifty cents per day, and that I must hang on until it was done. I began the job and gave it the first coat, and when that was done, I told him that it would take about two days to dry, during that time I proposed to him I would go home, and when it was ready for second coating I would return and do it—with a view to lighten his expenses; to which proposition he objected, upon the ground that I would not return, and said that he would find me another job during the time allowed for drying. So I asked him what it was; he told me I should go along with him, and he led the way into the cellar; the repository of his wine, cider, apples and so forth: to stop rat holes in the wall. He gave me privilege to use any thing, in any manner I pleased; so I began to stop rat holes, and while my laborer was bringing me stuff, I sat myself down on a lot of sand, and began to dig in it with my trowel, and at last I dug up a longed necked bottle, neatly sealed up. I held it up to the light, when the laborer came into the cellar, I asked him what he thought it was, he said it was wine, we agreed to decapitate the bottle and test its contents, and when we had drank it, sure enough it was wine of a very fine quality; he then asked me what was to be done with the bottle. I told him we would break it up and stuff the pieces of it into the rat hole, and in the course of an hour another bottle shared the same fate as the first, and after awhile we slaughtered a third one; by the time we had finished a third bottle, old Bunty he got pretty boozy, we also tried a few of father De Barth's apples; the cider we never disturbed it while we were stopping rat holes, we held the wine too high to have any thing to do with cider, and in the course of that day we finished stopping rat holes.—While we were in the cellar, father De Barth was called away and was absent about a day and a half; in that time I closed up all the rat holes in the cellar, and had tore away a book case which he wished removed in his room. While I was in the act of tearing away the book case I found two parcels of money wrapped up in paper, and they were both labelled in a language foreign to my own. I opened them and the one contained eighteen French crowns, and the other had five pieces of gold, the

145 The Conewago Chapel, built in 1787 in the village of Edge Grove, just outside Hanover (see Map 2), is the oldest stone Catholic church in the United States and is listed on the National Register of Historic Places. Otter was not plastering the chapel itself but the adjoining rectory, still also standing, though much enlarged. Fr. Louis De Barth was the superior at Conewago from 1820 to 1828. John T Reily, *Conewago: A Collection of Catholic Local History* (Martinsburg, W.Va., 1885).

value of which I also did not know; after I had seen their contents I wrapped them up again, and put them into my pocket until he should return; upon his return, I handed the money to him, he said that they were left by some of the Priests who had been there before him, and said that he knew nothing of it, he gave me five dollars for my finding it; in the morning after, he and I went into the cellar to see how I had stopped up the rat holes, he examined all as he went along, until we came into the wine cellar, he jocularly observed to me, that he hoped that I had not found out his wine. I laughingly replied, oh yes, I had found it out; he asked me did I drink any, I told him I had drank two or three bottles of it, he told me that was right, as he had given me full privilege to help myself to any thing that was in it.

I then put on the second coat in the room, and whitewashed it; after I had finished my job, father De Barth he planked down the cash, and I put out.

The next thing that came into the way that afforded me fun, was while I was plastering the big house for the Sisters of Charity;[146] an Irishman who had just landed from the sod, who, was in the employ of the Sisters of Charity as a farm hand, came to me one day, to the house from the field next to the house, where he was engaged in harrowing, he had there came across a terapin, which was a novelty to him, he took a stick and stuck it to the spot where he found the terapin, to find it again, said he to me, Bill I found a horse's foot down here and it is alive yet. I went with him to the field and when we came to the marked spot, the terapin was gone. We hunted about, and at last I found it. I invited his attention to him and he acknowledged that was it, why said I to him, my dear fellow this is a terapin; said he I was sure it was a horse's foot, and observed that he had never seen one before.[147]

I once worked at a job of plastering for an old gentleman near Waynesburg, who was excessively close and stingy. I let a war hawk slip at him, and he never felt it, but the sum and substance of the business is, that I got four chickens to eat and he got the broth; it was got up under the following circumstances: he happened to have an attack of diorrhae, and he complained to me about it. I sympathized with him and told him that I had

---

[146] The "big house" at the Sisters of Charity was the DuBois Building, demolished in 1965. The St. Joseph's Provincial House Archives, Emmitsburg, Maryland, contains the record of expenses for the "New building," dated 27 March 1826, showing a $253 payment to "Wm. Otter."

[147] This may be folklore. Later in the century, "Foolish Irishman tales" were widespread in the oral tradition; in one, for example, an Irishman mistakes a pumpkin for a mule's egg. Otter's story seems to fit quite closely within this genre. For a collection of such tales, see Richard M. Chase, ed., *American Folk Tales and Songs* (1956; rpt., New York, 1971).

suffered many inconveniences arising from it, and began a prescription for him; I advised that he should go to Waynesburg and get a box of Anderson's pills, and take three of them for a dose, he asked me where he could get them, I told him at Mr. Charles Smith's store, and if they did not operate in two or three hours, to repeat the dose and take three more, so off he started, got the pills, and took them as I had directed him, and they did not meet his wishes; I advised the other dose, he took them and they produced the effect desired. I then, to get a mess of chicken, advised him to take chicken broth; he had a chicken killed, we got the chicken for breakfast, and my patient took the broth. I suggested to him to have two more chickens killed, and to continue to take broth to work off the medicine he had taken, and as he had experienced a considerable relief from the first, he had two more chickens killed, and he stuck to the broth, and at dinner we ate the two chickens. I liked the sport of eating the chickens, and he was fully as well pleased as I was with broth, he expressed great satisfaction at the effects produced. I thought to spin my yarn as long as I could. I told him that if he would have another chicken killed and take the broth of that, that I would ensure him a sound man. So we had the chicken for supper and he held on to the broth, and it produced a very happy result. He allowed that he never experienced such efficacy of medicine in his life. I finished my old tunker's job,[148] he paid me for doing it, and I put out home.

About this time I opened a shop in Emmetsburg, and, as my circumstances were of an ordinary character, I had to buy my liquors by the gallon.[149] I used to get them from —————— ——————, he was very kind to me; others that I also held in esteem, who are, in the main, pretenders only. At length my good old friend told me he had a ten gallon keg; that I should take the whiskey by the keg; that he would lend me the keg; that it would come cheaper to me than by the gallon. I told him I was agreed, that if he would let me have the keg I would take good care of it. I then bought of him by the keg for better than a year. One day he suggested the idea to me that I should buy the keg from him. I told him it was hardly worth while, that I had it cheap

---

[148] Tunkers or Dunkards are a sect of German Baptists, the members of which settled in Southern Pennsylvania beginning in the eighteenth century.

[149] This "shop" was presumably the Otter tavern in Emmitsburg. The 1840 census showed ten adults and two children living in Otter's household, six of the adults were listed as "employed in manufacturing and trades"—perhaps Otter boarded some of his journeymen. Census Office, Sixth Census, 1840, manuscript, Election District No. 5, Frederick County, microfilm, National Archives; James A. Helman, *History of Emmitsburg, Maryland* (Frederick, 1906), p. 87; Meline and McSweeny, *Story of the Mountain,* p. 376

enough as it was. I took a notion to see how much the keg actually would hold, it was then just empty, I took a measure and measured it, and it held nine gallons and a half, scant measure. I took my keg over to have it filled, and I asked him if that keg held ten gallons, he said yes, he thought it did, that it was a ten gallon keg. I told him I thought it looked rather slim, that I did not think that it held ten gallons. I bet you, said he to me, the full of it that it does. I told him that I would not like to bet that much, that he knew its contents and I did not. He said no, that he had bought it for a ten gallon keg. Well, said he, will you bet it, that's the business. I told him I did not much care, that I would bet him that it did not hold ten gallons. He began to measure it, and laughingly observed that I would lose it. While measuring the keg, he began to be apprehensive that he might lose the bet. He used to leave some in the measure. Said I to him I'll either win or lose all, will you go the keg too? He said yes. Said I, well then, we will go the whiskey, keg, brass cock, and all. Agreed, said he, and I discovered the big business, that he was not exactly using fair play in measuring. Come said I, my boy, measure fair. At the end of the whole affair, the keg only held nine gallons and a half, and then I raised the laugh on him, shouldered the keg. Well, said I, I won the whole of the whiskey, keg, brass cock and all. Oh! Bill, said he, you will leave the keg. No indeed, not a hoop, said I to him, and walked home with my prize like a man, that's the way I fixed my friend.

While I was employed in the plastering the house of Mr. Abraham Krise, in Adam's county, there was in the neighborhood of Mr. Rhodes's mill, a house whose inmates were candidates in a matrimonial point of view. One evening we all started off on a rabbit hunt, and in our rambles we came to this house, and we found, what is not every where, or at all times to be met with, every girl in the house had a beau. When we had learned how things were, we began to look about to see if any subject for a little fun and sport, could be met with. At last I espied a gobler who was perched on an old stove chimney. Said I to the boys, if they would hide behind a stack of hay that stood about fifteen yards from the house, I would show them a piece of sport. All the lads fixed themselves, and I approached the gobler to seize him; he sung out quit, quit. Said I, I will directly. I seized him and socked him down the chimney. When he got in contact with the fire on the hearth he raised a terrible fright among the boys and girls; he lashed about the fire with his wings at such a rate that it took them some time to recover the panic they had been thrown into. They ran out of the house, and I got down while this general confusion prevailed, and went and laid myself along side of the fence near the house. At last they seen that it was the gobler; they came to the conclusion that it was the smoke that had brought him down the chimney. They took him and placed him on the roost again from whence he came, when all was quiet. I slipped out from the place of my concealment, and seized the gobler a second time and souzed him down the chimney a second time, left them to enjoy the sport, and put out.

While I was engaged in plastering at the college, Mr. Dubois requested me to take his horse and ride over the mountain to Mr. Reed and Bonebreak to engage for him two kilns of lime. On my way there I overtook a white man and a black man. The black man's arms were tied behind his back with a silk handkerchief. I asked the white man as I came up to them, if he had caught a runaway?[150] He said no, that the black man belonged to him. I asked him the reason why he had him tied? He said that he had him tied for fear of his making his escape from him on the mountains. I asked him how far he was going on that road? He told me he was going as far as Mr. Fisbury's, that he had some business there to settle. He asked me if my name was Otter? I told him yes, Otter was my name. I suppose, said he, you don't know me? I said to him that I did not. He asked me if I ever had worked at Millerstown? I told him I had. He then asked if I ever knew one George McCullough that worked there? The moment he mentioned his name I recognized the man, and answered him that I knew him. He then told me that he had caught that negro coming down the mountain, and that he believed him to be a runaway. He asked me what I would give him for him haphazard? I told him that I had no notion to buy him, not knowing if he was a runaway or that there was any reward on him.[151] He told me he wished me to ride along to the tavern and try to get out of the negro what he was and who he was. I went with him to the tavern, and when I was there I called the negro out and asked him who he belonged to? He told me that he belonged to one Mr. Gelwicks, in Virginia. I asked him how many children Mr. Gelwicks had? He said he did not know. Said I to him, you belong to no such man at all; and asked him to

---

[150] Maryland was, of course, a slave state. In this period, however, slavery was declining in most parts of Maryland and the free black population growing rapidly. In Frederick County the number of blacks had never been very large, but it was one of the few Maryland counties in which the slave population actually increased in the antebellum period: the number of slaves grew from 3,417 in 1790 to 3,913 in 1850 (compared with 3,760 free blacks and 33,314 whites in that year). Barbara Jeanne Fields, *Slavery and Freedom on the Middle Ground: Maryland during the Nineteenth Century* (New York, 1985), figures on p. 13.

[151] None of the censuses or the 1825 and 1835 Emmitsburg tax assessments show Otter owning a slave.

tell the truth, to whom he belonged? He said, well I belong to Mr. Goldsborough. To find my lad out, said I, does he live in the town or country? He told me Mr. G. lived in the town. I asked him how many slaves has Mr. G? He said he had a good many. How many, said I, to elicit a positive answer from him? He said he did not know rightly how many he had. I observed that it was not worth while to say another word to him as he was determined not to speak the truth about it. I took him into the bar room, and told George McCullough that I could get nothing out of him. He swore he would take him on to Baltimore and sell him. I told him that he dare not do that, for the laws of the country would punish him for such an act. He asked me to tie him, for, said he, you know more about it than I do. I told him if he would get me a rope that I would tie him. He asked the landlady for a piece of rope. She said she had none, but allowed that she could let him have a piece of home-made linen, if that would answer. I told her it would. She produced the linen, a strip about as broad as my hand, and I tied the negro's arms on his back. While I was tying the negro's arms I told him to try to make his escape from that man, for sure as guns he would take him to Baltimore and sell him to the Georgia traders, and if he effected his escape to take refuge in the mountains. He got considerably alarmed at the piece of intelligence which I had imparted to him. He promised faithfully that he would try to make his escape and flee to the mountains. I took him after he was tied into the bar room. George McCullough called for something to drink. I drank, and in turn called for half a pint of whiskey, which made my good old friend pretty well how come you so. I inquired at him where he was going to. He said he was going across the country, to a Mr. Fisher's. I wanted to go to Mr. Bonebreak's to buy lime; we went together until we came to the lane that leads to Mr. Fisher's. I bid him good bye. I pursued my road, and he steered his course for Mr. Fisher's. In about one hour's ride I came to Mr. Bonebreak's the man from whom I wanted to buy my lime. I went into the meadow where they were making hay, and I asked if Mr. Bonebreak was there? They told me no that the old man was not there, and that his two sons were in pursuit of a runaway negro who had bent his course toward the mountains. I asked them how the negro was dressed? They said that he had no hat on, and that he had two rags on his arms. I asked which way he went? They showed me the course, and I hitched my horse and started after the boys across the country. I went about half a mile, and I met the boys on the back track. I asked them if they had caught the negro? They said that they had not. I asked them the direction he went? They showed me, and I put out

after him with a dog of the spaniel breed to assist me in the pursuit, and on
whom I mainly depended as he was one among the finest of that species of
dog. I got on his track, and pursued him to a large barn at the foot of the
mountain, the barn was of logs, and rather in a state of dilapidation. The
gable ends were both open, and as I got up at the one gable end he got down
at the other, and he made for the woods, and I hissed my dog Ponto on him,
and as soon as the hiss was out of my mouth, my dog flew at him, and seized
him, and held on to him until I came up to him. When I came up to him I said
well you are here. He said yes. I asked him how he got away? He said that man
whose captive he was, called at a house and asked if Mr. Fisher was at home,
and being informed that he was not at home, he hitched the black man to
the post where horses were generally hitched, at the piece of linen which
I had tied his arms with, and Mr. McCullough laid himself down on the
bench, and the weather was very warm; he fell asleep, and I began chopping
the linen backwards and forwards until it broke in two, and when I was free I
started off and run through the orchard as hard as I could run, and lost my
hat in the orchard, and did not take time to pick it up. I asked him how he
liked to go home? He said he did not care much about it. I asked him if the
dog had bit him? He said no, that he held him by the trowsers. He admired
the dog's performance, and allowed that that dog was worth money. I said
yes he was so. I then asked him, if ever he had been at Emmetsburg? He said
he never was there, but that he knew a man there. I asked him who that man
was? He said Mr. McBride, the constable. I asked him where he learned to
know Mr. McBride? He said at his master's house, that Mr. McBride had
often been there. He still stuck to it that he belonged to Mr. Goldsborough. I
found that the black rascal was determined to lie. I marched him off to Mr.
Bonebreaks. I engaged my lime, and then started off and crossed the mountain that night with my runaway lad. I cautioned him not to try to run away
from me that if he did that my dog would tear him to pieces. He said he
would not make the attempt. I told him if he did not that I would not tie
him. So I marched over the mountains free from any fetters. When I came
home it was past one o'clock at night. I gave him something to eat, and put
him and the dog Ponto in a room and kept him there until morning. In the
morning I walked down to Mr. McBride's to walk up to see the black boy.
When he came into the room where he was I asked Mr. McBride if he knew
that negro? He said he did, that he belonged to Mr. H, in this county. I gave
the negro his breakfast and locked him and Ponto, his companion, up in a
room, mounted my horse, rode to Mr. H's house, and asked him if he had

lost a negro? He said he had, and walked out into another room. While he was gone out I discovered a bundle of handbills laying on the stove, and took one of them and put it into my hat. By this time he came into the room, and asked me where I lived? I told him that I lived in Emmetsburg, and asked him if it was his negro what he would give? He told me that he would pay me well for my trouble, and ordered his horse and we started for Emmetsburg. We came to my house, I opened the room, brought the negro out, and asked him if that was his negro. He said he was, and asked me where I got him? I told him that I apprehended him in Pennsylvania; that a man had him in possession, that he was going to sell him, that the negro runaway from him, and that I had caught him. He asked me what my charges were for the apprehension, and delivery of his negro? I told him I thought he knew what was right, judging that he would come up to the notch of his advertisement in which he offered a reward of twenty dollars. He said if he would give me ten dollars that that sum would be enough for my trouble. I told him that I felt no disposition to take up any man's runaway negro for that sum. He then said that ten dollars was all the money he had with him, and when he came to town again he would give me some more. I seen Mr. H. in Emmetsburg in about three weeks after that, approached him and hinted to him the balance that he owed me; and asked him how his negro man came on? He said he came on very well, but he would not be hinted at. Mr. H. came again in the course of a few weeks, and I was determined to bring our negro runaway business to a close, and went to him and asked him how his negro man come on? Very well, very well indeed. Then how is it about that little balance between you and I? Oh, said he, I paid you. Well, said I, you don't intend to pay me any more, that's all I want to know? He said he had paid me. I walked up town to a squire shop and took out a warrant against Mr. H. for a balance of ten dollars. The writ was placed into the hands of a constable, who, in short order, had Mr. H. before the magistrate. The squire opened the case, and read the charge preferred by me against Mr. H., a balance of ten dollars for catching a runaway negro. He said he had paid Mr. Otter all he owed him. The squire asked Mr. H. how much he had paid me? He said he had paid me ten dollars. The magistrate observed to him that the charge was a balance; to which he replied he had not made any contract for any more, and plead payment in full. The squire asked me if I could prove a contract? I told him I thought I could. He asked me where my witness was? I told him I believed I had him in my pocket. I put hand to pocket, pulled out Mr. H's. advertisement, and placed it before the magistrate as the evidence on which I

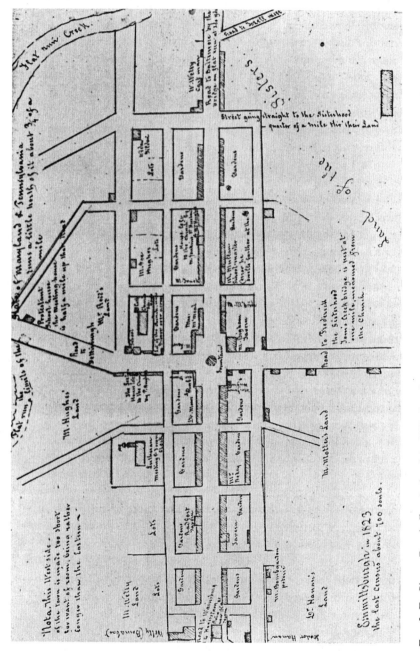

FIG. 9. Fr. Simon Bruté, *Emmitsburgh in 1823*. Otter's tavern was on the southwestern corner of the square. The Frederick County land records show that in 1827 Otter purchased a house on the south side of the Baltimore Road two blocks to the west (left) of the square. From Bruté, "Emmitsburg, 1823." Courtesy, St. Joseph's Provincial House Archives.

based my suit of action. The squire asked him if that was his advertisement and the reward therein offered? He said it was, but plead that he never put them up; to which I observed that I never had put it up, but that it was up now. The squire gave me a judgment for ten dollar against Mr. H., and when I had judgment against him he paid me like a man, and thus ended this spree.

I once got a parcel of conies, and they were, as all are, very pretty animals; and they are somewhat mischievous. I had to barricade the warren for fear of their being torn by dogs; and while I was engaged as above stated in repairing their warren, a certain Mr. M. M. came along, and he fell in love with their appearance, and asked me how many of them I had? I did not tell him the exact number. Said he to me, making the question as impressive as he could, well Bill, what will you take for a *him* and a *her*? I told him that I would take one dollar for a him and a her, repeating, his word. He allowed that a dollar was too much for a him and a her. I told him that I would not take any thing less for them.

Now for the celebrated Woodsborough spree, which took me a full half a day to get through and a good part of the night into the bargain. The way it commenced was as accidental to me as it was to the hands who were involved in it. It happened the day after the election in eighteen hundred and thirty four. As I was going on to Mr. Bowers to plaster his house for him, the town of Woodsborough lay in my way, and when I came to the town, I stopped at the tavern kept by the widow Yantis. Little did I think when I stopped, of cutting a single caper. As soon as I had put foot into the tavern, the political inquisitive fellows asked me the result of the election in the Emmetsburg district, I told them that the Jackson party had lost ground.[152] That piece of news pleased some, and others again it did not please. There were in the bar room two Clay men, who had not yet gone home from the election, they were a little touched with Jackson tea, and a Jackson man, who also had a rip.[153] He was a hanger on, for the whole three were farmers. The two Clay-

---

[152] Although the Democratic candidates for the four state assembly seats and for Congress carried Emmitsburg by a narrow margin, the Whigs did indeed run more strongly than in 1832. Overall, Frederick County was solidly Whig. *Frederick-Town Herald*, 11 October 1834 and 18 October 1834.

[153] Terms such as "Jackson Party" and "Clay men" were the typical party labels in this period; "Democrat" and "Whig" did not come into standard use until the late 1830s. William G. Shade, "Political Pluralism and Party Development: The Creation of a Modern Party System, 1815–1852," in *The Evolution of Modern Electoral Systems*, ed. Paul Kleppner (Westport, Conn., 1981), p. 80.

men appeared to be very liberal in their manners, and the Jackson-man was a very close, stingy, miserly sort of a fellow. One of the Clay-men asked the other who I was. He told him I was Otter, from Emmetsburg, the plasterer. He took a look at me, and allowed that I was very big fellow. He felt his keeping as I have already said. He told his comrade, notwithstanding my size, that he believed that he could whip me. All this conversation I overheard, but never let on I heard them. I thought to give him a hint. I told one of my comrades that the Clay-men, at least all those whom I knew, were such rascals, that the Jackson-men had no chance any more among them. He took the bait intended for him. He got up and said that was a lie, there were as good Clay-men as Jackson-men. I told him if there were any such, that I never knew them. His comrade begged him not to mind it, that he knew that I meant no harm in what I said, and that he knew me very well, which interposition of his comrade in my behalf, only had a tendency to raise his dander the higher. He said that he could whip me, even if I was as big as the house. I told him that I could not fight, and never did intend to fight, but I can beat any Clay-man belonging to the party in the whole United States, at *butting*.

This wide spread banter he could not brook. He pronounced it a lie. Those who wanted to see fun, urged him to take a butt with me. He said he was no bull, and could not stand it. Well, said I, I cannot stand fighting, so there is no danger of our hurting one another. He still kept harping on his favorite theme, that he would like to have a crack at me. At length some of the fellows worked upon him to give me a wiper. Well, said he, I don't care, I will take a butt with you anyhow. Well, said I, take off your hat. By this time I was fully determined to give him a good one. I caught hold on his two ears, and he caught hold on mine, and I gave him a rouser that sent him heels over head on the floor. This created a good deal of laughter among the spectators of the scene before them.

This performance raised his dander to the highest pitch, and I complained of my head very much. They urged him on to take another crack, and wanted to persuade him to try it again. I told them that I would rather not, that as soon as I butted one man down that I felt offish, and invited him up to the bar to take a drink, and make good friends. No, said he, I am not satisfied, you must give me another chance. I still pretended to be rather off, and told him that if he would treat I would give him another chance. He agreed to treat with a view to get another butting. I begged of him not to butt too hard. He said by swearing an oath, that he would butt all he knew.

We took our usual ear hold, and I butted all I knew and laid him flat on the floor a second time. When he got up, he appeared a little bewildered. His laboring under a kind of stupor, which was occasioned from the blow I gave him, gave his general phiz rather a comical kind of appearance, which created a great deal of laughter, sport, and much amusement to the company. I called on him to pay the treat he promised, and he swore he would whip me. He paid the treat, rolled up his sleeves, and was for making at me. I told him that if he struck me, that I would have another butt at him. His comrades persuaded him not to mind it. I got him up to the bar, and got the old Jackson-man, whom I have taken notice of in the commencement of the story. The company all were agreed that I should make that old fellow treat in turn. That he would drink until all was blue, when he could drink for nothing. So I asked him to drink, and sure enough he took his horn like a man. As it seemed by consent of the whole company, that I should get him to treat, I called in vain, he refused to treat, and said he had drank enough, thanked me, and did not wish to drink any more.[154] I told him in terms not to be misunderstood, that if he did not treat in turn and that the whole company, that I would be under the necessity of giving him a butting. He said I had better not. I told him that it was the sense of the whole company, that he should treat or take a butting. He said he had sufficient. Well, said I, are you going to treat or not. He answered me he would not treat. Well, said I, then you must take a butting, and I caught him by the ears, and gave him a tremendous butt and knocked him as stiff as a poker. He fell against the wall, and as he was in the act of falling, his eyes rolled in his head and a good deal of the white in them appeared. When he recovered a little, he went in quest of a magistrate to have himself righted. The squire refused to give him law for the butt he got, and I am at a loss to determine whether butting would at all be recognized in law, or not. The law defines an assault and battery very clearly, and am rather inclined to think that in its definition it does not reach butting, and I am sure that butting is no species of felony of any kind whatever. What the real cause was that he could get no law to protect him I

---

[154] As one guide for immigrants to America put it, treating "'good fellows' when we meet them, and receiving treats from *good fellows* in return" was the common procedure when drinking with others. To accept a treat and not to return it was an extremely serious breach of barroom ethics. Jack London, out of ignorance, once failed to treat: "*I had let him buy six drinks and never once offered to treat. . . .* The heat of my shame burned up my neck and into my cheeks and forehead. I have blushed many times in my life, but never have I experienced so terrible a blush as that one." Thomas Mooney, *Nine Years in America* (Dublin, 1850), p. 65; and London, *John Barleycorn: "Alcoholic Memoirs"* (1913; rpt., Oxford, 1989), p. 47

cannot tell. But the way I sent him against the wall was a caution. When I had stiffened my old Jackson-man, I turned on my Clay friend again. They urged him to give me another flyer at butting, that he should not think himself conquered. He allowed my head was too hard for his, and that inasmuch as I had failed in making the old Jackson-man treat, that I should pay a treat myself. Agreed, said I. Come all ye that thirst, and I treated the whole company.[155] I told him that I was very glad that the old Jackson-man was gone, that my head felt like a poor man's garret, that it was full of lumber. Yes, and God knows, says he, my head aches too. The company agreed that we should take another butt, and by mutual consent then should give it up. I told them that I was agreed, that my head could not ache worse after it than it does at present. They got him worked up to the sticking point, and we took another whack, and I knocked him against the bar table as stiff as a poker.

We all went up to the bar, and I insisted that it was his turn to treat the company, to be even with me, that the company drank last at my expense. We all came to the conclusion to give Mr. Lind, also a tavern keeper in Woodsborough, a call, and wind up our spree there. Mr. Lind lived about a quarter of a mile from Mrs. Yantis, and as soon as the idea was suggested to go to Mr. Linds, all hands were immediately agreed to the proposition. The two Clay-men felt a disposition to take a gig and ride down. I was full of frolic, and wished to shew out some of the blossoms of the wild oats, which I felt at this time disposed to sow, being a Jackson-man myself,[156] and the whole mess of us on a Jerry. I proposed to the two Clay-men that if they would pay me a bottle of French brandy when we came to Mr. Lind's tavern, that I would take the gig shafts and haul them down through the town myself. As soon as I made this proposition to haul them down myself, they agreed that they would pay me the bottle of French brandy. The bargain was struck, the gig was brought before the door. As soon as the gig was ready, I got into the shafts in good earnest, to let them see that nothing was wanting on my part. The passengers took their seats. The one he folded up his arms and laid them across his breast, his legs crossed, and leaning backwards as if determined to enjoy the ride in luxury. The other was more of a romp, he made

---

155 Otter probably has in mind John 7:37: "In the last day, that great day of the feast, Jesus stood and cried, saying, If any man thirst, let him come unto me and drink."

156 Otter became a naturalized American citizen on 25 September 1828, less than two weeks before the presidential election. I believe that Otter did this so he could vote for Jackson; see the commentary, p. 221.

no particular parade about the contemplated ride. After they were seated, I enquired of them in these words:

"Gentlemen are you ready," they responded in the affirmative. Said I stop a little till I spit in my hands, and, as I made the motion, aided by a small jerk at the shafts, and letting them go at the same time, my passengers took a sudden notion to go up, instead of down town, and heels over head they both went out of the hind part of the gig, and as the gig turned a summerset, one of them, the fellow who sat careless, seized the springs of the top part of the gig, landed himself by the aid of the spring and his powerful exertion, on his feet. Said he, that goes "pretty and nice." The other one fell on the back part of his head, neck, and shoulders and was terribly staved. He laid senseless on the street for a short time. We carried the old fellow into the tavern, sent for Dr. Sinners to examine him, he came, had no idea of our spree, allowed to wait a while, to see what the probable result might be. He left us, and after a short time came back, we then told him of our performance. He said, under such circumstances, the better plan was to let him remain as he was, labouring under some excitement, kept up from the free use of brandy and allowed, if necessary, to take some blood from him in the morning. Then came the time for censure, some said I done it purposely, and I alleged that I was not well broke to the shafts, and, for myself, ascribed the whole to the want of a belly band, so ended that spree, and it was the last. In it I sowed all my wild oats. I have arrived at an age when all men become grave. I feel that time is making his inroads on me as well as all other mortals, being now in the forty-seventh year of my age. In the course of my mechanical pursuits as a plasterer, working as master of my trade, I have kept a record of every house I plastered, as well as all other buildings, such as churches, colleges, academies, and so forth. I began for myself in the year 1810, during which time I plastered two hundred and three houses, including thirty-two churches, five colleges, two academies, and one market house, and all the money that they came to, was the neat sum of fifteen thousand three hundred dollars, and am still a poor man, without my earnings, having a large family, which run away with the beans to support them.[157]

---

[157] Otter's evaluation of himself as a "poor man" is exaggerated, but Big Bill clearly was not wealthy. Otter is not listed as owning property in the 1825 Emmitsburg tax records. The 1835 list assesses "William Otter Senr." for a lot with a frame house at $117 and "William F. Otter" for a lot without a house at $67. It is possible that the second lot was owned by William Otter, Jr., who was twenty-three years of age. The average property assessment in Emmitsburg in 1835

In the spring of eighteen hundred and thirty-five, the citizens of Em-
mettsburg conferred on me their best gift, elected me burgess of the town,
by a very handsome majority over my opponent, and have, as far as my
ability allows, discharged the duties entrusted to me, without favor, affection, or partiality.[158]

---

was $166; if William Otter, Sr., owned both lots, his worth would be $184, slightly above the
mean; if he owned only the lot with house, he would be considerably below average. See also the
commentary, p. 201. Commissioners of the Tax, Assessment Record, Real Property, 1825 and
1835, Emmitsburg, Frederick County, Hall of Records, Annapolis, Maryland. Maryland also
taxed personal property: in the 1835 personal tax assessment list there is one entry for "William
Otter Sr ," for $100, and three for "William F. Otter," totaling $268. As with real property, it is
impossible to be sure if "William F Otter" is Big or Little Bill. Commissioners of the Tax,
Assessment Record, Personal Property, 1835, Election District No. 5, Frederick County, Hall of
Records, Annapolis, Maryland.

[158] Burgess is the equivalent of mayor. Unfortunately, in the words of Emmitsburg's historian
James A. Helman, "The burgess' books prior to 1840 are not to be found, hence all is darkness."
The returns for Emmitsburg local elections are not given in the Frederick newspapers, nor is
there any information available in the Maryland Hall of Records. Hence no information exists
about Otter's term or terms as mayor After 1840 Otter held no elective office in Emmitsburg.
Helman, *History of Emmitsburg,* p. 65

POSTSCRIPT

After *History of My Own Times* was published in 1835, Otter continued to live in Emmitsburg until 1850. The Frederick County land records show that in 1837 Otter cosigned a note for $520 so that his son, William Otter, Jr., could buy a house in Emmitsburg. Little Bill had followed in his father's footsteps, becoming a plasterer, and seems to have taken over the tavern's stable, and possibly the tavern itself from his father at some point in the late 1830s.

In 1845 the Otter tavern was destroyed by fire. In 1849 Little Bill appears in the Baltimore City Directory; in 1851 William Otter, Sr., is listed as a "liquor dealer," living "s.w. corner Lomb. and Shroeder." Whether the fire was a factor in their decision to move from Emmitsburg is unknown but certainly possible. The 1850 Baltimore census lists Otter's age as sixty-seven (he was really sixty-three), born in England, occupation "innkeeper." His wife "Mary" was fifty-eight. Shortly after this, Big Bill fell ill with "consumption and dropsy." On 8 April 1856, William Otter, Sr., died in Baltimore. His wife survived him by many years and attended Little Bill's funeral in Baltimore in 1883.

The 1856 death notice for William Otter, Sr., in the *Baltimore Sun* was accompanied by the following obituary poem:

> If I had thought thou couldst have died
>   I might not weep for thee;
> But I forgot when by thy side
>   That thou couldst mortal be;
> It never through my mind had passed,

Thy time would e'er be o'er;
And I on thee should look my last,
    And thou shouldst smile no more;
And still upon that face I look
    And think twill smile again,
And still the thought I will not brook
    That I must look in vain;
But when I speak thou cost[?] not say
    What thou ne'er left unsaid,
And now I feel as well I may
    Sweet William, thou art dead.

If thou wouldst stay e'en as thou are,
    All cold and all serene,
I still might press the silent heart
    And where thy smiles have been;
While on the chill bleak corpse I look
    Thou seemest still mine own,
But there—I lay thee in thy grave,
    And I am now alone.

I do not think where'er thou art
    Thou hast forgotten me,
And I perhaps may soothe this heart
    In thinking too of thee;
Yet there was round thee such a dawn
    Of light ne'er seen before,
As fancy never could have drawn
    And never can restore.

Sources: Census Office, Sixth Census, 1840, manuscript, Emmitsburg District, Frederick County, microfilm, National Archives; Census Office, Seventh Census, 1850, manuscript, Wards 12 and 18, City of Baltimore, Maryland, microfilm, National Archives; Liber HS 5, pp. 450–451, 7 November 1837, Land Records, Records Room, Frederick County Courthouse, Frederick, Maryland; Ordinary License List, Frederick County License Book, 1845–1857, Hall of Records, Annapolis, Maryland; James A. Helman, *History of Emmitsburg, Maryland* (Frederick, 1906), p. 87; *Matchett's Baltimore Directory for 1849'50* (Baltimore, 1849); *Matchett's Baltimore Directory for 1851* (Baltimore, 1851); *Baltimore Sun*, 22 April 1856; and *Hanover Spectator*, 14 March 1883.

COMMENTARY

William Otter and the Society of Jolly Fellows
in the Early Republic

istory of My Own Times was the title Otter chose for his book. Why call it that? In what sense did Otter mean the title? Clearly, it is not a history in the usual sense of the word. Think of what is missing here: most of the great events of the period. No politician or great person is mentioned (except the references to Jackson and Clay "men"); and the War of 1812 is noted only in reference to cruel pranks. Nor is there mention of the Burr-Hamilton duel or the 1805 yellow fever epidemic, both of which happened while Otter was in New York City; the Louisiana Purchase; the 1824 presidential election and the "corrupt bargain"; or Fulton's invention of the steamboat. Cultural events in the new nation receive no attention whatsoever.

In short, this is simply not a history of Otter's time. Is Big Bill joking? I do not think so. Or at least I don't think he is entirely joking. To try and understand why Otter chose this title is to ask *why* he wrote this book. The title itself is almost certainly borrowed from another book with that name which was published in Frederick in 1832 by the Rev. Daniel Barber, an Episcopal minister who converted to Catholicism, who no doubt adapted it from the classic account of the Glorious Revolution: *Bishop Burnet's History of his own Time*. Barber, like his Connecticut ancestors before him, was "naturally fond of associating with people whose manner and conversation savored of piety," and Barber's *History* is an eclectic compilation of childhood reminiscences, accounts from his Revolutionary War service, a description of his conversion, and excerpts from his homilies. It is possible that Otter may simply have liked Barber's title, but given that Otter's book, with its drinking, brawling, and pranks, is almost the antithesis of Barber's devout, patriotic, and high-minded volume, I do not think so. I believe Big Bill was responding to Barber's book, that Otter was writing a *History of My Own Times:* that may be your history, Reverend Barber, but this is mine. I am describing a life, and milieu in every way different from yours, a profane life not a sacred one, and I do so without shame or apology.[1]

The unremorseful tone is significant. There are other works from this period that recount a rowdy, dissolute life-style—for example, the carpenter-turned-gambler Robert Bailey's 1822 autobiography or John Gough's 1845 temperance memoir. But these books are religious autobiographies; they recount a reckless past to highlight a reformed present. In Otter there is no sense that he expects us to condemn the "jolly fellows" or recoil from them.[2]

Bill Big may have been making some sort of subversive statement in his choice of title, but I doubt he would take the time and effort involved in writing a 357-page book merely as a retort to Barber. I suspect that, as in most things, there was probably not a single motive for writing *History*, no simple reason for an Emmitsburg, Maryland, plasterer to write his autobiography.

But what other motives might there have been? Otter's preface can be read as a parody of more genteel literature, which supports a subversive interpretation of the work but otherwise does little to illuminate *why* Otter

---

[1] The Rev. Daniel Barber, *The History of My Own Times*, 3 vols. (Washington, [D.C.,] and Frederick, Md., 1827–1832), quotation 1:9. After Barber's wife died, he "commenced a kind of pilgrimage state of life, wandering from place to place," spending some time "at the College in Georgetown" (3:11). At some point during his travels he visited Emmitsburg; there is in the Mount St. Mary's archives a letter from Barber to Fr. John McGerry, president of Mount St. Mary's, dated 21 November 1828, in which Barber writes: "I often very Often think how happy I should be to see you all again and come visit the foot of the Great Mountain the seat of wisdom and Pious Contemplation.—Remember me to all the sisters." Given the identical title (the only books with this title in the Library of Congress catalogue), the Frederick publication of the last volume, and Barber's past visit or visits to Emmitsburg and his desire to visit there again, it seems to me extremely likely that Otter had seen Barber's memoir and perhaps even met Barber.

[2] Robert Bailey, *The Life and Adventures of Robert Bailey* (Richmond, Va., 1822); Bailey's contrition, though often expressed, does not always seem heartfelt. John Gough, *An Autobiography* (Boston, 1845).

wrote it. He states in the preface that *History* "is not expressly for the use and instruction of children," but he is not very enlightening on the specific reasons for authoring the book, leaving readers "to their own conclusion." Certainly financial motives cannot be ruled out. Otter describes himself as "a poor man" and might have seen *History* as a way to make a few bucks. It is interesting to note that he finally settled Peter Winebrenner's 1819 judgment against him on 5 December 1834, so possibly Otter was under unusual financial strain in 1835. It is hard to assess this speculation because nothing is known about the book's publishing—was it Otter's idea or another's? Did Otter have subscribers before publishing *History*? Whatever his hopes may have been, the extreme rarity of the book indicates that not many copies were printed, and profits must have been very small if there were any at all.

Whatever monetary considerations may have existed, Otter surely understood that no book could succeed without a story people wanted to read. But what did Big Bill think readers would find fascinating? This autobiography is clearly highly selective, for there is little "history" in *History*, and Otter mentions his wife and family only in passing. The book focuses, as the preface promises, on "all the scrapes" Otter was in. That, indeed, is the organizing principle in *History*—one scrape per paragraph. To modern readers this seems an odd book to write, for these "scrapes" reveal Otter as a vicious, racist bully. It is likely, as I will explain, that many readers in the 1830s would not have found these episodes offensive; nevertheless, it is still an unusual focus for an autobiography. So why did Otter write a book with this peculiar slant?

One possibility is that he was counting on his reputation in the area; it seems clear that Big Bill was something of a local legend. In *History* he is referred to as the "celebrated plasterer" from Hanover, and the *Hanover Spectator* in 1883 described Otter as a man "who flourished in our town some half century ago, and who was famous as a wag and practical joker." John T. Reily in the comment I quoted in the Introduction called Otter a "peculiar man who did some very foolish things" and was "well known." Reily's spelling of the name as "Arter" strongly suggests that Reily's remarks were based on oral tradition regarding Big Bill. It seems clear that Otter was by no means a completely obscure man, and I suspect that he hoped many of the sales of his book would be to people who knew Big Bill's big reputation. So writing *History* may have served to elaborate Otter's local prominence and give it permanency; the focus is exactly on those "foolish things" that had made Otter notorious. And his stories may have been polished by constant retelling. According to the history of Mount St. Mary's College, Otter "kept the village tavern" and "entertained his bibulous guests with many 'adventures,' more or less credible and creditable, but clothed in language quite suitable to their taste and surroundings." So *History* may be "The Best of Big Bill Otter," written in the hope that people in the vicinity would be interested in hearing about the scrapes of this larger-than-life local figure, the Till Eulenspiegel of Frederick County.[3]

To raise this possibility, however, is not to exclude others. It is conceivable, for example, that some political motive was involved. In 1833, Harper Brothers of New York had published the allegedly autobiographical *Sketches and Eccentricities of Colonel David Crockett of West Tennessee* (probably written by Matthew St. Claire Clarke, a friend of Nicholas Biddle). Congressman Crockett was shifting at this point into the anti-Jackson camp, and this book was designed to publicize this *other* Tennessee politician. The point is that Crockett's putative autobiography—which had very strong sales—in its description of Crockett's "fondness for fun," comic anecdotes, and boasting, bears some resemblance to *History*. Otter was a self-described "Jackson man," elected burgess of Emmitsburg in 1834. Possibly, perhaps at the urging of others, he was hoping that *History* would give his budding political career a boost, just as *Sketches and Eccentricities* had helped Crockett.[4]

One of the most commonly cited reasons for writing autobiography is, as Roy Pascal puts it in *Design and Truth in Autobiography*, "a search for one's inner standing," a voyage of discovery through which self-knowledge is gained.[5] Otter was not an introspective man and made little effort in *History* to impose sense and purpose on his life. Such an element does enter, however. The book ends on a rather elegiac note: "I have arrived at an age when

---

[3] *Hanover Spectator*, 14 March 1883; and John T. Reily, *Conewago: A Collection of Catholic Local History* (Martinsburg, W.Va., 1885), p. 170. Otter may have expected other jolly fellows to buy *History* —his reference to "Mr. B., of Hanover, H.R., H.W., M.D." seems to be an in-joke (157). Otter's comments near the begining of the chapter on Cincinnati about his intended audience are rather ambiguous: "I am not now writing for a community that exactly is in the latitude of Cincinnati, and shall content myself to tell my readers who are residents of the Lord knows where." Mary M. Meline and Rev. Edward F.X. McSweeny, *The Story of the Mountain: Mount St. Mary's College and Seminary, Emmitsburg, Maryland* (Emmitsburg, 1911), 1:376.
[4] The publishing history and background of David Crockett's *Sketches and Eccentricities* is given in James Atkins Shackford, *David Crockett: The Man and the Legend*, ed. John B. Shackford (Chapel Hill, N.C., 1956), pp. 253–264. For "fondness for fun," see Crockett, *Sketches and Eccentricities of Colonel David Crockett of West Tennessee* (New York, 1833), p. 75.
[5] Roy Pascal, *Design and Truth in Autobiography* (Cambridge, Mass., 1960), p. 182.

all men become grave. I feel that time is making his inroads on me." Otter is suggesting that he has come to realize that he is getting too old to continue as the Big Bill who did "very foolish things," and sees this book, perhaps, as a kind of summing up to prepare him for the next stage as the respected burgess of Emmitsburg. Whether or not we find the suggestion entirely convincing—as with a drunkard who swears off liquor time and again, this statement may represent more a public affirmation of hope than a realistic plan for change in his life-style—it does raise yet another motive Otter may have had for writing *History*.

He therefore may have had several reasons, those mentioned and perhaps others at which one cannot even guess. From reading and researching *History*, I have established certain possibilities, but finally, it is impossible to know why Otter wrote *History*. This uncertainty of motive makes it hard to judge his perspective and thus leaves the book something of a mystery.

I am convinced, however, that Otter was not completely joking in calling this a history of his times; the book provides a powerful sense of time and place. It is a strange history to be sure—one with an Emmitsburg plasterer at its center, and the concentration on sprees is odd, indeed almost unique. Yet I would argue that this very quality makes it useful to our understanding of the past; it gives us an unusual look at life in the early Republic. *History* is interesting for more than its historical significance. It is also an adventure story, a comic tale, and a study in psychology. Yet it would not be worth reprinting, to my mind, unless it gave some insight into the American society of the period. I believe it does so. Before we can analyze Otter's *History* as history, however, it is necessary to answer two questions: How accurate is it? and How typical was Otter?

Accuracy and Typicality

The difficulties in understanding Otter's motives in writing *History* contribute to the problem of assessing its accuracy. Did the events he recounts really happen? Otter, of course, presents this as a true story, stating at its beginning that his friends "would, if called upon, bear him out in the sincerity, and the sovereignty of truth, of the 'History of his Own Times.'" Should we take him at his word? Or is this one more of his pranks?

As with Otter's intentions, the truthfulness of *History* cannot be settled definitively. It is clear that it is not a novel; many of the events and people

were real. It might seem tempting to view Otter as a naïve writer unacquainted with literature to any significant degree who is simply relating his
life and sprees in a straightforward, guileless way. This is impossible to
credit. It is certainly true that *History* does not follow established literary
conventions—there are no chapters, and some of the paragraphs are ten and
twelve pages long. The inconsistent spelling and use of vernacular, such as
"done" for "did," reinforce this impression. But I doubt that Otter was
as unknowledgeable about literature as the organization of the book
might suggest. Otter was not very well schooled, but he portrays himself
reading for recreation (163). Despite the overly complex, at times even
convoluted, sentence structure, *History* is actually rather well written,
though the possibility that Otter dictated all or part of it to someone else
cannot be ruled out.

My feeling is that Otter conceived *History* quite consciously as an autobiography. He had probably read other autobiographies—perhaps Cellini's,
or Franklin's—and was familiar with the genre. I tend to doubt, however,
that he was following a precise model. Obviously, the tone of *History* is
different from that of Franklin; indeed, it is almost an inversion of this most
famous of American autobiographies.[6]

Nor do I think that Otter was significantly influenced by another genre to
which *History* bears a certain resemblance, that of picaresque literature.
Typically in picaresque novels such as Alain-René Le Sage's *Gil Blas*, Henry
Fielding's *Tom Jones*, and Tobias Smollett's *Roderick Random*, the hero is
forced into being an outcast from society, a traveler, who lives by his wits,
becoming a trickster, even a petty criminal. In some ways Otter's story, with
its pranks and adventures of the road, fits the genre. Certainly, the episode
involving "Dr. Vanpike," whom Otter humiliates at fencing before pissing in
his face (near the end of "Hanover") sounds right out of Smollett. Yet, there
is a key difference between Otter's book and picaresque literature. Although
the picaresque hero never questions the social order, most novels in the
genre are works of social criticism, and usually the target of the rogue-hero's
pranks is a powerful person: an aristocrat, priest, or unfair master. In *Histo-*

---

[6] Working-class autobiographies were a minor genre in the nineteenth century. On English
workers' autobiographies see David Vincent, *Bread, Knowledge, and Freedom: A Study of Nineteenth Century Working Class Autobiography* (London, 1981). There is no similar study for the
United States, but W. J. Rorabaugh, *The Craft Apprentice: From Franklin to the Machine Age*
(New York, 1986), bases his book on an extensive reading of first-person accounts.

ry, by contrast, Otter's targets are less often powerful than powerless—blacks, the Irish, widows, and domestic animals.[7]

It is possible that Otter read picaresque literature, but I doubt *History* was modeled on it. There are similarities, just as there are similarities to the often ferocious American Southwestern humor of such mid–nineteenth-century writers as George Washington Harris, creator of the Sut Lovingood stories. I would argue, however, that most of this similarity stems from that in the milieu in which these works were produced. People in the streets of eighteenth-century London really could have bedpans emptied on them, and ordinary Americans really did drink and brawl. These works, like Otter's, did not focus on refined society.[8]

If we conclude that Otter was not following a fictional model, does that mean we can put more faith in his account? Yes, but this hardly means we can accept *History* as the truth. No autobiography can be completely true in the historical sense. As Pascal explains, "Autobiography is . . . an interplay, a collusion, between past and present; its significance is indeed more the revelation of the present situation than the uncovering of the past."[9] The truth is in the telling; even if Otter is genuinely trying to be accurate, his memory of the past cannot help but be influenced by subsequent events.

A minor example suggests how, as Pascal puts it, the present penetrates the past. Otter claims that the statue in the center of Delacroix's Vauxhall was of the Virgin Mary (41). Contemporary evidence makes clear, however, that it was of George Washington. Otter's years of living in Emmitsburg, one of the early centers of American Catholicism, had apparently influenced his recollections. The example is a minor one, to be sure, but it illustrates how

[7] Picaresque literature is classified in Frank Wadleigh, *The Literature of Roguery* (Boston and New York, 1907), 2 vols. The meaning of this literature is discussed in Robert Alter, *Rogue's Progress: Studies in the Picaresque Novel* (Cambridge, Mass., 1964). One eighteenth-century reader complained of *Roderick Random:* "I cannot read Smollett anymore. . . . For no reason at all people are hurt and humiliated even skinned; even those who help him to perpetuate fun. Jokes about hunchbacked people. . . . Pissing for no reason." These comments could very easily be applied to *History.* Quoted in Paul-Gabriel Boucé, introduction to *The Adventures of Roderick Random,* by Tobias Smollett (1748; rpt., Oxford, 1979), p. xxiii.

[8] For an example of an apprentice cabinetmaker in early nineteenth-century New York City who was influenced by picaresque literature in writing his autobiography, see Samuel Seabury, *Moneygripe's Apprentice: The Personal Narrative of Samuel Seabury III,* ed. Robert Bruce Mullin (New Haven, Conn., 1989).

[9] Pascal, *Design and Truth in Autobiography,* p. 11.

unreliable memory can be. This and other minor errors—for example, the way Otter collapses time in his New York City years—I point up in footnotes. More worrisome are major errors that may exist undetected. Is the "tone" of *History,* with its combination of pranks, violence, and racism, a product of the 1830s that Otter projected into the earlier years? Such problems are the inevitable result of writing autobiography. Historians are wary of oral history (which Otter's account may be) and autobiography because they recognize how inaccurate and self-serving memory can be. Yet historians also recognize the value of oral history as a means to get at the texture of life in the past in ways impossible with other sources.[10]

Most autobiographers are therefore inadvertent liars. But there is an additional problem: Otter may also have been an intentional liar. He seems to be giving us a story crafted, in part, to enhance his reputation as an outcast from genteel society, the jolliest of the jolly fellows. Could he really have been so triumphantly victorious in virtually every encounter? No one gets the better of Big Bill here. Now some boasting is probably unintentional— Otter genuinely believes in his own invincibility and remembers things in a way that validates it. But, there is no reason not to wonder whether Big Bill consciously embellished his accounts of his sprees when he retold them in his tavern. Otter was a storyteller in a period when the tall tale was admired.[11]

One way to try to assess how truthful, both consciously and unconsciously, Otter was is to check his story against documentary evidence. The evidence I found is in the footnotes. And the story largely checks: as far as I can determine, Otter was where he says he was, most of the names are those of real people and events, and such incidents as his violent encounter with Jacob Witter (94–95) really happened. But, of course, much of what is most interesting in Otter cannot be checked—most of the book involves personal stories and "scrapes" involving jolly fellows. Take for example, the "Great Dog Massacre" (147–148). The people involved were real; there actually was a Ben Yingling, and John Grabill did own a mill with a pond on Middle Creek near Emmitsburg. Yet did Otter actually drown that dog? James Doogan was a journeyman chairmaker in Gettysburg, but did Big Bill really

---

[10] See footnote 39 in the text.

[11] Some of the issues involved in "conscious and unconscious misrepresentation" in autobiography are discussed in Timothy Dow Adams, *Telling Lies in Modern American Autobiography* (Chapel Hill, N.C., 1990), pp 1–16.

pull a ladder out from under him? (99) Confirming the existence of the people involved gives us more confidence in Otter's veracity, but in the end we can never know for sure if these episodes actually happened.

All this being said, my opinion is that most of what Otter describes really happened or that he embellished on actual events. Otter's reputation as a person who "did some very foolish things" must have more basis than tavern bombast. I realize this judgment is subjective, but let me give an example. When Otter meets those menacing "three sturdy fellows" near Cadiz, Ohio, when returning east from Cincinnati, I expected some dramatic denouement. Otter and his companion stop for the night, they put a knife in the door latch, and Otter keeps his loaded pistols handy. Yet nothing climatic happens, and Otter relates that he learned the three men were later captured. In his preface, Otter says that "those amongst whom he has spent the last twenty years of his life" will confirm the truth of *History*. None of these acquaintances could possibly know about the Cadiz incident, so Otter was essentially free to say whatever he wanted without fear of contradiction. Yet instead of a dramatic saga, the tale Otter tells is rather banal.

History is not a novel, yet how truthful it is remains an open question. The vast majority of incidents in the book cannot be factually confirmed. I believe that most of what Otter recounts actually happened; to me, the Cadiz incident rings true. I feel that *History* tells an amazing story, offering an interesting, perhaps unique, insight into life in the early nineteenth-century United States.

Historians who read *History* will probably ask, first, Is it true? and, second, Is Otter typical? Obviously, the value to social historians of Otter's account is greater if he is describing a life that resembles those of others, if Otter's experience is characteristic of life in this period. This question can be answered more definitely than the question about truth—Otter was almost certainly not "typical." To an extent, the notion of typicality in social history is extremely problematic. Almost everyone is typical in some ways and not in others. Indeed, my guess is that a "typical" artisan who became a journeyman at an average age, made an average income, was no more or less involved in trade unions than were most other artisans, went to the tavern as often as others, and so on, was in fact in a small minority of artisanal workers. In many ways the search for a typical experience in the past is a chimera.

Even if we accept the notion that the typical is probably exceptional, however, it is hard not to be struck by how unusual Otter was. In a way, of course, any person who writes a book is unusual, especially when that person is a manual worker. And the boasting delight with which Otter writes about his brutal pranks is certainly unusual, even if, as I will argue, this sort of mentality was common. But I believe *History* does have value for social historians, a significance beyond being simply an interesting story of a "peculiar man." Three points can be made in this regard.

First, some things about Otter were *not* at all unusual. He was an immigrant in a period when foreign-born workers were common; he made the traditional (though not routine) transition from apprentice to journeyman to master; he was a rural artisan in a time when more than 90 percent of the American population lived outside towns and cities; and like so many other Americans, Otter was a "man in motion," moving steadily west. In some respects, Otter's life was quite "normal."

Second, even when Otter is being his peculiar self, at many points we see in the background of his stories the elements of ordinary life. For example, the seasonality of both work and life comes through very clearly: "The time of year was arrived when mechanics of my profession are obliged to lay upon their oars. I was spending my time in all sorts of fashions" (115). Or the incidental remark that "I was riding and the rest of the hands were on foot" (151), which gives a nice sense of the differences between being a master and being a journeyman.

Third, I would argue that *History* is significant because Otter's brawling, jesting behavior was odd more in degree than in kind. Other people were almost always taking part in Otter's sprees. His drowning of a dog "for a piece of sport" is surely one of the most shocking episodes in the book, a story that few modern readers would find at all amusing, yet Otter has an accomplice—the "boss painter" Benjamin Yingling, and probably Grabill as well. Although Otter was usually the motive force in most of the sprees and pranks, others were there to help him. It was the audacity with which Otter acted that made him a star among the tavern crowd—the things he did, bizarre as they were, brought him a kind of infamous honor. Otter attracted attention not because his actions outraged and disgusted the tavern crowd but because he did things which the jolly fellows delighted in watching but which they lacked the boldness to do themselves. So, although Otter was clearly unusual, many of his actions were embedded in a tavern subculture that looked favorably on such unconventional comportment; in that group, his unruliness made him king.

Otter's very atypicality—his readiness to do what others only talked about—bestowed leadership in this milieu. One of the main points of interest in *History* is, I think, an inside account of this rough, masculine, tavern-based subculture, which, I will argue, was a significant part of American life in this period. One could say, therefore, that *History*'s atypicality is a benefit: whereas this sort of unrespectable behavior may actually have been rather common, only a singular individual such as Otter had the audacity to commit it to print.

It would, of course, be nice to conclude that everything in the book is true and that Otter was a typical rural artisan of the early nineteenth century, neither of which can be affirmed completely, unfortunately. So with these qualifications in mind, let us inspect *History* to see what can be learned from it about American society and culture in the nineteenth century.

Work

Clearly Otter's occupation is important to him and forms part of his identity. From other records (see note 149) we know that Otter opened a tavern in Emmitsburg in the 1830s. And he worked as tavernkeeper for a time before that, probably as early as 1808 or 1809 (86). Even though Otter spent a good deal of his time and earned income as a tavernkeeper, he seems to prefer to identify himself to readers as "Big Bill the Plasterer."[12]

Although there exist a number of fine histories of urban artisans in the early nineteenth century, much less is known about the considerably greater number of rural artisans. Less than 10 percent of America's population in this period lived in towns with more than twenty-five hundred inhabitants, so Otter's residence in Hanover and Emmitsburg for most of his life puts him in the majority of artisans. Within the rural artisanry, the construction trades were especially numerous. And within the construction trade were a substantial number of plasterers, an occupation far from unusual. Although there was only one other plasterer among the heads of households in Han-

---

[12] The evidence on Otter's career as a tavernkeeper is given in footnote 25 below.

over in 1820, in Marietta, Pennsylvania, where Otter worked in 1808 and met his wife, there were, out of 261 taxable males in 1814, 29 in the construction trades, including 5 plasterers. Perhaps Marietta was unusual, but it is clear that plastered walls were becoming more common in ordinary homes in the early 1800s.[13]

Plastering was a skilled occupation. Generally, the early nineteenth-century houses that were plastered received three coats: a base or scratch coat (usually strengthened with horsehair), a second coat, and a finish coat. The plasterer first had to lath, that is, attach wooden strips one-fourth inch thick and one to one and a half inches wide to the frame of the house to hold the plaster. It cannot be known if Otter always did his own lathing, but he sometimes did (70). Mixing the plaster from water, sand, and lime, the plasterer knew by feel the correct consistency for each coat. Plastering, in short, requires considerable experience and judgment. Otter could not make cornices and considered himself "a very good plain workman." But he did know how to work with plaster of paris and overall was proud to consider himself "a jam hand at my business" (72).[14]

Because plastering methods remained about the same from the 1700s to the end of the nineteenth century, Otter was engaged in a trade that was only modestly affected by change and would remain so for some time. York County, Pennsylvania, and Frederick County, Maryland, where Otter lived, were not the backcountry but rapidly developing areas, thus experiencing increased wealth and a growing demand for plastered interiors. So Otter was

---

[13] Perhaps the most interesting book on rural artisans in this period is Charles F. Hummel, *By Hammer and Hand: The Dominy Craftsmen of East Hampton, New York* (Charlottesville, Va., 1968). In 1820 of the 3,015 "manufacturers" (which were mostly artisans) in Frederick County, Maryland, only 520 were in Frederick City. See Census Office, *Census for 1820* (Washington, 1821); and Census Office, Fourth Census, 1820, Population, manuscript, York County, Borough of Hanover, microfilm, National Archives. On Marietta, see the 1814 tax list reprinted in Franklin Ellis and Samuel Evans, *History of Lancaster County, Pennsylvania* (Philadelphia, 1883), p. 262. The population of Marietta in Donegal Township, Lancaster County, cannot be determined from the census but was likely under one thousand

[14] For Otter's mentions of his work abilities, see near the beginning and the end of "Philadelphia." Evidence on plastering comes from Edward Hazen, *Popular Technology; or, Professions and Trades* (1836; rpt., New York, 1850), pp. 125–127, Harley J. McKee, *Introduction to Early American Masonry: Stone, Brick, Mortar, and Plaster* (Washington, 1973), pp. 81–89; and Charles E. Peterson, ed., *Building Early America: Contributions toward the History of a Great Industry* (Radnor, Pa., 1976), pp. 71–72. The "Articles of an Agreement between Rev. John DuBois and William Otter, 11 October 1823" in the Appendix calls for three coats but allows Otter to use "two coats only on the Exterior back walls."

rather lucky, for economic change spurred demand for his work yet did not undermine his skill.[15]

There was much in Otter's experience as a plasterer that was quite ordinary. Like many American artisans, Otter had been an apprentice in several trades. In New York, he had begun learning shoemaking, venetian blind making, and carpentry before being bound as a plasterer. In labor-scarce America it was rather simple to get an apprenticeship, unlike in England, where the apprentice's family had to pay a premium to have a son bound. An English worker who had emigrated to New York explained to his British readers "that during the seven years that a boy is apprenticed in England the young American has gained a smattering of three or four occupations."[16]

After Otter was formerly bound, however, he remained a plasterer. My guess is that even while a tavernkeeper in Emmitsburg, he continued to plaster when the weather was suitable; only in 1850, when he was identified in the Baltimore city directory as a "liquor dealer" and in the census as an "innkeeper," is it likely he abandoned plastering. By 1850 Otter was sixty-three, in failing health, and no longer able to meet the physical demands of the craft.

Although Otter seemed to have served most of his four-year apprentice-ship with master plasterer Kenith King in New York and remained a plasterer for most of his life, he lacked the skill to make cornices, an important feature of plastering in this period. According to Edward Hazen, "In all well-finished rooms, cornices are run at the junction of the wall and ceiling." Whether this inability to "cornish" was because Otter had not finished his apprenticeship or had simply apprenticed as a plain plasterer is not clear. In his lack of complete skill Otter was also typical. A Scots traveler to America explained: "In a new country like this . . . there is not the demand for the labour of those who work in the fabrication of luxuries as there is for hands to be employed on works of sheer utility." Although Otter found good-paying work in New York and Philadelphia, it may be that his decision to settle in rural Pennsylvania was influenced by the expectation that his inabil-

[15] Diane Lindstrom, *Economic Development in the Philadelphia Region, 1810–1850* (New York, 1978); and Diane Shaw Wasch, "City Building in Frederick, Maryland, 1810–1860," Master's thesis, George Washington University, 1990.

[16] *London v. New York*, "by an English Workman" (London, 1859), p. 10. On this point see Richard B. Stott, *Workers in the Metropolis: Class, Ethnicity, and Youth in Antebellum New York City* (Ithaca, N.Y., 1990), pp. 98–101.

ity to "cornish" would make less difference there. My guess is that it would have been more difficult for him to become a boss in a city without this ability.[17]

European-trained artisans were stunned at how fast American artisans worked. Mechanics in the United States would "drive business" when they labored, and foreign-born workers had to learn to labor at the American "railway pace," as it was sometimes called. Clearly, Otter was in this mold of the speedy American artisan; he was even faster than many native-born plasterers, or so he claims. While in Valley Forge in 1807, Otter's fast work for Mr. Pennypacker elicits the question of whether "all hands worked with such extraordinary speed in the city—to which I replied, that they did not, only some of them" (72). Otter claimed he could plaster fifty yards a day (128), providing in *History* several examples of how fast he worked, with perhaps the most impressive being when he plasters in two hours a ceiling that others had been working at for two weeks and were still far from finishing. Clearly not all American artisans were fast workers (Otter notes that these plasterers admitted "they did not understand the business," 108).[18]

Otter is clearly very proud of being a "jam hand" in plastering, by which he seems mainly to have meant his quickness. It was how fast he could plaster of which he was proudest: people are constantly expressing astonishment to Otter on his unbelievably rapid manner of working. Such valuation on speed of work was quite common among American artisans; as one English emigrant guide explained, in the United States, "Excellence is only a secondary consideration, . . . a man is principally esteemed for his speed, or, in other words, for the task he can perform."[19]

It also seems that such fast work, not just physical labor itself, was part of the definition of manliness in this period. It is clear that much of the behavior of the jolly fellows can be viewed as an assertive masculinity—the drinking, brawling, and vicious pranks. The ability to do hard, physical, fast-paced work was part of the equation. When Otter's hod carrier at Mr. Pennypacker's was able at first to keep up with Big Bill, Otter notes he "began to feel himself a man" (71). It seems Otter is proud of his superiority over slower men, lesser men, who were "ashamed of their work" (109). From this perspective, Otter's fast pace of working and his rowdy comportment off

[17] Hazen, *Popular Technology*, p. 126; and John Prentice, "Letter to the Working Classes of the City of Edinburgh," *Scotsman*, 16 April 1834.

[18] "Drive Business," *New York Tribune*, 5 September 1845; and Stott, *Workers in the Metropolis*, pp. 128–140.

[19] *The British Mechanic's and Labourer's Hand Book* (London, 1840), p. 17.

the job are connected; they are part of what being a man meant in the jolly fellows' subculture.

In any case, as a fast worker, Otter was a typical American artisan. Although he may have viewed his exceptionally rapid manner of working as a way of asserting his superior manhood over slower, less robust men, there is little sense here that plastering itself was anything more than an occupation. In England and in France, dense tradition and ritual characterized artisanal life. Among the rich customs of English artisans were the waygoose in the spring when candles were no longer required for work as well as the elaborate system of ritual fines under the "Strong Beer Act" for such things as wearing a dirty shirt. American artisanal life was less ritualistic, but trade associations in New York City, Philadelphia, and other cities fostered a collective sense of pride in artisanship.[20]

Here, the difference between the American countryside and the city emerges clearly. The early national period was the zenith of artisanal craft cultures in American cities, perhaps best exemplified by the great processions to celebrate major events. As described by Howard Rock and Sean Wilentz, the artisans in these parades would march behind banners identifying the craft and often carried objects symbolizing the solidarity of the trade and its importance—ship caulkers carried hammers, for example, or printers walked behind a printing press mounted on a wagon. Otter does not mention such rituals in recounting his life in New York, which is hardly remarkable considering that he was an apprentice, although the utter absence of "artisan republicanism" anywhere in *History* is rather surprising. In Cincinnati, the plasterers of the city were sufficiently organized and unified to visit Otter at work, and "every one of the craft made themselves acquainted with me, and told me that I done the work too cheap." In the countryside, no such organization exists: nothing in *History* suggests any customs or any special fraternity among plasterers. Indeed, Otter never even mentions Hanover's other plasterer, Alexander McElwain. For Otter, the trade seems to have had little mystery; his pride at being a plasterer is as an individual, not as part of a group of men with a special skill.[21]

---

[20] On English artisanal rituals see John Dunlop, *Artificial and Compulsory Drinking Usages of the United Kingdom* (London, 1844); see also E. J. Hobsbawm, "The Transformation of Labour Ritual" in Hobsbawm, *World of Labour: Further Studies in the History of Labour* (London, 1984), pp. 66–82.

[21] On New York City artisans see Rock, *Artisans of the New Republic: The Tradesmen of New York City in the Age of Jefferson* (New York, 1979); and Wilentz, *Chants Democratic: New York City and the Rise of the American Working Class, 1788–1850* (New York, 1984). On Cincinnati see Steven J. Ross, *Workers on the Edge: Work, Leisure, and Politics in Industrializing Cincinnati,*

The term "artisan" does make sense—it seems clear that Otter's self-identification as a plasterer is more significant to him than was his status as apprentice, journeyman, or master within the profession. Otter did accomplish the artisan's ideal in his achievement of master status. Yet, he tells us this in an offhand way: in 1810, when Otter plastered the White House for the Sisters of Charity he mentions he did it with "my partner, Mr. Samuel Agnew" (93). At that time Otter was only twenty-three years old. The Sisters of Charity records show, however, that payment was made to Agnew, thus suggesting that Otter may have been a junior partner or perhaps still an employee. Otter refers to the 1824 Mount St. Mary's plastering as "the very first job I done in my line of business," apparently meaning in Emmitsburg. Then thirty-seven, Otter had "many good hands at work under my charge" (see near the beginning of Emmitsburg and the contract in the Appendix). The image of Otter riding back from a job while "the rest of the hands were on foot" is that of a successful master. Otter trained his son William Otter, Jr.—known, perhaps inevitably, as "Little Bill"—in his trade, perhaps with the intent of passing the business on to him.[22]

But it does not seem that Otter considered his upward mobility very significant, for he does not emphasize it in *History*. Otter always seems to have had a strong sense of his autonomy, so perhaps being an employer seemed less significant. It is also probable that, as has often been argued, the line between boss and employee was in fact far less delineated in the artisanal system than was the case after the Industrial Revolution: in small shops, the master knew his workers as individuals, all were engaged in manual work, and all faced the vicissitudes of an economy subject to sharp seasonal and cyclical downturns. This is, of course, not to say that the line is invisible— Otter as a boss sometimes had "a piece of sport" with his journeymen but as

---

1788–1890 (New York, 1985). See also Thomas R. Winpenny, *Bending Is Not Breaking: Adaptation and Persistence among Nineteenth Century Lancaster Artisans* (Lanham, Md., 1990). McElwain's identification comes from Census Office, Fourth Census, 1820, Population, manuscript, Borough of Hanover; the census taker helpfully recorded the occupations of everyone in Hanover. 22 Payment record of seventy dollars to "Sm. Agnew, plasterer," 28 August 1810, Saint Joseph's Provincial House Archives, Emmitsburg, Maryland; and "Articles of an Agreement between Rev. John DuBois and William Otter, 11 October 1823." William Otter, Jr., is listed as a plasterer in Baltimore directories in the 1850s and in the 1850 Baltimore census. The information that he was called "Little Bill" is from Cornelia A. Howard, letter to Rev. John McCaffrey, 10 May 1838, Mount St. Mary's College Archives. My thanks to Prof. Kelly Fitzpatrick, director, Archives and Special Collections, Mount St. Mary's College, for making available to me both photocopies and typescripts of these documents.

an apprentice and journeyman never played pranks on his master. The difference in power between those who did the laying off and those who were laid off is considerable.

Still, we see scant evidence that Otter felt any particular antagonism toward bosses when he was a journeyman or any solidarity with other masters regarding journeymen. In New York Otter was part of "our gang," quite possibly the infamous Highbinders, which might represent a primitive form of class consciousness since most of its members were young and either apprentices or journeymen. Still, even in New York and Philadelphia there is little sense of solidarity with other manual employees against bosses. One would hardly expect to find class consciousness in rural Pennsylvania and Maryland in the early 1800s, so its absence there is no surprise. In Hanover and Emmitsburg the social group that was most significant to Otter was a masculine society of jolly fellows that, as the section on society will show, transcended social class.

Another possible explanation for Otter's seeming lack of interest in his social status is that he remained in his own eyes, as he says at the end of the book, "a poor man," even after building a substantial plastering business. Although wages and fees for plastering are often given in *History,* it is difficult to determine the accuracy of Otter's subjective assessment of his economic situation. Although he mentions wages, he does not often tell us how steadily he worked, and in the early nineteenth century, wage rates were probably less important in determining income than was regularity of employment. All work in this period was unsteady, and plastering was especially subject to seasonal variation because it cannot easily be carried on below a temperature of forty-five or fifty degrees: "Mrs. C. asked me one day, what was I going to do that winter? I told her that I was not going to do any thing that I knew of" (86). When Otter decided "to hook it" from New York to Philadelphia in 1807, his "particular croney," John Lane, who is interested in accompanying Otter, proposes they leave in March, but Otter demurs: "I told him, that the tenth of March would be too early for me, that I could get no work at that time" (51).[23]

So it seems quite likely that Otter was able to work at his trade only seven or eight months a year, perhaps less. Thus when he lists his wages, he is referring to income that was available only part of the year; in several places

[23] On seasonality in nineteenth-century manufacturing, see Stott, *Workers in the Metropolis,* pp. 110–119. On temperatures needed for plastering, see John R. Diehl, *Manual of Lathing and Plastering* (n.p., 1960), p. 62.

in *History*, Otter mentions "the time of the year" when mechanics "are obliged to lay upon their oars."

Nor can it be assumed that Otter worked full-time even during the season. One year he was paid twenty-four dollars a month "during the season," but at other times he worked at individual jobs. It is clear from *History* that Otter spent a considerable amount of time traveling between jobs. He seems to be constantly on the move, and several of his anecdotes take place while traveling, such as the attack by Witter's dogs during his return to Hanover in 1810 after plastering the White House for the Sisters of Charity in Emmitsburg. No doubt part of the reason for the prominence of the tavern in *History* stems from Otter's peripatetic life-style during the plastering season.

Otter's income as a master is equally problematic. Otter tells us at the end of his book that as a master, between 1810 and 1835 he plastered 203 houses and buildings for which he earned $15,300. A few of the jobs, such as the 1824 plastering at Mount St. Mary's, were quite substantial. Others involved plastering an ordinary house, for which $80 was a typical payment, and some, no more than a room or two. The $15,300 comes from an average of 8.1 jobs per year, $75.37 per job, for a yearly total of $612. But this figure probably represents total payments to Otter, out of which he had to pay his journeymen and hod carriers, as the contract in the Appendix suggests.[24]

It might still be possible to attempt an estimate of Otter's income as a journeyman and master if it could be assumed that plastering was his sole source of income, but such was not the case. As a journeyman, Otter began working in the off-season as a bartender. Apparently Big Bill continued to keep bar during the winter, even after becoming a master. At some point, perhaps as early as the 1810s, certainly by 1825, he had his own tavern. By the 1830s, Otter's tavern in Emmitsburg seems to have been a rather substantial establishment.[25]

[24] For an ordinary house, Otter mentions being paid eighty dollars for plastering a "very large house" in Oxford, Pennsylvania, in about 1808 (near the end of "Pennsylvania"), the same figure Jacob Englebrecht, a Frederick tailor, paid to plaster his two-story house in 1826. *The Diary of Jacob Englebrecht, 1817–1878*, ed. William R. Quynn (Frederick, Md., 1976), vol. 1, 26 September 1826.

[25] Reily, *Conewago*, p. 170, states that Otter "kept a tavern in Hanover," but he is not found in the tavern license list in the Historical Society of York County, York, Pennsylvania, nor in Daniel Lange's 1818 list of Hanover tavernkeepers which is reprinted in George R. Prowell, *History of York County, Pennsylvania* (Chicago, 1902), 2:846. On 2 November 1825, Otter sold Isaac Baugher "Sixteen chairs, Four Tables [and] Bar Furniture," Liber SS 23, pp. 404–405, Land Records, Records Room, Frederick County Courthouse, Frederick, Maryland. On the Otter tavern in Emmitsburg, see James A. Helman, *History of Emmitsburg, Maryland* (Frederick, 1906), pp. 48, 76; and Meline and McSweeny, *Story of the Mountain*, 1:376.

In addition to tending bar, Otter apparently owned a livery business, presumably connected with his tavern, in the late 1820s and early 1830s. He also occasionally tracked runaway slaves for the reward, thus the proceeds from plastering were only a part, though surely the largest part, of Otter's income.[26]

So what can we say about Otter's earnings? First, his story suggests the complexity of "income" and especially how unusual year-round labor at one occupation was for artisans, and not just in the countryside. The American climate in the North was considerably colder than Europe, and immigrants to the New World were often stunned to discover that although wages in their trade were higher than in the Old World, the flow of such income was also more variable.[27]

The components, therefore, of Otter's income were complex, and it is almost impossible to calculate how much he earned from plastering and from other sources. That being said and in full awareness of these problems, I think that Otter's income was probably rather good. Journeymen in New York City, according to the Census of Manufactures, averaged $312 a year.[28] If Otter worked thirty weeks a year as a plasterer (admittedly a big if), his Philadelphia wages at age twenty would have brought him $240 plus board. In Columbia, Pennsylvania, where Otter made $25 a month all season, working thirty weeks would give him $187.50. The Philadelphia figure is comparable to that for New York, the Columbia totals considerably lower, but living expenses outside the city were also lower. Of course, it is not possible to be sure Otter made this much, but even if his income was somewhat less, it seems to me that he was doing pretty well for someone in his mid-twenties.

As a master, the $612 he received yearly for plastering was probably gross, not net earnings. But even if Otter kept only half of it, that plus his tavern business and livery earnings would probably provide him with a handsome

---

[26] In *History* Otter does not directly refer to his livery business, though he mentions that during his brief residence in Baltimore in 1821, "I also attended to the selling of horses" (see the text at note 131). The existence of Otter's livery business is made clear in the following documents: Payment to William Otter for providing a gig and horses for Dr. Agans, 15 October 1828, Mount St. Mary's College Archives, Emmitsburg, Maryland; Liber JS 41, p. 609, 26 March 1832, Land Records, Frederick County Courthouse, Frederick, Maryland, which records the sale of all or part of Otter's livery business, horses, wagons, etc., to Joseph Danner; and Cornelia A. Howard, letter to the Rev. John McCaffey, 10 May 1838, Mount St. Mary's College Archives, requesting her son be driven home to Baltimore "in Little Bill Otter's best small barouche with two quiet horses."

[27] Stott, *Workers in the Metropolis,* pp. 110–119.

[28] Ibid., p. 36.

income. It is impossible to be certain about this, but it would seem quite unlikely that by moving to the countryside to carry on his trade, Otter suffered financially, and he may even have gained. For a "plain workman," the evidence suggests that Otter made a good deal of money in Hanover and Emmitsburg.

Given a plastering business that was substantial enough to do the 1824 Mount St. Mary's job, his tavern, and his stable, not to mention his slave catching, one might assume that Big Bill was a successful entrepreneur, a man on the make in the age of Jackson. This, however, seems to me to be misleading. Although Otter was a hard worker, the evidence suggests that he was not a good businessman. At the end of *History*, after proudly telling us his total income from plastering came to "the neat sum of fifteen thousand three hundred dollars," Otter adds that he is "still a poor man, without my earnings, having a large family, which run away with the beans to support them." Otter rarely mentions saving money, and when he does it is soon spent. As a journeyman, he clearly shared the "easy come, easy go" mentality toward money, an outlook that seems to have been quite widespread among workers in this period: "I earned money fast [in Philadelphia], and I expended a reasonable share of my earnings in good clothing, of which I had got for myself a very decent set, the balance of my money went for the first three months, light come, light go" (58).[29]

As a master, Otter may have been a bit more careful with his money, but there is little evidence that Big Bill was much of a capitalist. He seemingly lacked the bourgeois virtues that are so often associated with upward mobility. Not a religious man, Otter spent his time drinking and gambling in taverns. At one point, Mr. Pennypacker presumes that a hardworking man such as Otter must be laying all his "money out in houses." Otter readily agrees: "He took it for granted that I was expending my money in the purchase of houses . . . [but] the houses in which I laid out my money were ornamented with a sign and sign-post" (75).

Otter's own subjective assessment of himself as a poor man cannot be taken at face value, but the tax records clearly indicate that he was far from wealthy. Of course, tax records are only a rough measure of wealth because only land and houses—plus in Pennsylvania, cows and horses, and in Mary-

---

[29] When Otter wrote that he was "still a poor man" in 1835, his children were adults; see note 118. "'Come easy, go easy' seems to be the maxim by which nearly all classes of workingmen . . . regulate their conduct," wrote James Dawson Burn, who worked in the United States as a hatter during the Civil War, in his memoir *James Burn; the "Beggar Boy"* (London, 1882), p. 280.

land, slaves and silver plate—were assessed. In Hanover in 1821–1822 Otter was valued at $410 for his house, lot, and cow, compared with an average assessment of $555. In Emmitsburg he may have done slightly better: in 1835, at age forty-eight, Otter owned one lot with a frame house (presumably his home) and possibly a second lot. If he owned both lots, his assessment was $184, compared with an average village real estate assessment of $166. Otter did not own the building in which his tavern was located. To label Otter, with a skilled craft, house, and tavern business, a "poor man" is clearly an exaggeration, but it does seem that the fruits of his hard labor, at least as measured by the tax records, were rather meager.[30]

Otter's "live for today" outlook prevented him, even with his manly pleasure in hard work, from prospering. Despite a fairly considerable income, Otter thought himself a poor man and spent his declining years as a liquor dealer in Baltimore.

Play

In a sense it is misleading to treat work and play separately, because one of the striking features of *History* is how they interpenetrate. Still, although many of Otter's pranks occur at work, many others originated in the tavern. The line between the two, while blurred, is discernable.

Clearly "play" includes many things in *History*. Otter's recreation included reading, playing cards, dominoes, and taking trips to scenic sights such as Black Rock. But his main center of recreation was the local barroom; time and again we see him in the tavern. No doubt one reason for his affinity for taverns was his job, which called on him to travel and be away from home a good bit. Still, Otter certainly deeply enjoyed congregating with other men in taverns. Indeed, *History* is organized largely as a series of sprees, many of which originated in taverns, and the book may be in part a collection of anecdotes whose telling was polished in taverns.

I think the salience of the tavern in Otter's life was probably not typical of most men; Otter's family plays virtually no role here. Although the tavern

[30] In Hanover in 1821–1822 Otter was assessed $250 on his house and lot, $50 for his occupation, and $10 for his cow. It appears that property was assessed at approximately 40 percent of full value. In earlier years the Hanover assessments show Otter owning a horse, but otherwise his wealth was the same. He disappears from the Hanover assessments in 1823. Tax List, 1821–1822, Borough of Hanover, York County, microfilm, Hanover Public Library, Hanover, Pennsylvania. On Otter's wealth in Emmitsburg, see footnote 157 in the text.

may have had an exaggerated role in *History*, it should be emphasized that taverns were exceptionally important in early American society, which the numbers alone suggest: in 1810 there were sixty-one taverns on the sixty-six–mile pike between Philadelphia and Lancaster. The town of Hanover, with eight hundred residents, had eight taverns in 1818; so significant were taverns in Pennsylvania that several towns such as King of Prussia and Red Lion were named after them. Emmitsburg in 1823, according to Fr. Simon Bruté, had seven hundred inhabitants and "4 principales tavernes—et peut-être 7 à 8 tippling shops."[31]

Taverns filled many roles, serving as places to stay for travelers, centers for information, and sources of entertainment (the baboon at Lititz, for example). Their most important function, however, was as a social center, certainly the main role they served for Otter. Drinking was obviously a very significant part of the tavern's appeal, but not, or so it seems in *History*, the only one. Alcohol does play a major role in Big Bill's tales: "We had drank as much as we wanted, and more too," writes Otter of his visit to Clark's tavern in Valley Forge. The number of slang terms for liquor in *History* is astonishing, and in many of the sprees the participants had been "warmed with a little steam" (112). But drinking is not really the focus of the book, and Otter actually describes himself as a restrained drinker, "although I never poured it into my shoes, neither" (85).

It was not drink that was the tavern's greatest attraction but the chance to shoot the breeze with other jolly fellows. Many men would visit a tavern in the course of a day, but for Otter and the other regulars, it was their special milieu. It is no surprise to learn that Otter ended up a tavernkeeper in Baltimore.

But to Otter, even more than the camaraderie, the tavern meant a spree: "John Barts [a tavern in Hanover] was my place of general rendezvous for sport" (120), he writes. It was in taverns that the "sprees" and "scrapes"— the true focus of *History*—were planned and often occurred. No doubt the frolics not only reflected the conviviality of the "tavern crowd" but also helped strengthen the group by uniting them in a common endeavor, the result of which could be retold and laughed at in the future.

---

[31] Kym S. Rice, *Early American Taverns: For the Entertainment of Friends and Strangers* (Chicago, 1983). John T. Faris, *Old Roads Out of Philadelphia* (Philadelphia, 1917), p. 123. On Hanover, see Prowell, *History of York County*, 1:846, and on Emmitsburg, Fr. Simon Bruté, "Emmitsburg, 1823," manuscript, Box 7-3-1-1, St. Joseph's Provincial House Archives, Emmitsburg.

"Sprees" or "frolics" were an important part of life in antebellum America. Target-shooting exhibitions, "water frolics," horse races, and wrestling matches between local champions all fell under the heading of "spree." Among workers in New York, these frolics were often characterized by loud, boisterous behavior and quite commonly a few fistfights. Cornelius Mathews described New York City workers "on a Sunday outing . . . always in a wonderful state of commotion . . . pushing and pulling each other freely and indulging in a good deal of vigorous horse-play." German immigrant Jonas Heinrich Gudehaus, who traveled through rural Pennsylvania in 1822 and 1823, discovered that "before such a frolic or vendue begins there is especially much talk about who wants to fight at the same, for that is their chief pleasure. . . . One always hears the people say: 'You, John, Pitt, Sam, haven't you heard who's going to fight at the frolic?'"[32]

The book is organized by sprees, one per paragraph. Otter's fascination with "scrapes," "sprees," "fracases," "affairs," "jokes," and "rumpuses," as he calls them, will perhaps strike readers as interesting, but not in itself shocking. The thing that is unsettling is that for Otter, the merriment of sprees came mostly from inflicting pain on others. And it is the way laughter and violence were intertwined that most surprises modern readers about *History*.

Laughter is a recurring theme in *History*. But it is cruel laughter, at others. The jokes of Otter and the jolly fellows almost always aim at hurting, physically or mentally, or at least at irritating, other human beings or animals. Their own sense of honor seemed derived from dishonoring others. On rare occasions the target was a respectable person who was humiliated (the Vanpike episode; more often it was a black, a "very saucy Irishman," one of Otter's journeymen, a drunk, a nearsighted man, a widow, a chained baboon, or an overly trusting "friend." Big Bill's victims were more likely to be powerless than powerful. Certainly, at six feet four inches and 252 pounds, Otter could be confident that few of the butts of his pranks would try to retaliate physically.

To be considered fun, the violence usually involved some subterfuge. It was the way Otter and Mr. Yingling mentioned the nonexistent handbills for

[32] Stott, *Workers in the Metropolis*, pp. 229–230, 245; Mathews, *A Pen-and-Ink Panorama of New-York City* (New York, 1853), p. 89, and see also pp. 137–140, and Gudehaus, "Journey to America," in *Ebbe fer Alle-Ebber, Ebbes fer Dich, Something for Everyone—Something for You: Essays in Memoriam of Albert Franklin Buffington*, trans. Larry M. Neff, Publications of the Pennsylvania German Society (Breinigsville, Pa., 1980), 14:292–293.

a diving dog that make the dog drowning "a piece of sport." In his account of the attack on the black church in Philadelphia, Otter includes the byplay involving the goat, which I think serves to make it a spree and not just an assault. Most of the time, however, it was the violence that seemingly most appealed to Otter, not the deceit leading up to it. One episode revealing of Otter's mentality comes at the beginning of the "Hanover" section when Mr. Overbaugh mistakes for a pitcher of cold water a pot of hot coffee, "which terribly scalded his throat. . . . It was fun for me, and death to Mr. Overbaugh." Nothing whatever clever exists in this, merely delight in another's pain.

In several episodes there is no practical joke or prank. Splashing lime at a baboon "bip into his eyes" shows little shrewdness; nor is there much humor in persuading a drunken "friend" to sit on a flax hackle. Yet Otter's reaction to others' suffering, whether the result of a prank or not, is always amusement. Some of his victims are "only" pissed on, given a laxative, or subjected to beer poured in their pocket. Others, however, are seriously hurt: "[I] hit him on the jaw and knocked him down . . . his jaw was fractured and pretty much shattered" (51); "my friend [who sat on the flax hackle] who had a light colored pair of pantaloons on, he was all over blood from his heels up to the false seat of honor" (126); he "fell on the back part of his head, neck, and shoulders and was terribly staved" (177).

Yet all these are fun to William Otter. Big Bill pulls the ladder out from under journeyman chairmaker James Doogan as he is coming out a second floor window, then writing: "Poor Jim who by the way had a very hard fall, he came crawling on his hands and knees towards me, making his way homewards as well as he could, every yard or two he would mutter the words O Lord, which tickled me most prodigiously, I almost killed myself laughing at him" (99). Few modern readers will find this funny, yet to Otter it was hilarious. Otter shared "the basic premise of the practical joker: that the 'guy' is inferior to you, and deserves everything he is stupid enough to take." Otter evinces no sympathy for the victim, only pride in his ability to make others suffer.[33]

Our initial response will probably be to conclude that Otter was simply a bit unhinged, a sadist. Yet, although I do think Otter was psychologically abnormal, it is clear that others were amused by these pranks and often took

---

[33] E.F. Bleir, introduction to *Peck's Bad Boy and His Pa*, by George W Peck (1883; rpt., New York, 1958), p. v. The "humor" in this enormously popular book is quite similar to much of that in Otter—mean-spirited and often vicious.

part in them. Indeed, it seems that such humor was a characteristic of American society in this period. Scholars since Constance Rourke and Bernard De Voto in the 1930s have noted the "emphatic, coarse, vivid, violent, uproarious" strain in American humor. This type of comic literature, which centered according to Rourke on "vast practical jokes," began appearing in the decade or so after *History* was published in 1835 (thus Otter was not imitating these works). Found in journals such as the *Spirit of the Times*, these tales were written by such popular dialect humorists as Augustus B. Longstreet, Joseph Baldwin, T. B. Thorpe, and Henry Clay Lewis.[34]

That other Americans in the first half of the nineteenth century shared a comic sensibility similar to Otter's is suggested by the enormous popularity of Tennessee humorist George Washington Harris's Sut Lovingood tales, which began appearing in the *Spirit of the Times* in 1845. When I first read *History*, I was struck by its similarity to Harris's Lovingood stories. F. O. Matthiessen believed that Harris "brings us closer than any other writer to the indigenous and undiluted resources of the American language, to the tastes of the common man himself."[35]

But what tastes! As in Otter, humor and violence seemed inextricably bound: in a typical story, Sut disrupts a "nigger" camp meeting with a giant stink bomb and a swarm of angry bees. And also as in Otter, some of the most memorable episodes in the Lovingood stories involve cruelty to animals. One scholar has described "skinned carcasses or the bloody parts of butchered animals" as one of the recurring images in the tales. In one of the most popular Lovingood stories, one widely anthologized in the nineteenth century, Sut feeds a dog a sausage skin filled with gun powder.

> I hearn a noise like bustin sumthin, an his tail lit atop ove my hat. His head wer way down the hill and hed tuck a death holt onter a root. His fore laigs wer fifty feet up the road, a makin runnin moshuns, and his hine ones a straddil ove the fence. His innerds were hangin in links onter the cabin chimley, sept about a yard in mam's bussum, and his paunch cum down permiscusly like rain. Es tu the dog hisself, *es a dog*, I never seed him agin.

---

[34] Joan Shelly Rubin, *Constance Rourke and American Culture* (Chapel Hill, N.C., 1980), quotation p. 150; Constance Rourke, *American Humor: A Study of the National Character* (1931; rpt., New York, n.d.), quotation p. 69; Bernard De Voto, *Mark Twain's America* (1932; rpt., Cambridge, Mass., 1951). Rourke tended to downplay the crudity, cruelty, and violence that characterizes this type of humor; see Rubin, *Constance Rourke*, pp. 150–154.

[35] F. O. Matthiessen, *American Renaissance: Art and Expression in the Age of Emerson and Whitman* (London, 1941), p. 637.

M. Thomas Inge, who in 1967 republished the Lovingood tales, expresses wonder that "Sut's famous dog story" was so often reprinted and adds that "one is hard put to explain exactly why the nineteenth-century reader found it humorous." Edmund Wilson in *Patriotic Gore* calls Harris's work "by far the most repellent book of any real literary merit in American literature," memorably describing Sut as "a dreadful half-bestial lout . . . a peasant squatting in his own filth."[36]

Wilson describes this "crude and brutal humor" with its "tradition of the crippling practical joke" as an American institution in the nineteenth century. Harris was part of an established literary genre labeled "Southwestern humor," and the Lovingood tales are by no means the most savage. Other Americans therefore shared Otter's delight in pain inflicted on others—humor and violence *were* closely linked. In the tavern, with its collection of jolly fellows, Otter found a milieu that regarded his sadism as entertaining and worthy of acclaim. In this subculture that valued sprees and vicious practical jokes, Big Bill's inclination for violence made him prominent.[37]

Society

Not just the humor but also the society Otter describes is clearly different from our own. The ambit of human behavior as described in *History* was astonishingly large—brutality was open and respected, yet one finds examples of great kindness as well. While walking from London to Hull, the young Otter is given a place to sleep and food by strangers; Captain Clark

[36] George Washington Harris, *Sut Lovingood's Yarns* (New York, 1867). Milton Rickles, "The Imagery of George Washington Harris," in *The Frontier Humorists: Critical Views*, ed. M. Thomas Inge (Hamden, Conn., 1975), p. 158; George Washington Harris, "Sut Lovingood at Bull's Gap," in *High Times and Hard Times: Sketches and Tales by George Washington Harris*, ed. M. Thomas Inge (Knoxville, Tenn., 1967), p. 150; M. Thomas Inge, introduction to "Sut Lovingood's Yarns," in *High Times and Hard Times*, ed. Inge, pp. 110–111; and Edmund Wilson, *Patriotic Gore: Studies in the Literature of the American Civil War* (New York, 1962), pp 509, 510.

[37] Wilson, *Patriotic Gore*, p. 509. The most ferocious "humorist" of the antebellum Southwestern school was Louisianan Henry Clay Lewis. In these 1840s tales a mule is set on fire as a prank, a doctor pours burning alcohol over an Irishman, and a medical student steals a dead black baby from its dead mother's arm to practice dissection, only to drop the corpse accidentally on a busy street. *Louisiana Swamp Doctor: The Writings of Henry Clay Lewis*, ed. John Q. Anderson (Baton Rouge, La., 1962). Kenneth S. Lynn remarks that Lewis's sadistic book "was considered a humorous work is amazing but true"; Lynn, *Mark Twain and Southwestern Humor* (Boston, 1959), p. 104.

and Captain Leeds go to considerable trouble and some risk to get him across the Atlantic. In the New World, such acts of kindness are less common—perhaps the higher American standard of living eroded the interdependence caused by scarcity; in America it was easier to live as an individualist.

Still, even in America, people seem surprisingly open and unsuspicious. Time and again Otter is able to succeed with his pranks because the victims trust Big Bill; people are unprepared for his duplicity and aggression. Despite the evidence of kindness and naïveté, however, it is Otter's viciousness and his sharply etched portrait of a rough, profane masculine world that will attract most readers' attention.

This society of jolly fellows seems to have existed in cities and in the countryside. Indeed, the terms "jolly fellows" or "jovial companions" had a specific connotation in this period. P. T. Barnum remembered Bethel, Connecticut, in the early 1820s:

In nearly every New-England village at the time of which I write, there could be found from six to twenty social, jolly, story-telling, joke-playing wags and wits, regular originals, who would get together at the tavern or store, and spend their evenings and stormy afternoons in relating anecdotes, describing their various adventures, playing off practical jokes upon each other, and engaging in every project out of which a little fun could be extracted by village wits whose ideas were usually sharpened at brief intervals by a "treat," otherwise known as a glass of Santa Cruz rum, old Holland gin, or Jamaica spirits.[38]

Although the rural jolly fellows, according to the accounts of both Barnum and Otter, appear to be widespread, even universal, they were not, as Otter's New York and Philadelphia sections make clear, confined to a single geographical area. Clearly there were urban-rural differences. In New York City, Otter is part of a gang that was composed mostly of young men. The collective brawling and rioting of the Highbinders has no equivalent in the countryside, where the violence is mostly individual. In addition, the sections on New York and Philadelphia are more dynamic—there is a greater sense of the passage of time. By contrast, the Hanover and Emmitsburg

---

[38] P. T. Barnum, *The Life of P. T. Barnum* (New York, 1855), p. 29. Barnum later refers to the Bethel crowd as a "jolly company"; see p. 56.

sections are more episodic, providing largely a list of the pranks Otter played.

Still, it does seem that Otter moved from the city to rural Pennsylvania and Maryland rather easily. In both, Big Bill found a tavern culture into which he fitted smoothly: the jolly fellows were everywhere. Alexander Saxton has argued that there flourished in the nineteenth century a permissive male life-style that was found in cities as well as on the frontier, noting that "in both East and West, the male population was concentrated in factories, boarding houses, and in construction and mining camps." Otter's account might seem to support Saxton's seminal interpretation on the cultural links between cities and the West.[39]

I think that Saxton's point is generally correct and that he offers a useful perspective for understanding antebellum American society. York County, Pennsylvania, and Frederick County, Maryland, however, cannot be called "the frontier" or "the West" in the early nineteenth century. Hanover was laid out as a town in 1763, and the area had been settled some years earlier; Emmitsburg was founded in 1786, and visitors today can see the Lutheran church built in 1797. Indeed, this region was one of the most economically advanced of the United States—the land was mostly good, and the numerous turnpikes in the area allowed farmers and artisans to become extensively involved in market production. Many of the saddles made in Hanover in this period were shipped to Baltimore for sale.[40]

Indeed, one could argue that the jolly fellows flourished in part *because* of the region's development. The sixty-one taverns on the Lancaster Pike were a result of the extremely heavy traffic on the road, and the large number of teamsters and boatmen at places on the Susquehanna such as Columbia no doubt contributed their share of jolly fellows. Plastering itself is not an activity that is usually associated with the backcountry—Otter's large amount of work reflected the economic maturity of the area. There clearly were still some rough edges: a dozen beds in a single tavern bedroom and

---

[39] Saxton, "Blackface Minstrelsy and Jacksonian Ideology," in *The Rise and Fall of the White Republic: Class, Politics, and Mass Culture in Nineteenth-Century America* (London, 1990), quotation p. 171.

[40] John Gibson, ed., *History of York County, Pennsylvania* (Chicago, 1886), p. 574; Helman, *History of Emmitsburg, Maryland*, pp. 20–21; James T. Lemon, *The Best Poor Man's Country: A Geographical Study of Early Southeastern Pennsylvania* (Baltimore, 1972); Paul G.E. Clemens and Lucy Simler, "Rural Labor and the Farm Household in Chester County, Pennsylvania, 1750–1820," in *Work and Labor in Early America*, ed. Stephen Innes (Chapel Hill, N.C., 1988); Lindstrom, *Economic Development;* and *Hanover Herald*, 15 January 1887.

hog butchering in a tavern's front yard, for example. But when Otter visits the real West during his 1819 trip to Cincinnati, the story of his encounter with the bandits near Cadiz, Ohio, has a wildness and menace not found in his tales of life in Pennsylvania and Maryland.

The tavern subculture of jolly fellows was not confined to cities or the frontier. So what can be said about this tavern-based society that seems so widespread? First, and perhaps most obvious, it was a masculine subculture. This generalization needs a qualification, however. Although women played little role in this book, we cannot automatically assume that lack of mention equals lack of importance. This is, after all, a book about Otter's pranks, not a general narrative of his social life.

It is surprising how insignificant women are in *History*—Otter's wife and family receive very little attention. Near the end of the section on Pennsylvania, Otter describes in some detail his courtship of "my little Dutch girl" and his triumph over two rival suitors; after that, however, his spouse tends to fade out of the story. Indeed, he never gives his wife's name or those of his children. Both the tavern and the work of plastering were male preserves; plastering required a good deal of travel, and Otter was often away from home. The picture that emerges from *History* is not one of triumphant domesticity.

But ambiguities remain. At the end of his long description of his confrontation with Witter, after which Otter is arrested and brought to trial, he adds, "My wife knew nothing of this performance until court time came on" (98). Why? Did Otter simply feel that this matter was none of her business? Was he ashamed to tell her? It is curious behavior for Big Bill, who usually is far from circumspect.

In addition, not only is there little about wife and family, but sex plays little role here. One might have expected Otter, so boastful in so many other ways, to have often shown himself lucky in love as well. The autobiography of Jacques-Louis Ménétra, an eighteenth-century Parisian glazier, is quite similar to Otter's, with its structure based on pranks (and in that Ménétra's wife is rarely mentioned). Unlike Otter, however, Ménétra brags of his sexual exploits. It might be objected that Ménétra did not intend his life story to be published, whereas Otter wrote for publication. Yet even by standards of genteel literature, Otter seems rather restrained, and nongenteel writers such as the Southwestern humorists were far more open. Otter rarely treads near sexual matters and when he does uses uncharacteristic discretion, as in the references to what were very likely New York City houses of prostitution as "dance halls." Again, it is hard to know why. Was Otter worried about what his friends and neighbors would think? It seems odd that a man who gloats about drowning a dog and getting "a friend" to sit on a flax hackle would worry about openly mentioning prostitutes.[41]

Still, despite these enigmas, a picture emerges of a male world. That it was as central to Otter's life as it is to *History* is unclear, but Otter does present a memorable description of a masculine subculture that flourished in both city and countryside in the early Republic. Unlike later in the century, when male workers drew on their "manhood" in identifying themselves as virtuous, upright craftsmen, it seems obvious that for Otter masculinity was the negation of respectability. What is especially striking, in contrast to the later nineteenth century, is the absence of a respectable middle class. It is possible that such may have been there but went unrecorded by Otter. Still, Big Bill, despite his violence and crudity, seems to have received surprisingly little censure. In fact, he appears to have been something of a hero, for he was even elected burgess of Emmitsburg.[42]

One might object that Otter's election shows only that he was popular with a majority of the community; perhaps more respectable elements shunned him. But when we actually look at who the jolly fellows were, we see that they were not the local riffraff, "good old boys," but some of the most distinguished men in the area. There do seem to be some "good old boys" around, given the suggestions that the Pigeon Hills outside of Hanover were not a center of genteel society. But many of the people mentioned in *History* as cronies of Otter were quite prominent in the local community.

Jacob Eichelberger, the Hanover tavernkeeper who Otter jocularly describes as "a perfect gentleman in every respect, and one of the laziest men in York county" (114), was the second wealthiest man in Hanover (assessed at $5,355), was elected chief burgess of Hanover four times, and was considered one of the town's most distinguished citizens, "a true representative of

---

[41] Jacques-Louis Ménétra, *Journal of My Life*, ed. Daniel Roche (New York, 1986). Exclaims Sut Lovingood on seeing the beautiful Sicily Burns: "Sich a bizzim! Jis' think ove two snow balls wif a strawberry stuck but-ainded into bof of em"; George Washington Harris, "Blown Up with Soda," in Harris, *Sut Lovingood's Yarns*, p. 75.

[42] Labor historians have come increasingly to understand that definitions of masculinity have an important role in male working-class consciousness. Most of the research along these lines, however, has argued that "manhood" contributed to craft respectability. But for Otter and his friends, masculinity is an assertion of scorn for respectability and later became a dividing line between the jolly fellows and the emerging middle class (see below). The importance of constructions of gender for both male and female workers is emphasized in Ava Baron, ed , *Work Engendered: Toward a New History of American Labor* (Ithaca, N.Y., 1991).

the gentlemen of olden time." John Bart's tavern Otter describes as "my place of general rendezvous for sport"; it is Bart who gives Otter the hog's eye in the prank on the man from "Pigeon Hill country"; Bart was town constable. Bernhardt Gilbert puts Otter up to smashing Dr. Vanpike's gin flask and later was witness to Big Bill pissing on the good doctor: "Whenever Barney Gilbert sees me, this spree occurs to him, and has a hearty laugh at it"; Gilbert was Adams County sheriff from 1821 to 1824, later county prothonotary and treasurer, and one of the richest men in Gettysburg. John Grabill, the distiller who schemes with Otter to get John Brown (Grabill's employee) and Brown's wife drunk, was the wealthiest man in the area, the owner of five slaves and a prominent citizen of Emmitsburg who presented a barrel of rye whiskey to Lafayette on his visit to Frederick on 29 December 1824.[43]

The rural jolly fellows were not simply what people in colonial America called "the meaner sorts"—it was not a counterculture. Interestingly, none were primarily farmers. Despite his modest wealth, Otter himself was a master plasterer with resources to undertake major projects such as the 1824 work at Mount St. Mary's. Probably Otter's plastering brought him into contact with the rural elite in a period when more modest homes were unplastered. And like Eichelberger, Bart, and Gilbert, Otter was elected to public office. This is not to suggest that all jolly fellows were notables or that all members of the local elite were jolly fellows. Caleb Bailes, Otter's partner in pranks, "one of the wonders of the world," was a man of modest wealth, not prominent in local records. In addition, the local histories of Hanover and Emmitsburg mention other distinguished men who do not appear in *History.* Samuel Agnew was from one of the most distinguished families in the region and Otter's plastering partner but not his associate in sprees.[44]

The jolly fellows, then, seem to have transcended social status, being unified by laughter. The tavern was their milieu. Barrooms were important social institutions in the nineteenth century, so perhaps the prominence they receive in Otter's account is not surprising. The tavern appears unusually significant to the jolly fellows, however, and the best evidence of this is how many of the people mentioned most often by Otter, such as Bart and Gil-

---

[43] On Eichelberger, see footnote 99 in the text, quotation from the *Hanover Herald,* 15 January 1887. On Bart, see footnote 106 in the text. On Gilbert, see footnote 110 in the text. On Grabill, see footnote 135 in the text, Commissioners of the Tax, Assessment Record, Personal Property, 1835, Election District No. 5, Frederick County, Hall of Records, Annapolis, Maryland; and T.J. Williams and Folger McKinsey, *History of Frederick County* (1910; rpt., Baltimore, 1967), p. 183.

[44] On Bailes see footnote 94 in the text. *History of Cumberland and Adams Counties,* p. 215.

bert, were or became tavernkeepers. No doubt part of the political success of the jolly fellows was due to their tavern ownership. As Tammany Hall later discovered, drinking places were ideal forums in which to mobilize political support in an all-male electorate.

Although membership in the jolly fellows was not limited to a single economic group, the same openness did not apply to sex, ethnicity, or race. No woman plays a significant role in any of the sprees, and Otter, a man who boasts of his own and other men's drinking, expresses strong disapproval of women who were "fond of the drops," a character weakness "utterly un-sufferable in the female" (74). Equally sharp was the jolly fellows' exclusion of blacks and the Irish.

It would be surprising in the early Republic if racism was not present in such a group. One might hesitate to label Otter's behavior "racist," because he does many of the same things to the Irish that he does to blacks; both were outsiders to the jolly fellows and, as such, targets for violence. This point is significant: a line was clearly drawn, on the wrong side of which stood blacks and the Irish. But I do think that in *History* blacks usually come in for harsher, more extreme treatment than do the Irish. What is perhaps surprising is the absence of any verbal expressions of antiblack hostility by Otter—it seems that to him violence against blacks was simply part of the natural order, requiring no particular explanation or justification. Otter is not entirely without sympathy, for he refers to the Negro oyster shuckers beaten "into a jelly" by the "lads" during a brawl in New York City as "poor d———ls" (50). And later, in Hanover, Otter complies with the escaped "negro" (a term Otter usually uses for a slave) Congo's request for a drink and urges another slave to try and escape to the mountains to avoid being sold to "Georgia traders" (113, 169). Otter at times can relate to his black victims on a human level. Even though *History* was written at a time of growing abolitionist sentiment, like most Americans of the period, Otter never questioned the institution of slavery or the morality of returning blacks to their owners.

The Irish are also routinely victimized. Although Otter was an immigrant, he seems to have aligned himself with native Americans quite easily. Indeed, Otter assimilates almost effortlessly, with the only prejudice he encounters from people mistaking him for an Irishman: "Irish Rascals," J. Witter yells at Otter and Agnew during their confrontation. Why this English immigrant plasterer fitted in so readily is not clear; even during the War of 1812 Otter recounts no prejudice. His entrance into the jolly fellows assured his acceptance, but why did he find this entrance so easy? Part of the answer may have been his personality, his willingness to do the things others only talked of. Perhaps the exclusionary line was drawn around blacks and the Irish, while others, even the English, were on the "right" side.

Examples of Otter's actions toward the Irish abound in *History:* he demolishes an Irish-owned tavern during the Augustus Street Riot; in Philadelphia, Otter doses his "raw Irishman" hod carrier with jalap to win a bet (63); he plays the prank on the "very saucy" Irish tollgate keeper such as "to make his berth a burden to him" (151); and he beats up "an Irishman of the name of McHenry" (161). Several other victims, such as James Doogan, who Otter pulls the ladder out from under, may have been Irish, though not specifically identified as such. One might have thought that being denigrated as an "Irishman" would have given Otter a certain sympathy toward Hibernians, but this was not the case.

The position of Germans in relation to the jolly fellows is uncertain. Caleb Bailes pinches "a Dutchman" and starts a brawl (104), but the Germans are generally not objects of pranks. Indeed, Bailes may not even have known until they awoke that the persons he pinched were German. Most of the jolly fellows themselves were non-German, but Bernhardt Gilbert and Jacob Eichelberger (who was only, it seems, on the fringe of the tavern crowd) were of German extraction.

In a sense, the world of the jolly fellows resembles the individualistic, egalitarian society that Tocqueville and other visitors to America saw; it was open to men of different social backgrounds. Women, blacks, and the Irish, however, were excluded. In fact, it may be that in nineteenth-century America, equality for white males could be achieved *only* by excluding unpopular races and ethnic groups and women. White equality and racism appear to have been inextricably bound together.

The America Otter describes here is the one foreign visitors saw—not just Tocqueville but Dickens and Frances Trollope as well. It was a rough, raw, and rowdy society. We do not have to rely on only Europeans to confirm Otter's portrait, for many American writers of the period portrayed a similar social life, from the Southwestern humorists to Robert Bailey's picaresque 1822 autobiography and the acerbic, opinionated travel accounts of Anne Royall. Some of the artists of the period, such as George Caleb Bingham, also depicted the rough-hewn nature of nineteenth-century America.[45]

[45] Bailey, *Life and Adventures.* Anne Royall, a Virginian, wrote a series of books recounting her travels and battles with evangelical Christians; see, for example, Mrs. Anne Royall, *Mrs. Royall's Pennsylvania, or Travels Continued in the United States* (Washington, 1829). Elizabeth Johns, *American Genre Painting: The Politics of Everyday Life* (New Haven, 1991).

Otter puts himself in this genre not only by the story he tells but also by the way he tells it. The use of the vernacular, which was later to become the hallmark of American regional humor, clearly sets the context within a demotic subculture. The repeated use of "I seen" and "them days" and colloquialisms such as "in the suds" (mistaken), "warmed with a little steam" (drunk), and "Suse had been fixed for slow travelling" (pregnant) is a bit unusual in American literature of this period. These earthy and humorous expressions give *History* a vitality that sets Otter apart from the attempts at dialect by genteel writers of the period such as Washington Irving.

With its association of humor and violence the world of the jolly fellows resembles in some aspects that of traditional European popular culture. Similarities exist between Otter's account and the life story of Ménétra, the Parisian glazer, especially in the emphasis on pranks and grotesque laughter. Robert Darnton calls this culture "Rabelaisian," a term that might also be applied to Otter. Yet the differences between Ménétra's *Journal of My Life* and *History of My Own Times* are notable. Ménétra's preoccupation with sex is not reproduced in *History*. Nor is there the same emphasis on death. In Ménétra's world, death is omnipresent: people are drowned, blown up, poisoned, and discovered dead on the roadside. The Southwestern humorists also routinely detail death. In Otter death plays a much less salient role—none of the human victims of his pranks are killed, nor is anyone else in *History* (with the exception of the cook on the *Nonesuch*). People die mostly from natural causes, without influence or comment from Otter. The presence of superstition in Ménétra's work also contrasts with its absence in Otter's. Big Bill's world is devoid of folklore—there is a down-to-earth, pragmatic outlook in *History* which leaves little room for superstition. It may well be that laughing at the supernatural in the form of both superstition and, as will be noted, religion was integral to the rough, masculine outlook of the jolly fellows.[46]

---

[46] On European popular culture, see Peter Burke, *Popular Culture in Early Modern Europe* (New York, 1978). Compare Ménétra's account of when his master slips while carrying panes of glass on his head—"his head went through the panes, he was caught. The pieces of glass tore at his collar; the slightest movement caused him intense pain. . . . I couldn't prevent myself from laughing and telling him that he ought to wear a hat" (*Journal*, 116)—with Otter's "poor Jim who by the way had a very hard fall, he came crawling . . . towards me . . . every yard or two he would mutter the words O lord, which tickled me most prodigiously, I almost killed myself laughing at him" (99). On the term "Rabelaisian," see Darnton, foreword to *Journal*, by Ménétra, p. xv. "Bodies of the lynched, murdered and grotesquely killed are the stock devices in this humor," De Voto writes of the Southwestern humorists in *Mark Twain's America*, p. 152.

Traditional as it may have been, this masculine, violent, joking attitude was coming under attack in the early nineteenth century. One of the most profound and perplexing questions in American history is the connection between the growth of the middle class and the Second Great Awakening. Whatever that relationship, something was changing in the first three decades of the century. According to Daniel Walker Howe, the evangelical movement "reshaped the cultural system of the Victorian middle class in Britain and America. . . . The reforms it inspired profoundly affected society and politics in both countries." Howe emphasizes the importance of women in creating this new culture, the hallmarks of which were strict morality and discipline combined with a Christian emphasis on improving human self-development. Characteristic reforms included temperance; antislavery; Sabbatarianism; opposition to physical violence, the "campaigning against corporal punishment of children, wives, sailors and prisoners"; and, for the most radical, women's rights.[47]

It is hard to fix exactly the date when this new movement became a significant force in America, but one key event seems to have been the genesis of the Sabbatarian movement that began in 1807 in the village of Washington in western Pennsylvania. The attempt to halt Sunday mail delivery gradually worked its way east and became one of the most important symbolic issues of the period. In southern Pennsylvania where Otter lived, the Second Great Awakening was clearly well underway by the 1820s, with Methodists holding protracted meetings and other denominations being revitalized.[48]

Otter and the jolly fellows supported just about everything that the emerging Victorian culture was against. One term frequently used by evangelicals to sum up what they opposed, and a keyword of the period, was "licentiousness," which found its expression in swearing, drinking, brawling, gambling, and whoring. Clearly Otter fitted the indictment connoted by this

[47] On the question of relationship between the growth of the middle class to the Second Great Awakening, see Paul Johnson, *A Shopkeeper's Millennium: Society and Revivals in Rochester, New York, 1815–1837* (New York, 1978); and Mary P. Ryan, *The Cradle of the Middle Class: The Family in Oneida County, New York, 1790–1865* (Cambridge, 1981). Daniel Walker Howe, "The Evangelical Movement and Political Culture in the North during the Second Party System," *Journal of American History* 77 (1991), 1218

[48] Richard R. John, "Taking Sabbatarianism Seriously: The Postal System, the Sabbath, and the Transformation of American Political Culture," *Journal of the Early Republic* 10 (1990), 517–567; and Terry Billhartz, *Urban Religion and the Second Great Awakening: Church and Society in Early National Baltimore* (Rutherford, N.J., 1986), pp. 86–87.

term. He was not a religious man, for example, he turns down an invitation to go to church, adding, "I had not got much in the habit of attending . . . and I feel a pretty strong prediliction never to get myself much into that habit" (68). The only church service Otter mentions attending ends up in a "general fight" after his drunken friend insults the minister (85). Otter was, of course, a drinker—indeed, he seems to have spent many Sundays drinking in taverns (73)—as well as a gambler, a slave catcher, and a brawler. He was not domestic, spending most of his time traveling from job to job or in taverns. In short, he was the evangelicals' worst nightmare—without self-discipline, licentious.[49]

This sort of comportment was the target of reformers as an attempt not simply to end drinking and other licentious behavior but to reform the individual as well. And they succeeded to a degree, though I suspect standards of gentility were never quite as high in the countryside as among the urban middle class. It is inconceivable to me that in the second half of the century someone like Otter could have been considered a small-town dignitary, elected to public office. As Victorian culture organized following the Second Great Awakening, the days when local notables, men like Gilbert, Bart, and Otter, could sit around the tavern planning violent sprees and still be considered respectable were numbered.[50]

It was more than just a change in behavior that the Victorian reformers were after: it was a change in attitudes. Thomas Haskell has used the term "humanitarian sensibility" to describe the great wave of reform sentiment that spread throughout Europe and North America in the eighteenth and early nineteenth centuries. "Sensibility" seems the right word—there was an

[49] On "licentiousness" see Richard J. Carwardine, *Evangelicals and Politics in Antebellum America* (New Haven, 1993), pp. 57–58 Otter writes on page 74, "I was a quaker long ago." But this reference is presumably a joke. In any case, it seems that Otter had no religious affiliation at the time he wrote *History*

[50] The rural jolly fellows did not disappear with the onset of the evangelical–middle-class campaign for respectability: note, for example, the "House of Commons" crowd that gathered at the Mansfield, Connecticut, general store in the early 1870s, described in Wilbur L. Cross, *Connecticut Yankee: An Autobiography* (New Haven, Conn., 1943), pp. 28–36; the "House of Commons," however, seems rather tame compared with Otter's jolly fellows. The struggle of "evangelical culture" to tame "male culture" in the South is traced in Ted Ownby, *Subduing Satan: Religion, Recreation, and Manhood in the Rural South, 1865–1890* (Chapel Hill, N.C., 1990). See also Grady McWhiney, *Cracker Culture: Celtic Ways in the Old South* (Tuscaloosa, Ala., 1988), pp. 127–137, 146–170; and Elliott J. Gorn, "'Gouge and Bite, Pull Hair and Scratch': The Social Significance of Fighting in the Southern Backcountry," *American Historical Review* 90 (1985), 18–43.

alteration not only in the way people acted but also in how they felt, which is why, I believe, so many episodes that Otter considers humorous no longer seem funny. Writing of Ménétra, Darnton notes that "laughter does not echo unambiguously across the ages. When it reaches us from the distant past, it makes us sense the gap" between our time and theirs. I would suggest that in America the Second Great Awakening and the subsequent humanitarian reforms helped create this "gap."[51]

Not only are the sort of sprees that Otter recounts today proscribed by law and public opinion but they also no longer seem attractive or amusing to us. What is so funny about Mr. Overbaugh scalding his throat with boiling coffee? Such incidents, especially the beating of blacks and the torturing and killing of domestic animals, strike us as repulsive, not as entertaining. We are on the other side of this change in sensibility and have an instant, spontaneous reaction totally divergent from Otter's pleasure in Mr. Overbaugh's pain.

In *History* it is the cruelty to animals that perhaps delineates the divide most clearly and indicates something of the coherence of the humanitarian sensibility. The campaign against cruelty to animals in the United States and England emerged, according to James Turner, "from the milieu of humanitarian reform" in the early nineteenth century. As with antislavery, many of the early leaders of the movement were Quakers, and also as with antislavery, women took a prominent role. In England Wilberforce led the crusade against bearbaiting, and in America Harriet Beecher Stowe was a leading supporter of the animal welfare movement in the 1860s. Violence against animals was a hallmark of those who lacked self-control, who were licentious, and the opposition stemmed according to Keith Thomas from "a combination of religious piety and bourgeois sensibility."[52]

This "modern sensibility," as Thomas calls it, was part of what the Victorians called progress. To put it this way is not to imply that I question whether this change was a "good" thing. But it is interesting to speculate on this transformation: Is it possible that there was a price to be paid? That what was lost was an openness, a friendliness, a spontaneity, a *fraternity* that

[51] Thomas L. Haskell, "Capitalism and the Origins of the Humanitarian Sensibility," in *The Antislavery Debate: Capitalism and Abolitionism as a Problem in Historical Interpretation,* ed. Thomas Bender (Berkeley, 1992), pp. 107–160; and Darnton, foreword to *Journal,* by Ménétra, p. xiv. See also on this point Gorn, "'Gouge and Bite,'" esp. pp. 34–38.
[52] Turner, *Reckoning with the Beast: Animals, Pain, and Humanity in the Victorian Mind* (Baltimore, 1980), p. 36; and Thomas, *Man and the Natural World: A History of Modern Sensibility* (New York, 1983), p. 159.

I think comes through in Otter's *History*? The instinctive sympathy Otter receives from strangers on his travel back to Hull and the innocent, trusting attitude of the victims of some of his pranks suggest such traits. One of the most striking things about *History* is the juxtaposition of brutality and benevolence; the range of human conduct was very broad. In Otter's world, a very sharp boundary existed between insiders and outsiders; those within could expect a camaraderie and empathy that strikes us as unusual, whereas those beyond the boundary were fair game. Could it be that our greater tolerance today is achieved at the cost of a certain indifference?

Haskell argues that this humanitarianism was due less to the growth of the bourgeoisie itself than to the nature of capitalism that caused "an expansion of the conventional limits of moral responsibility." In this regard it is perhaps significant to point out that Otter, despite being a very hard worker, does not seem to have been a very good capitalist, remaining "still a poor man." Is it possible that Otter's spontaneous cruelty and his poor business sense are in some way connected, that he lacked the self-controlled outlook, the "modern personality," as Richard D. Brown calls it, needed for financial success? Could it be that the jolly fellows' lack of bourgeois traits left them ill-suited for the rational, regimented world that was emerging, ensuring their economic decline and marginalization?[53]

This is speculation. What does seem clear is that this change was underway as Otter was writing. The world of the jolly fellows was becoming marginalized. I would suggest that the growth of Victorian culture not only marginalized this world, but also, in a way, focused it. That is, as jolly compartment became defined as unacceptable in society at large, those places where rowdy behavior remained took on added importance. I am thinking here of what was emerging in mid–nineteenth-century America as the two bastions of this older cultural style, the Bowery and the frontier.[54]

Which brings us back to Alexander Saxton's point about the linkage of

---

[53] Haskell, "Capitalism and the Origins of the Humanitarian Sensibility," p. 133; and Brown, *Modernization: The Transformation of American Life, 1600–1865* (1976; rpt., Prospect Heights, Ill., 1988). Stuart M. Blumin in his study of nineteenth-century Kingston, New York, concluded from Mercantile Agency reports that "there is a fairly close correspondence between 'good habits'" and future success; men with "questionable habits" tended to fail. See Blumin, *The Urban Threshold: Growth and Change in a Nineteenth-Century American Community* (Chicago, 1976), p. 208.

[54] Ownby, *Subduing Satan.* For a sense of how this ethos has continued on the margins of American society, note the "Lumberjack Code," with its valuation on "unslacking prodigious toil," drinking, and brawling, in Richard M. Dorson, *Bloodstoppers and Bearwalkers: Folk Traditions of the Upper Peninsula* (Cambridge, Mass., 1952), pp. 186–188.

the city and the frontier. Both the Bowery and the frontier were predominantly young and male, and here continued drinking, swearing, brawling, and wenching. But there is more to it, perhaps, than that. Is it possible that these masculine spaces took on a specific meaning *only* when Victorian culture began to define this type of conduct as illicit? Otter's account clearly suggests that there were plenty of rowdy young men in New York in the early 1800s, but no Bowery. The sort of behavior Otter describes was quite traditional, but its sole "purpose" seems to have been to stigmatize outsiders.[55]

The Second Great Awakening and the development of middle-class notions of respectability labeled such comportment subversive. In a "feminized" American cultural mainstream, to use Ann Douglas's term, this brawling masculine subculture now had a meaning. The Bowery and the frontier became places "outside" propriety and middle-class morality. Men who therefore gravitated to the Bowery or visited gold rush California were, in a way, making a cultural statement by rejecting Victorian ideology. It was here that the jolly fellows became a counterculture. I would suggest that the Bowery, which emerged in the 1840s, could have done so only *after* the Second Great Awakening had defined the city's rowdy male subculture as sinful.[56]

By the 1840s, the jolly fellows were under attack, and it was only in cities among workers and in parts of the West and the backcountry of the South that the subculture could function almost fearlessly. Even in those milieus there were large, perhaps growing numbers of respectable workers and miners who repudiated the tavern ethos. One might speculate that Otter's move from Emmitsburg to Baltimore in 1850 was made in part because he hoped that in a city his "propensity for fun" might be less subject to condemnation.[57]

In focusing and giving coherence to this subculture, the Second Great

[55] On the Bowery see Peter Buckley, "To the Opera House: Culture and Society in New York City, 1820–1860," Ph.D. diss., S.U.N.Y. at Stony Brook, 1984. On the frontier see, for example, Hubert Howe Bancroft, *California Inter Pocula* (San Francisco, 1888); and Dee Brown, *Wondrous Times on the Frontier* (Little Rock, Ark., 1991).

[56] Ann Douglas, *The Feminization of American Culture* (New York, 1978). On the "outside" status of gold rush California, see Richard Stott, "The Geography of Gender in Nineteenth-Century America: Youth, Masculinity, and the California Gold Rush," Paper delivered at the Organization of American Historians Meeting, Louisville, Kentucky, April 1991.

[57] I do not suggest that the middle class was successful in eradicating this sort of behavior; Ownby makes clear that such was not the case in the South. But "male culture," as Ownby calls it, was clearly on the defensive; see his *Subduing Satan*.

Awakening *politicized* the jolly fellows' comportment. There is seemingly little about politics in *History*, which is not really very surprising—most of the period covered by the book was an era during which voter turnout was low and popular interest in politics was muted. It was with the genesis of the second party system in the 1830s that politics became a national obsession and voter turnout increased to over 80 percent of eligible voters. And only at the end of the book in his account of the "celebrated Woodsborough spree," "the day after the election in 1834," does Otter reveal himself as a "Jackson man."[58]

Perhaps more important, from our point of view, is the way culture became politicized during the second party system. In the 1830s and 1840s the campaign against licentiousness was identified with the Whig Party. According to Daniel Walker Howe, "The Whig Party's electoral campaign formed part of the cultural struggle to impose in the United States standards of morality we usually term Victorian." Those in opposition to this view tended to gravitate toward the Democrats. Culture and politics became intertwined: whereas mainline Protestant churches tended to support the Whigs, minstrelsy, with its racist egalitarian stance, was aligned with the Democratic Party.[59]

Only when the jolly fellows' behavior takes on political meaning as the antithesis of bourgeois middle-class culture does it begin to work its way onto the stage—and into literature. Kenneth Lynn has noted that the original Southwestern humorists of the 1830s and 1840s, such as Augustus B. Longstreet, were Whigs who described the male subculture to denounce it and uphold the Whig "self-controlled" (i.e., not licentious) gentleman as critical to "stabilizing a lawless and violent society." Then beginning in the mid- to late 1840s, Democratic writers such as George Washington Harris entered the field not to criticize male frontier rowdiness but to glorify it. Thus, by giving a meaning to mayhem (to borrow a phrase from Elliott J. Gorn), the Second Great Awakening made male licentiousness both a cultural and a political statement.[60]

But what of Otter? Much of what I have been discussing took place after

---

[58] Joel H. Silbey, *The American Political Nation, 1838–1893* (Stanford, 1991).

[59] Howe, *The Political Culture of the American Whigs* (Chicago, 1979), p. 33. See also Carwardine, *Evangelicals and Politics;* and John, "Taking Sabbatarianism Seriously," pp. 655–677. On the creation of minstrelsy see Robert C. Toll, *Blacking Up: The Minstrel Show in Nineteenth Century America* (New York, 1974), pp. 30–31. On the Democratic orientation of minstrelsy, see Saxton, "Blackface Minstrelsy," pp. 174–175.

[60] Lynn, *Twain and Southwestern Humor,* pp. 46–72, quotation p. 118. Gorn, *The Manly Art: Bare-Knuckle Prizefighting in America* (Ithaca, N.Y., 1986).

History was published in 1835. In Hanover in the 1810s and 1820s, I can discover no clear political alignment of the jolly fellows. The alignment between life-style and politics was beginning to emerge when Otter wrote, and I suspect that the story Otter tells has more of a political significance than might be readily apparent.

Otter was naturalized an American citizen on 28 September 1828 in Frederick, Maryland, almost certainly so he could vote for Jackson. The 1828 election saw a tremendous upsurge in voter interest. According to the *Frederick-Town Herald*, "Numbers, who, though advanced in years had never before voted, with others who have not been to an election in many years, came out Monday" (6 October 1828). Nationally, turnout increased from 27 percent in 1824 to 58 percent in 1828: like so many of his fellow Americans, Otter was drawn into the political system in support of Old Hickory. Later, he was elected burgess of Emmitsburg, presumably as a Jacksonian. Indeed, I earlier raised the possibility that *History* itself may have been some sort of campaign biography akin to *Sketches and Eccentricities of Colonel David Crockett of West Tennessee* (1833). For Otter, political affiliation probably had more to do with life-style than issues, thus suggesting why he does not explain what made him a "Jackson man."[61]

Otter, then, gives us a portrait of a world that, if not lost, was at least becoming marginalized. We might, in fact, add this to the list of possible reasons Otter had for writing *History:* to memorialize the world of the jolly fellows in the face of modernization. Although this subculture was being stigmatized by middle-class society, the life-style, as it became more focused and coherent, would provide an outlook upon which later writers such as Whitman and Twain drew to criticize mainstream American culture.[62]

Personality

In many ways the outlook of the jolly fellows was not unique in the early Republic. Otter was part of this group and seems to have been admired

[61] Naturalization Ledger, 25 September 1828, Record Room, Frederick County Courthouse, Frederick, Maryland, which shows a surge of naturalizations in late September and early October. Eight hundred more voters were recorded in Frederick County than in 1824; *Frederick-Town Herald*, 11 October 1828. The poll books for the 1828 and the 1832 elections are missing, but later poll books do show Otter voting; Election Judges' Polls Books, Presidential Electors, 1840 and 1844, Emmitsburg District, Frederick County, Hall of Records, Annapolis, Maryland. Silbey, *American Political Nation*, p. 29.

[62] On Twain and Whitman and this subculture, see Stott, "Geography of Gender."

within it. Yet I am reluctant to reduce him to being simply a representative of a certain mentality and comportment.

Otter, to borrow a phrase from the book's subtitle, was "altogether original," and the Reily description of him as "a peculiar man" suggests that he was widely recognized as such. I do not think, however, that recognition of Otter as sui generis contradicts the view of Otter as illustrative of a pattern of behavior in the early nineteenth century.

I believe Otter had a disturbed personality. Note, again, the Woodsborough head-butting spree, which fits in perfectly with the notion of a masculine, rowdy subculture—it could come right out of Sut Lovingood or one of the Crockett almanacs. But in telling it, Otter writes: "He fell against the wall, and as he was in the act of falling, his eyes rolled in his head and a good deal of the white in them appeared" (175). Otter has no compelling reason to provide such a detailed description, for it adds little to the narrative. Here and in other places, he seems to rejoice not just in the cruelty of the event itself but also in the precise details of brutality: the monkey Otter roasts "rolled his eyes about in his head at a frightful gait, lolled out his tongue" (153). To me, these very specific accounts of the effects of his violence suggest sadism.

The origin of this psychological abnormality, if Otter was sick, is impossible to know. Although it is a cliché to attribute a personality disorder to an unhappy childhood, the evidence provided in *History* can certainly be interpreted in that way. At the beginning of his text, Otter runs away to sea after receiving a "flagellation" from his father. Although he crosses the Atlantic to be reunited with his family and his meeting with "my mother, sisters and brothers" was so joyful that "language is too weak to express the sensations we labored under," Otter's description of meeting his father seems curiously unemotional.[63]

I also suspect that Otter's experience as a seaman in the Royal Navy may have contributed to his personality. The British Navy in the decade of the Spithead Mutiny (1797) was a tough masculine world and not exactly the place to unlearn any lessons in cruelty which Otter had received from his father. Otter had violence inflicted on him as a child and later inflicted it on others. He does not appear to have expected any favors from others and

---

[63] Although I think *History* generally suggests a distinct coolness toward his father, it should be noted that Otter and his wife named their first child, born 9 March 1811, Edward. "Church Records of Emanuel's Reformed Church, Hanover, York County, Pennsylvania," copied by William J. Hinkle, typescript in the Historical Society of York County, York, Pennsylvania.

indeed views those outside his circle as potential targets for vicious pranks. There seems to have been an innate viciousness about him, which is, I would argue, what made him a star among the jolly fellows.[64]

I feel that few of the jolly fellows dared to do the things Otter did—it is he who is constantly taking the lead, propelling the action, whereas others merely cooperate with him, laughing at Big Bill's exploits. He was "one of the boys," yet also a real character, literally a larger-than-life figure. They shared with Otter a delight in witnessing mayhem, but it took Big Bill himself, with his size and vicious temperament, actually to instigate it.

One might suggest that the jolly fellows' subculture typically functioned in this manner, with widely shared values but sport instigated by only a subset of members. To return to my earlier point, the great change is not just that this type of behavior was defined as illicit and marginalized but also, over time, that sensibilities have changed so that it no longer seems amusing. Thus I believe that an individual such as Otter, extraordinary as he was, enlightens us about past mentality and conduct. *History of My Own Times* is history in ways both intended and unintended.

[64] On the social world of sailors, see Marcus Rediker, *Between the Devil and the Deep Blue Sea: Merchant Seamen, Pirates, and the Anglo-American Maritime World, 1700–1750* (Cambridge, 1987).

APPENDIX

Articles of an Agreement between
Rev. John DuBois & William Otter
11 October 1823

Articles of an agreement Entered into by and between William Otter of the City of Baltimore on the one part and the Rev. J. DuBois President of mount St. Mary's Seminary Frederick County Maryland on the other part. Witnesseth that Said William Otter Engaged to Said John DuBois to plaster his new Stone house 95 feet by 44 three Stories high, to be divided below into five rooms and a passage—Seven rooms and two passages in the 2nd Story Seven rooms and two passages in the third Story and the Same divisions in the garret Part, the whole to be Lathed where it will be wanting & Plastered all over with three coats everywhere also to plaster the Outside back part of the building's walls where the three galleries are to be Erected, but the ceiling next to the roof alone to be plastered, the whole to be done in a Compleat workmanlike manner—all the materials to be furnished by the Said Rev. J. DuBois, viz the Sand for the two first Coat out of the bank Shewed as a Sample to him in presence of Francis Marshall, t'other Coat to be done out of Sand either brought from Baltimore or out of any other a Sample of which Shall be previously shown to & approved by Said William Otter the Said Rev. J. DuBois is to board all hands Employed by Said William Otter, reserving still to himself Said John DuBois the right of Expelling Said Tenders in case of misbehaviour—but he is to furnish no liquors—Said William Otter is also to be consulted about the Lime, that no blame can be attached to the Plaisterers on acct of the bad quality of the Lime. It is understood between the Said parties that the Carpenters work will be ready to receive the plaistering on or before the 1st of October or gradually for the work so as not to Stop him, that the Counterceiling will be done by a hand Employed by the Revd. J. DuBois—in consideration where-of the Said Rev. J. DuBois is to pay unto the Said William Otter four hundred and fifty dollars out of which he will advance him from time to time whatever he may want for the support of his family & the payment of his tenders to any amount not Exceeding two hundred dollars the Surplus to be paid after the work is Compleated—Should the work not be done according to the agreement in a Workmanlike manner, it is understood that said William Otter will forfeit any further Claim than the money advanced to him as Specified above—it is understood between the Said parties that the Said William Otter is at Liberty to put two coats only on the Exterior back walls between the Galleries, but is answerable for the Solidity & neatness of the wall as it is by his advice & opinion that Said plaistering is reduced to two Coats as most Solid, that Said William Otter will make the Plaistering of the backwall nearly similar in Colour to the front & divide it, by joisting, in regular Courses that Said William Otter shall furnish a wire Sifter for which if new, he will be paid two dollars & fifty cents, or less in proportion if it is 2d hand, to be used in preference by the hand employed by Rev. J. DuBois to Sift the Sand—also that Said John DuBois will furnish about 15 Bushels of Plaister of Paris to render the work more Substantial.

In Confirmation whereof the Said Parties have hereunto Set their hands and Seals this 11th Day of August Eighteen hundred and twenty three.

Witness Present	Wm. Otter (seal)
F. Marshall	John DuBois (seal)

it is further agreed and it is to be inserted in the double Copy of this agreement that the whole work is to be Compleated before the last of June 1824

Witness Present	Wm. Otter (seal)
F. Marshall	John DuBois (seal)

October 22nd 1823—the above Parties on reconsidering the above agree-ment, & seeing that the Sifting of the Sand had been left to the Charge of the above Contractor Rev. J. DuBois through mishapprension—Said Wm.

Otter releases Said John DuBois from Said Condition & reduced his Demands for all Expenses to four hundred and fifty dollars in full of all demands.

J. DuBois   Wm. Otter

Patrick Quinn

Source: Mount St. Mary's College Archives, Emmitsburg, Maryland. My thanks to Professor Kelly Fitzpatrick, director, Special Collections and Archives, Mount St. Mary's College, for making a typescript of this document.

INDEX

DOCUMENTS IN AMERICAN SOCIAL HISTORY
Edited by Nick Salvatore

*Their Lives and Numbers: The Condition of Working People
in Massachusetts, 1870–1900*
edited by Henry F. Bedford

*We Will Rise in Our Might: Workingwomen's Voices from
Nineteenth-Century New England*
by Mary H. Blewett

Dutch American Voices: Letters from the United States, 1850–1930
edited by Herbert J. Brinks

Peter Porcupine in America: Pamphlets on Republicanism and Revolution
by William Cobbett, edited and with an Introduction by David A. Wilson

*Invisible Immigrants: The Adaptation of English and Scottish Immigrants
in Nineteenth-Century America*
by Charlotte Erickson

Keepers of the Revolution: New Yorkers at Work in the Early Republic
edited by Paul A. Gilje and Howard B. Rock

News from the Land of Freedom: German Immigrants Write Home
edited by Walter Kamphoefner, Wolfgang Helbich, and Ulrike Sommer

History of My Own Times
by William Otter, edited by Richard B. Stott